# HOW LINUX WORKS

# HOW LINUX WORKS

## What Every Superuser Should Know

by Brian Ward

**NO STARCH
PRESS**

San Francisco

Publisher: William Pollock
Managing Editor: Karol Jurado
Cover and Interior Design: Octopod Studios
Technical Reviewer: Scott Schwartz
Copyeditor: Andy Carroll
Compositor: Wedobooks
Proofreader: Stephanie Provines

For information on book distributors or translations, please contact No Starch Press, Inc. directly:

No Starch Press, Inc.
555 De Haro Street, Suite 250, San Francisco, CA 94107
phone: 415-863-9900; fax: 415-863-9950; info@nostarch.com; http://www.nostarch.com

The information in this book is distributed on an "As Is" basis, without warranty. While every precaution has been taken in the preparation of this work, neither the author nor No Starch Press, Inc. shall have any liability to any person or entity with respect to any loss or damage caused or alleged to be caused directly or indirectly by the information contained in it.

*Library of Congress Cataloguing-in-Publication Data*

Ward, Brian.
  How Linux works : what every superuser should know / Brian Ward.
       p. cm.
  Includes index.
  ISBN 1-59327-035-6
  1.  Linux. 2.  Operating systems (Computers).  I. Title.
    QA76.76.063 W3654 2004
    005.4'32--dc22

                                                                  2004002692

# BRIEF CONTENTS

# CONTENTS IN DETAIL

## 1
## THE BASICS

# 2

# DEVICES, DISKS, FILESYSTEMS, AND THE KERNEL

# 3

# HOW LINUX BOOTS

# 4
# ESSENTIAL SYSTEM FILES, SERVERS, AND UTILITIES

# 5
# CONFIGURING YOUR NETWORK

# 6

# NETWORK SERVICES

# 7
# INTRODUCTION TO SHELL SCRIPTS

# 8
# DEVELOPMENT TOOLS

# 9
# COMPILING SOFTWARE FROM SOURCE CODE

# 10
# MAINTAINING THE KERNEL

# 11

# CONFIGURING AND MANIPULATING PERIPHERAL DEVICES

# 12

# PRINTING

# 13

# BACKUPS

# 14

# SHARING FILES WITH SAMBA

# 15

# NETWORK FILE TRANSFER

# 16

# USER ENVIRONMENTS

# 17
# BUYING HARDWARE FOR LINUX

# 18
# FURTHER DIRECTIONS

# A
# COMMAND CLASSIFICATION
# 331

# INDEX
# 337

# PREFACE

This book is about learning how a Linux system works so that you can be an effective systems administrator, programmer, home user, researcher, or just someone who likes to have fun with their computer. If you want to know what you can do when you have root access, then this book is for you.

The first part of this book shows you the basic layout and workings of a Linux system, including the directory structure and boot process. From there, you will learn the basics of networking.

The next part of the book is dedicated to programming tools. You may wonder why programming tools are important to system operation; after all, other systems don't come with development software. Unix-like systems such as Linux are different; not only is it not at all unusual to build your own version of popular software, but shell scripts and similar tools are closely intertwined with the system.

With the basic topics out of the way, the last half of the book is dedicated to more specialized information, such as the kernel, printing, and user environments. In addition, there is a very special chapter dedicated to purchasing hardware suitable for Linux systems.

One of the nice things about Linux is that the system doesn't make any effort to hide itself from you. You don't have to worry about strange undocumented binary formats, catch-all configuration databases (such as the Windows Registry), and frustratingly opaque GUI setup tools. Furthermore, like its BSD cousins, Linux retains its users because it gives them the chance to customize their systems to a degree impossible on other platforms. This book shows you how.

## Prerequisites

You do not have to know much about Linux or Unix to understand this book. Basic computer knowledge is more important than specifics. Here are the bare essentials:

- You should know what files and directories are.
- You should have Linux installed on a computer of your own, superuser (root) access, and a regular user account. The distribution that you choose does not matter. You need to be able to experiment with your machine as you read this book.

In addition, it helps if you have a little experience with the Unix shell. Without this background, it may take some time to get through the first chapter. You may also want to review binary and hexadecimal number systems for a few sections of the book.

## Kernel Chapter

Some time ago, I wrote a document called the Kernel-HOWTO. Due to increased demands on my time, I had to give up maintainership, but I haven't forgotten the first Linux-related thing I ever wrote. Chapter 10 is all-new material on how to configure and compile the Linux kernel. Furthermore, you are free to copy and distribute Chapter 10 as if it were a regular HOWTO document.

## Acknowledgments

Thanks go to James Duncan, Douglas N. Arnold, Bill Fenner, Ken Hornstein, Scott Dickson, Dan Ehrlich, Felix Lee, Scott Schwartz, Gregory P. Smith, Dan Sully, Gina Steele, and, of course, everyone at No Starch Press.

Brian Ward
San Francisco, CA

# 1

# THE BASICS

This chapter is a guide to the Unix commands and utilities that you must know to get anything out of this book. This is preliminary material, and you may already know a substantial amount. Even if you think you're up to speed, though, take a few seconds to flip through the sections just to make sure.

You may be asking yourself, "I thought this was a book about Linux, not Unix?" Don't worry; this chapter is just getting you ready for working with the Linux system. Linux is a Unix flavor at heart. You will see the word "Unix" in this chapter more than "Linux" because you can take the information straight over to Solaris, BSD, and other Unix-flavored systems. Special care has been taken to avoid too many Linux-specific user interface extensions, not only so you will have a better background with other operating systems, but also because these extensions tend to be extremely unstable. You will be able to adapt to new Linux releases much more quickly if you know the core that does not change.

Although the material here may seem sparse, you need to convince yourself that *Unix is not hard*. Yes, most reports from the field are to the contrary, but in the end, Unix is nothing but a bunch of files and a few commands for manipulating those files. If you are familiar with other operating systems, you shouldn't have a problem. However, if you find the information in this preliminary chapter somewhat lacking, there are books with much more detail for beginners, such as *UNIX for the Impatient* [Abrahams] and *Learning the UNIX Operating System* [Peek].

## 1.1 About /bin/sh

The shell is one of the most important parts of a Unix system. A shell is a program that runs commands. For example, one of the shell's duties is to run the commands that users type. Shells also serve as small programming environments. Unix programmers often break common tasks into little components and rely on the shell to manage tasks and to piece things together.

Many important parts of the system are actually *shell scripts* — text files that contain nothing but shell commands. If you have worked with MS-DOS, shell scripts may seem similar to .BAT files, but the shell is far more powerful. Chapter 7 is a small guide to shell scripts, and you can peruse it anytime after finishing this chapter.

As you progress through this book, you will learn how to manipulate commands with the shell. One of the best things about the shell is that if you make a mistake, you can look at what you typed, see what went wrong, and then try again quickly. *Do not be afraid to try new things.* The only way to learn the shell is to use it.

There are many different Unix shells, but all derive many of their features from the *Bourne shell*, or /bin/sh. Every Unix system needs the Bourne shell to function correctly, as you will see throughout this book.

Linux uses an enhanced version of this shell, called bash, or the "Bourne-again" shell. bash is the default shell for most Linux distributions, and /bin/sh is normally some sort of link to bash on a Linux system. You should use the bash shell when running the examples in this book.

You may not have bash if you're using this chapter as a guide for a Unix account at an organization where you are not the systems administrator. You can change your shell with chsh or ask your systems administrator for help.

## 1.2 Using the Shell

When you installed Linux, you set up a root (superuser) password, and hopefully you also made at least one more regular user for yourself. For this chapter, you should log in as the regular user.

The first thing you need to do after logging in is to bring up a shell window. After starting a shell, its window contains a prompt at the top that usually ends with a dollar sign ($). On Red Hat Linux, the prompt looks like [*name@host path*]$. If you know Windows, you will find that the shell window looks vaguely similar to the command prompt.

**NOTE**    *You may hear the shell window referred to as the* terminal *window. The terminal window is the part of the user interface that accepts keystrokes from the windowing system and draws the characters on the screen. You can think of the terminal as a middleman between the shell and the user.*

Now type the following command and press ENTER:

```
cat /etc/passwd
```

The command prints a couple of lines that start with usernames, and then you get your shell prompt back. If you can't read the text very well, manipulate the font settings to your liking. You're going to be spending a good part of your time with this book in the shell, so you should be comfortable with it.

The cat command is a great one to start with because it's one of the easiest Unix commands. Its syntax is as follows:

```
cat file1 file2 ...
```

When you run this command, cat prints (and concatenates) the contents of *file1*, *file2*, and any additional files you desire (denoted by ...) and exits.

If you do not specify any input files, cat reads from the standard input, which in this case is the keyboard. To see this at work, type cat and press ENTER. Unlike the earlier example, you do not get your shell prompt back because cat is still running. Now type some stuff (it doesn't matter what). After you press ENTER at the end of each line, cat repeats the line you typed. When you're sick of this, press CONTROL-D on a line by itself to terminate the cat command and return to the shell prompt.

**NOTE**    *Do not confuse CONTROL-D and CONTROL-C. CONTROL-D on a line by itself stops the current standard input entry (and often terminates a program). CONTROL-C terminates a program regardless of its input or output.*

You have now experienced *standard input* (stdin) and *output* (stdout), two important components of the Unix shell environment. Standard input is a program's default input source. When you ran cat without any arguments, it didn't give up because there were no arguments; instead, cat switched to standard input instead of going after some files. Here, standard input was the stuff that came from your keyboard. Standard output, on the other hand, is where a program's output goes by default. In this case, that location is the terminal window running the shell. The best feature of standard input and output is that you can easily send them to places other than their defaults, as described in Section 1.14.

## 1.3 Basic Commands

It's time to learn some other Unix commands. Most of the following programs take multiple arguments, and some have so many options and formats that an unabridged listing would be pointless. This is a simplified list; you don't need to know all of the details just yet.

### 1.3.1 ls

The ls command lists the contents of a directory. The default is the current directory. Use ls -l for a detailed (long) listing and ls -F to display file type information (for more on file types and the permissions in the left column, see Section 1.17). Here is a sample long listing:

```
total 3616
-rw-r--r--   1 juser   users      3804 Apr 30   2000 abusive.c
-rw-r--r--   1 juser   users      4165 May 26   1999 battery.zip
-rw-r--r--   1 juser   users    131219 Oct 26   2000 beav_1.40-13.tar.gz
-rw-r--r--   1 juser   users      6255 May 30   1999 country.c
drwxr-xr-x   2 juser   users      4096 Jul 17  20:00 cs335
-rwxr-xr-x   1 juser   users      7108 Feb  2   2001 dhry
-rw-r--r--   1 juser   users     11309 Oct 20   1999 dhry.c
-rw-r--r--   1 juser   users        56 Oct  6   1999 doit
drwxr-xr-x   6 juser   users      4096 Feb 20  13:51 dw
drwxr-xr-x   3 juser   users      4096 May  2   2000 hough-stuff
```

### 1.3.2 cp

In the first form shown below, cp copies the contents of *file1* to *file2*. In the second form, it copies all files to the *dir* directory:

```
cp file1 file2
cp file1 ... fileN dir
```

### 1.3.3 mv

In the first form below, mv renames *file1* to *file2*. In the second form, it moves all files to the *dir* directory:

```
mv file1 file2
mv file1 ... fileN dir
```

### 1.3.4 touch

The touch command creates a file. If the file already exists, touch does not change it, but it does update the timestamp you see with the long listing that you get with the ls -l command.

```
touch file
```

### 1.3.5 rm

To delete (remove) a file, use rm. After you remove a file, it's gone. Do not expect to be able to "undelete" anything.

```
rm file
```

### 1.3.6 echo

The echo command prints its arguments to the standard output:

```
echo Hello there.
```

The echo command is very useful for finding expansions of shell wildcards and variables that you will encounter later in this chapter.

## 1.4 Using Directory Commands

Unix has a directory hierarchy that starts at /, sometimes called the *root*. The directory separator is the slash (/), *not* the backslash (\). There are several standard subdirectories in the root directory, such as /usr (you'll learn all about them in Section 2.1).

A directory specification is called a *path*, and one that starts at the root (such as /usr/lib) is a *full* or *absolute* path. Similarly, a filename with a full path in front (such as /usr/lib/libc.a) is a *full pathname*.

The path component identified by two dots (..) specifies the parent of your shell's current directory, and one dot (.) specifies the current directory. For example, if the current working directory of your shell is /usr/lib, the path ../bin refers to /usr/bin. A path beginning with .. or . is called a *relative pathname*.

The following sections describe the essential directory commands.

### 1.4.1 cd

The cd command changes the shell's current working directory to *dir*:

```
cd dir
```

If you omit *dir*, the shell returns to your home directory.

### 1.4.2 mkdir

The `mkdir` command creates a new directory, *dir*:

```
mkdir dir
```

### 1.4.3 rmdir

The `rmdir` command removes the directory *dir*:

```
rmdir dir
```

If *dir* isn't empty, this command fails. However, if you're impatient, you probably don't want to laboriously delete all the files and subdirectories inside *dir* first. You can use `rm -rf` *dir* to delete a directory and its contents, but be careful. This is one of the few commands that can do serious damage, especially if you run it as the superuser. The `-r` option specifies recursive delete, and `-f` forces the delete operation. Don't use the `-rf` flags with wildcards such as a star (*). Above all, always double-check your command.

### 1.4.4 Shell Wildcards

The shell is capable of matching simple patterns with files in the current working directory. The simplest of these is the star character (*), which means match any number of arbitrary characters. For example, the following command prints a list of files in the current directory:

```
echo *
```

After matching files to wildcards, the shell substitutes the filenames for the wildcard in the command line and then runs the revised command line. Here are some more wildcard examples: `at*` matches all files starting with `at`; `*at` matches files that end with `at`; and `*at*` matches any files that contains `at`. If no files match a wildcard, the shell does no substitution, and the command runs with literal characters such as * (for example, try a command such as `echo *dfkdsafh`).

If you're used to MS-DOS, you might instinctively type `*.*` as a wildcard to match all files. Break this habit now. In Linux and other versions of Unix, you must use * to match all files. In the Unix shell, `*.*` matches only files and directories that contain the dot (.) character in their names. Unix filenames do not need extensions and often do not carry them.

Another shell wildcard character is the question mark (?), instructing the shell to match exactly one arbitrary character. For example, `b?at` matches `boat` and `brat`.

If you do not want the shell to expand a wildcard in a command, enclose the wildcard in single quotes (' '). For example, the command `echo '*'` prints a star. You will find this handy in a few of the commands described in the next section, such as grep and find. Quoting is a somewhat tricky matter, so don't get too involved with it just yet — you'll learn more much later, in Section 7.2.

This isn't the end to a modern shell's pattern-matching capabilities, but * and ? are what you need to know.

## 1.5 Intermediate Commands

The following sections describe the most essential intermediate Unix commands beyond the basics that you saw earlier in this chapter. There are many more commands where these come from; check out Appendix A for a large list of commands on your system.

### 1.5.1 grep

grep prints the lines from a file or input stream that match an expression. For example, if you want to print the lines in the /etc/passwd file that contain the text root, use this command:

```
grep root /etc/passwd
```

The grep command is extraordinarily handy when operating on multiple files at once, because it prints the filename in addition to the matching line when in this multiple-file mode. For example, if you want to check on every file in /etc that contains root, you could use this command:

```
grep root /etc/*
```

Two of the most important grep options are -i (for case-insensitive matches) and -v (which inverts the search; that is, it prints all lines that *don't* match). There is also a more powerful variant called egrep.

grep understands patterns known as *regular expressions* that are grounded in computer science theory and are ubiquitous in Unix utilities. Regular expressions are more powerful than wildcard-style patterns, and they have a different syntax. The two most important things to remember about regular expressions are these:

- .*   to match any number of characters (like the * in wildcards)
- .   to match one arbitrary character

The grep(1) manual page contains a detailed description of regular expressions, but it can be a little difficult to read. To learn more, you can try *Mastering Regular Expressions* [Friedl], or look at the regular expressions chapter of *Programming Perl* [Wall]. If you like math and are interested in where these things come from, look up *Introduction to Automata Theory, Languages, and Computation* [Hopcroft].

### 1.5.2 more and less

When a command's output is long, it can scroll off the top of the screen, and it's annoying to use a scrollbar to view such output because you have to move your hands around. You sometimes may also want to look at a large text file without starting a text editor. Two standard commands for text navigation are more and less.

To page through a big file like /usr/dict/words, use a command such as more /usr/dict/words. When running more, you will see the contents of the file, one screenful at a time. You can press the space bar to go forward in the file and the b key to skip back one screenful. To quit more, type q.

The less command performs the same function as more, but it is far more powerful and widely used. Use less --help to get a good summary of its operations.

As you will learn in Section 1.14, you can send the output of nearly any program directly to another program's input, enabling operations such as this (try it to see what it does):

```
grep ie /usr/dict/words | less
```

### 1.5.3 pwd

This program's name stands for "print working directory," and the command outputs the current working directory. That's all that pwd does, but it's useful. Some Linux distributions set up accounts with the current working directory in the prompt, but you may wish to change that because the current working directory takes up a lot of space on a line.

### 1.5.4 diff

To see the differences between two text files, use diff:

```
diff file1 file2
```

There are several options that can control the format of the output, such as -c, but the default output format is often the most comprehensible (for human beings, that is).

### 1.5.5 file

If you see a file and are unsure of its format, try using file to see if the system can guess, based on a large set of rules:

```
file file
```

You may be surprised to see how much this innocent-looking command can do.

### 1.5.6 find

It's frustrating when you know that a certain file is in a directory tree somewhere, and you just don't know where. Run find to find *file* in *dir*:

```
find dir -name file -print
```

Like most programs in this section, find is capable of some fancy stuff. However, don't try options such as -exec before you know the form shown here by heart, and you know why you need the -name and -print options. The find command accepts wildcard characters, such as *, but you must enclose them in single quotes ('*') to protect the wildcard characters from the shell's own wildcard features (recall from Section 1.4.4 that the shell expands wildcards before running commands).

### 1.5.7 head and tail

To quickly view a portion of a file or stream, use the head and tail commands. For example, head /etc/inittab shows the first ten lines of this system configuration file, and tail /etc/inittab shows the last ten lines. You can change the number of lines to print by using the -n option, where n is the number of lines you want to see. If you want to print lines starting at line n, use tail +n.

### 1.5.8 sort

The sort command quickly puts the lines of a text file in alphanumeric order. If the file's lines start with numbers, and you want to sort in numeric order, use the -n option. The -r option reverses the order of the sort.

## 1.6 Changing Your Password and Shell

On large commercial sites, it is important to change your password when you first log in. At home, you may not even have a password, but you should. Use the passwd command to change your password. It asks for your old password and then prompts you for your new password twice.

As any other manual will tell you, choose a password that does not include any real words in any language. Don't try to combine words, either. One of the easiest ways to get a good password is to pick a sentence, produce an acronym from it, and then modify the acronym with a number or some punctuation. All you have to do is remember the sentence. For example, Ayht8irt is a modification of the previous sentence.

### 1.6.1 chsh

You can change your shell with the chsh command, but keep in mind that this book assumes that you're running bash.

## 1.7 Dot Files

Change to your home directory and take a look around with ls, and then run
ls -a. At first, you will not see the configuration files, which are also called *dot
files*. Dot files are nothing more than files and directories whose names begin
with a dot (.). Common dot files are .bashrc and .login. There are some dot
directories, too, such as .mozilla.

There is nothing special about dot files or directories. Some programs
just don't list them by default, so that you don't see a complete mess when
listing the contents of your home directory. For example, without the -a
option, ls doesn't list dot files. In addition, shell wildcards don't match dot
files unless you explicitly use a pattern such as .*.

**NOTE**      *You can still run into problems with wildcards because .\* matches . and .. (the
current and parent directories). Depending on what you're doing, you may wish to
use a pattern such as .[^.]\* or .??\* to get all dot files except the current and
parent directories. This isn't a perfect solution, but it usually works.*

## 1.8 Environment and Shell Variables

The shell can store temporary variables, called *shell variables*, that store the
values of text strings. Shell variables are very useful for keeping track of state
in scripts, and some shell variables control the way the shell behaves (for
example, the PS1 variable controls the prompt). To assign a value to a shell
variable, use the equal sign (=):

```
STUFF=blah
```

The preceding example sets the value of the variable named STUFF to blah.
To access this variable, use $STUFF (for example, try running echo $STUFF).

An *environment variable* is like a shell variable, but is not specific to the
shell. All programs on Unix systems have environment variable storage. The
difference that you will notice is that the operating system passes all of your
shell's environment variables to programs that the shell runs, whereas shell
variables are not accessible by the commands that you run. Some programs
use environment variables for configuration and options. For example, you
can put your favorite less command-line options in the LESS environment
variable, and less will use these when you run it. Many manual pages contain
a section marked ENVIRONMENT that describes these variables.

You can assign a new environment variable just as you would a shell
variable, except that after creating the variable, you must run the export
operation to transfer the variable to the shell's environment variable storage.
The following sequence of commands assigns a value to STUFF and changes
it into an environment variable:

```
STUFF=blah
export STUFF
```

## 1.9 The Command Path

PATH is a special environment variable containing the *command path* (or *path* for short). A command path is a list of system directories that the shell looks in when trying to locate a command. For example, if you try to run the ls command, the shell searches the directories listed in PATH for the ls program. If programs with the same name appear in several directories in the path, the shell runs the first program that matches.

If you run echo $PATH, you'll see that the path components are separated by colons (:). Here's a simple example:

```
/usr/local/bin:/usr/X11R6/bin:/usr/bin:/bin
```

To make the shell look in more places for programs, you can change the PATH environment variable. You can add a directory *dir* to the beginning of the path so that the shell looks in *dir* before looking in any of the other PATH directories with this command:

```
PATH=dir:$PATH
```

As an alternative, you can append a directory name to the end of the PATH variable, causing the shell to look in *dir* last:

```
PATH=$PATH:dir
```

**NOTE** *Exercise caution when modifying the path, because you can accidentally wipe out your entire path if you mistype $PATH. Don't panic if this happens, because it isn't permanent (for a lasting effect, you need to mistype it when editing a certain configuration file, and even then it isn't difficult to rectify). One of the easiest methods to get back to normal is to exit the terminal window that you're using and start another.*

## 1.10 Special Characters

If you know people who are into Linux, and you have some inexplicable desire to discuss it with them, you should know a few names for some of the special characters that you'll encounter. If you are infinitely amused by this sort of thing, look at the Jargon File (http://catb.org/~esr/jargon/html/) or its printed companion, *The New Hacker's Dictionary* [Raymond].

Table 1-1 on the next page lists a select set of the special characters, what they are, what people call them, and their uses. You have already seen many of these characters in this chapter. Not all meanings of each character are identified because there are too many to list. Some utilities, such as the Perl programming language, use nearly every one of these special characters! Also, keep in mind that these are the American names for the characters.

**Table 1-1:** Special Characters

| Character | Name(s) | Uses |
|---|---|---|
| * | star | Regular expression, wildcard character |
| . | dot | Current directory, file/hostname delimiter |
| ! | bang | Negation, command history |
| \| | pipe | Command pipes |
| / | (forward) slash | Directory delimiter, search command |
| \ | backslash | Literals, macros (*never* directories) |
| $ | dollar | Variable denotation, end of line |
| ' | tick, (single) quote | Literal strings |
| ` | backtick, backquote | Command substitution |
| " | double quote | Semi-literal strings |
| ^ | caret | Negation, beginning of line |
| ~ | tilde, squiggle | Negation, directory shortcut |
| # | hash, sharp, pound | Comments, preprocessor, substitutions |
| [ ] | (square) brackets | Ranges |
| { } | (curly) braces | Statement blocks, ranges |
| _ | underscore | Cheap substitute for a space |

**NOTE** *You will often see control characters marked with a caret; for example, ^C for CONTROL-C.*

## 1.11 Command-Line Editing

As you play around with the shell, you may notice that you can edit the command line with the left and right arrow keys, as well as page through previous commands with the up and down arrows. This is as good as standard on almost any Linux system.

However, you should forget about the arrow keys and use control key sequences instead. If you learn and practice the ones listed in Table 1-2, you will have a great advantage when entering text in the many Unix programs that use these standard keystrokes.

**Table 1-2:** Command-Line Keystrokes

| Keystroke | Action |
|---|---|
| CONTROL-B | Move cursor left |
| CONTROL-F | Move cursor right |
| CONTROL-P | View previous command (or move cursor up) |
| CONTROL-N | View next command (or move cursor down) |
| CONTROL-A | Move the cursor to the beginning of the line |
| CONTROL-E | Move the cursor to the end of the line |

**Table 1-2:** Command-Line Keystrokes (continued)

| Keystroke | Action |
|-----------|--------|
| CONTROL-W | Erase the preceding word |
| CONTROL-U | Erase the entire line |

# 1.12 Text Editors

Speaking of editing, it's time for you to learn an editor. To get serious with Unix, you must be able to edit text files without damaging them. Most parts of the system use plain-text configuration files (for example, those in /etc). It's not too difficult to edit files, but you will do it so often that you need a serious, powerful tool for the job.

You should make a serious attempt to learn one of the two *de facto* standard Unix text editors, vi and emacs. Most Unix wizards are religious about their choice of editor. Don't listen to them. Instead, choose for yourself. If you choose an editor that matches your personality, you will find it easier to learn:

- If you want an editor that can do almost anything and has extensive online help, and you don't mind doing some extra typing to get these features, try emacs.

- If speed means everything to you, give vi a shot; it "plays" a bit like a video game.

*Learning the vi Editor* [Lamb] can tell you everything you need to know about vi. For emacs, use the online tutorial: Start emacs from the shell prompt or a GUI menu, type CONTROL-H, and then type t. If you want a book, look at *GNU Emacs Manual* [Stallman].

You might be tempted to bumble around with a "friendlier" editor, such as pico or one of the myriad GUI editors when you first start out, but if you're the type of person who tends to make a habit out of the first thing that you use, you don't want to go down this route.

Incidentally, the editing text is where you will first start to see a difference between the terminal and the GUI. Editors such as vi run inside the terminal window, using the standard terminal I/O interface that you are now starting to learn. However, GUI editors start their own window and present their own interface, independent of terminals.

# 1.13 Getting Online Help

Linux systems come with a wealth of documentation. For basic commands, the *manual pages* (or *man pages*) tell you what you need to know. To access this manual, use the man command. For example, to see the manual page for the ls command, run man as follows:

```
man ls
```

Most manual pages concentrate primarily on reference information. They may contain some examples and cross-references, but that's about it. Don't expect a tutorial, and don't expect an engaging literary style. For programs with many options, the manual page often lists the options in some systematic way (for example, alphabetical order). It won't bother to tell you what the important ones are. If you are patient, you can usually find what you need to know. If you're excessively impatient, ask a friend, or pay someone to be your friend so that you can ask them.

To search for a manual page by keyword, use the -k option:

```
man -k keyword
```

This is helpful if you don't quite know the name of the command that you want.

NOTE    *If you have any additional questions about any of the commands described in the previous sections, you can find the answers with the* man *command.*

Manual pages fall into numbered sections. When someone refers to a manual page, the section number appears in parentheses next to the name — ping(8), for example. Table 1-3 explains the section numbers:

**Table 1-3:** Online Manual Sections

| Section | Description |
| --- | --- |
| 1 | User commands |
| 2 | Low-level system calls |
| 3 | Higher-level Unix programming library documentation |
| 4 | Device interface and driver information |
| 5 | File descriptions (system configuration files) |
| 6 | Games |
| 7 | File formats, conventions, and encodings (ASCII, suffixes, and so on) |
| 8 | System commands and servers |

Sections 1, 5, 7, and 8 are good supplements to this book. Section 4 may be of marginal use. Section 6 would be great if only it were a little larger.

You can select a manual page by section. This is sometimes important because man displays the first manual page that it finds for a particular search term. For example, if you want to see the /etc/passwd file description (as opposed to the passwd command), you can insert the section number before the page name:

```
man 5 passwd
```

Manual pages cover the essentials, but there are many more ways to get online help. If you're just looking for a certain option for a command, try typing a command name followed by --help or -h (the exact option varies from command to command). You may get a deluge (as in the case of ls --help), but you may find just what you're looking for.

Some time ago, the GNU Project decided that it didn't like manual pages very much and switched to another format called info (or texinfo). Often, this documentation goes further than a typical manual page, but it is sometimes more complex. To access an info page, use info with the command name:

---
info *command*
---

Some packages dump their available documentation into /usr/share/doc with no regard for online manual systems such as man or info. Have a look in this directory on your system if you find yourself searching for documentation. And as ever, don't hesitate to look for help on the Internet if you have a connection.

## 1.14 Shell Input and Output

Now that you are familiar with basic Unix commands, files, and directories, you are ready learn the shell's I/O tricks. You can redirect the standard input and output. Let's start with standard output.

If you wish to send the output of *command* to a file instead of the terminal, use the > redirection character:

---
*command* > *file*
---

The shell creates *file* if it does not already exist. If *file* does exist, the shell erases the original file first; this is called *clobbering* the file. Some shells have parameters that prevent clobbering. For example, you can type set -C to avoid clobbering in bash.

If you don't want to overwrite a file, you can append the output to the file instead with the >> redirection syntax:

---
*command* >> *file*
---

This is a handy way to collect output in one place when repeatedly executing a variant of the same command.

To send the output of a command to the input of another command, use the pipe (|). To see how this works, try these two commands:

---
head /proc/cpuinfo
head /proc/cpuinfo | tr a-z A-Z
---

You can send output through as many piped commands as you wish; just add another pipe (|) before each additional command.

### 1.14.1 Standard Error

Occasionally, you may redirect standard output but find that the program still prints something on the terminal. This is *standard error* (stderr), an additional output stream for diagnostics and debugging. Try this command, which produces an error:

```
ls /fffffffff > f
```

After completion, f should be empty, but you still see the following error message on the terminal as standard error:

```
ls: /fffffffff: No such file or directory
```

You can redirect the standard error if you like. If you want to send standard output to f and standard error to e, use the following command:

```
ls /fffffffff > f 2> e
```

The number 2 specifies the *stream ID* that the shell modifies. Stream ID 1 is standard output (the default), and 2 is standard error.

You can also send the standard error to the same place as stdout with the >& notation. For example, to send both standard output and standard error to the file named f, try this command:

```
ls /fffffffff > f 2>&1
```

### 1.14.2 Standard Input Redirection

It is also possible to channel a file to a program's standard input with the < operator. Here's an example:

```
head < /proc/cpuinfo
```

You will occasionally run into a program that requires this sort of redirection. However, because most Unix commands accept filenames as arguments, this redirection isn't very common. For example, the preceding command could have been written as head /proc/cpuinfo.

## 1.15 Understanding Error Messages

When you encounter a problem on a Unix-like system such as Linux, you *must* read the error message. Unlike messages from other operating systems, Unix errors usually tell you exactly what went wrong.

Most Unix programs generate and report the same basic error messages, but there can be subtle differences between the output of any two programs. Here is an example that you'll certainly encounter in some form or other (the error message is in boldface):

```
$ ls /dsafsda
ls: /dsafsda: No such file or directory
```

There are three components to this message:

- The program name, ls. Some programs omit this identifying information, which can be annoying when you are writing shell scripts, but it's not really a big deal.
- The filename, /dsafsda, which is a more specific piece of information. There's some problem with this path.
- The specific error, No such file or directory, indicates the problem with the filename.

Putting it all together, you get something like "ls tried to open /dsafsda but couldn't because it does not exist." This may seem kind of obvious, but these messages can get a little confusing when you run a shell script that includes an erroneous command under a different name.

Always address the first error first. For example, some programs report that they can't do something before reporting a host of other problems. For example, let's say you run a fictitious program called scumd, and you see this error message:

```
scumd: /etc/scumd/config: No such file or directory
```

Following this is a huge list of other error messages that looks like a complete catastrophe. Don't let those other errors distract you. You probably just need to create /etc/scumd/config.

**NOTE** *Do not confuse error messages with warning messages. Warnings often look like errors, except that they contain the word "warning." A warning usually means something is wrong but that the program will try to continue running anyway. To fix a problem noted in a warning message, you may have to hunt down a process and kill it before doing anything else (you'll read about processes in Section 1.16).*

## 1.15.1 Common Errors

Many of the errors that you will encounter in Unix programs result from things that can go wrong with files and processes. Here is the error message hit parade:

### No such file or directory

This is the number one error. You tried to access a file that does not exist. Because the Unix file I/O system does not discriminate between files and directories, this error message occurs everywhere. You get it when you try to read a file that does not exist, when you try to change to a directory that isn't there, when you try to write to a file in a directory that does not exist, and so on.

### File exists

In this case, you probably tried to create a file that already exists. This is common when you try to create a directory with the same name as a file.

### Not a directory, Is a directory

These messages pop up when you try to use a file as a directory, or a directory as a file. You may have to hunt around a little after you see the error message. Here is an example:

```
$ touch a
$ touch a/b
touch: a/b: Not a directory
```

Notice that the error message only applies to the a part of a/b. When you encounter this problem, you may need to dig around a little to find the particular file that is being treated like a directory.

### No space left on device

You're out of disk space. See Section 2.4.7 for information on how to manage this.

### Permission denied

You get this error when you attempt to read or write to a file or directory that you're not allowed to (that is, you have insufficient access privileges). This includes the case when you try to execute a file that does not have the execute bit set (even if you can read the file). You will read more about permissions in Section 1.17.

### Operation not permitted

This usually happens when you try to kill a process that you don't own.

### Segmentation fault, Bus error

A segmentation fault essentially means that the person who wrote the program that you just ran screwed up somewhere. The program tried to access some part of memory that it was not allowed to touch, and the operating system killed it. A bus error is similar, except that it tried to access some memory in a particular way that it shouldn't. When you get one of these errors, you might be giving a program some input that it did not expect.

## 1.16 Processes

A *process* is a running program. Each process on the system has a numeric *process ID* (PID). For a quick listing of the processes that you're running, just run the ps command on the command line. You should get a list like this:

```
  PID TTY STAT TIME COMMAND
  520 p0  S    0:00 -bash
  545 ?   S    3:59 /usr/X11R6/bin/ctwm -W
  548 ?   S    0:10 xclock -geometry -0-0
 2159 pd  SW   0:00 /usr/bin/vi lib/addresses
31956 p3  R    0:00 ps
```

This is an abridged listing; yours will be much longer if you're running a windowing system. The fields are as follows:

- **PID**  The process ID.

- **TTY**  The terminal device where the process is running (don't worry about this for now).

- **STAT**  The process status; that is, what the process is doing at the given time and where its memory resides. For example, S means sleeping and R means running. Check the ps(1) manual page for all the symbols.

- **TIME**  The amount of CPU time (in minutes and seconds) that the process has used so far. In other words, this is the total amount of time that the process has spent running instructions on the processor.

- **COMMAND**  This one might seem obvious, but be aware that a process can change this field from its original value.

If you're interested in all processes on the system (not just the ones you're running), use ps ax, and if you'd like a more detailed report on process characteristics, use ps u. As with other programs, you can combine options, as in ps aux. Another important option that works in conjunction with a is w, which tells ps to print the full command name if it's too long to fit on one line.

To check on a specific process, add its PID to the argument list of the ps command. For example, one way to inspect the current shell process is with ps u $$ ($$ is a shell variable that evaluates to the current shell's PID).

You'll find information on two handy administration commands called top and lsof in Section 4.8. These can be useful when locating processes, even when doing something other than system maintenance.

### 1.16.1 Killing Processes

To terminate a process, send it a *signal* with the kill command. In most cases, all you need to do is this:

```
kill pid
```

There are many types of signals. The default signal is TERM, or terminate. You can send different signals by adding an extra option to kill. Let's say that you don't want to terminate the process, but rather, freeze it with the STOP signal. Use this command:

```
kill -STOP pid
```

A process stopped in this manner is still in memory, ready to pick up where it left off. Use the CONT signal to set the process on its way again:

```
kill -CONT pid
```

As you may recall from Section 1.2, CONTROL-C terminates a process running in the current terminal. This is the same as using kill to end the process with the INT (interrupt) signal.

The most brutal way to terminate a process is with the KILL signal. Other signals give the process a chance to clean up after itself, but KILL does not — the operating system terminates the process and forcibly removes it from memory. Use this as a last resort.

**WARNING** *Don't kill processes indiscriminately, especially if you don't know what they're doing. This can be akin to shooting yourself in the foot.*

### 1.16.2 Job Control

Shells also support *job control*, a way to send STOP and CONT signals to programs by using funny keystrokes and commands. For example, you can send a STOP signal with CONTROL-Z and start the process again by typing fg or bg.

Despite the habits of many experienced users, job control is not necessary and can be confusing to beginners — it is not uncommon for the user to press CONTROL-Z instead of CONTROL-C and have many suspended processes sitting about.

If you want to run multiple shell programs, you can either run each program in a separate terminal window, put non-interactive processes in the background (explained in the next section), or learn to use the screen program.

### 1.16.3 Background Processes

Normally, when you run a Unix command from the shell, you do not get the shell prompt back until the program has finished executing. However, you can detach a process from the shell and put it in the "background" with the ampersand (&); this gives you the prompt back. For example, if you have a large file that you need to decompress with gunzip (you'll see this in Section 1.18), and you want to do some other stuff while it's running, run the command as in this gunzip example:

```
gunzip file.gz &
```

The shell responds by printing the PID of the new background process, and the prompt returns immediately so that you can continue working. The process also continues to run after you log out, which comes in particularly handy if you have a program that does a lot of number crunching that you need to run for a while. Depending on your setup, the shell may notify you when the process completes.

The dark side to background processes is that they may expect to work with the standard input (or worse). If the program wants to read something from the standard input when it is in the background, it can freeze (try fg to bring it back), or it may terminate. If the program writes to the standard output or standard error, the output can appear in the terminal window with no regard to anything else running there.

The best way to make sure that a background process doesn't bother you is to redirect its output (and possibly input) as described in Section 1.14.

If spurious output from background processes gets in your way, you should know how to redraw the content of your terminal window. bash and most full-screen interactive programs support CONTROL-L to redraw the entire screen. If a program is reading from the standard input, CONTROL-R usually redraws the current line. Unfortunately, pressing the wrong sequence in the wrong situation can leave you in an even worse situation than before. For example, CONTROL-R at the bash prompt puts you in an annoying mode called reverse isearch.

## 1.17 File Modes and Permissions

Every Unix file has a set of *permissions* that determine whether you can read, write, or run the file. Running ls -l displays the permissions. Here's an example of such a display:

```
-rw-r--r-- 1 juser  somegroup   7041 Mar 26 19:34 endnotes.html
```

The first column represents the *mode* of the file, and it is shown in bold. The mode represents the file's permissions and some extra information. There are four parts to the mode; Figure 1-1 on the next page illustrates the pieces.

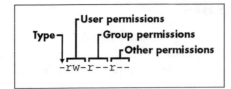

Figure 1-1: The pieces of a file mode

The first character of the mode is the *file type*. A dash (-) in this position, as in the example, denotes a *regular* file, meaning that there is nothing special about it. This is by far the most common kind of file. Directories are also common, carrying d in the file type slot. The rest of the file types are listed in Section 2.3, but you don't need to know about them just yet.

The rest of a file's mode contains the permissions, which break down into three sets: the *user, group,* and *other* permissions, in that order. For example, the rw- characters in the example are the user permissions, r-- are the group permissions, and r-- are the other permissions.

Four basic things can appear in each permission set:

- r Means that the file is readable
- w Means that the file is writable
- x Means that the file is executable (that is, you can run it as a program)
- - Means nothing

The user permissions (the first set) pertain to the user who owns the file. In the preceding example, that's juser.

The second set, group permissions, are for the file's group (somegroup in the example). Any user in that group can take advantage of these permissions. (Use the groups command to see what group you're in, and see Section 4.3.2 for more information.)

Everyone else on the system has access according to the *other* permissions. These are sometimes called *world* permissions.

NOTE    *Each read, write, and execute permission slot is sometimes called a* permission bit. *Therefore, you may hear people refer to parts of the permissions as "the read bits."*

Some executable files have an s in the user permissions listing instead of an x. This indicates that the executable is *setuid*, meaning that when you execute the program, it runs as the file owner instead of you. Many programs use this setuid bit to run as root to get the special privileges they need to change system files. One example is the passwd program, which needs to change the /etc/passwd file.

## 1.17.1 Modifying Permissions

To change permissions, use the chmod command. First, pick the set of permissions that you want to change, and then pick the bit to change. For example, say that you want to add group (g) and world (o, for "other") read (r) permissions to *file*. You can do it with two commands:

```
chmod g+r file
chmod o+r file
```

Or you can do it all in one shot like this:

```
chmod go+r file
```

To remove these permissions, use go-r instead of go+r.

**NOTE**    *Obviously, you shouldn't make your files world writable because it gives anyone on your system the ability to change them. But would this give anyone connected to the Internet a chance to change your files? Probably not, unless your system has a network security hole. In that case, file permissions aren't going to help you.*

You may sometimes see people changing permissions with numbers, for example:

```
chmod 644 file
```

This is called an *absolute change,* because it sets all of the permission bits at once. To understand how this works, you need to know how to represent the permission bits in octal form (each numeral represents an octal number and corresponds to a permission set). If you're curious about this, look at the chmod(1) manual page or the info page.

It is actually not that important to know how to construct absolute modes; it is easier to just memorize the modes that you use. Table 1-4 lists the most common absolute modes.

**Table 1-4:** Absolute Permission Modes

| Mode | Meaning | Used For |
|------|---------|----------|
| 644 | user: read/write; group, other: read | files |
| 600 | user: read/write; group, other: none | files |
| 755 | user: read/write/execute; group, other: read/execute | directories, programs |
| 700 | user: read/write/execute; group, other: none | directories, programs |
| 711 | user: read/write/execute; group, other: execute | directories |

Directories also have permissions, as you can see from the preceding list. You can list the contents of a directory if the directory is readable, but you can only access a file inside if the directory is executable. One common mistake people make when setting the permissions of directories is to accidentally remove the execute bit when using absolute modes.

Finally, you can specify a set of default permissions with the umask shell command that are applied to any new file you create. Without going into too much detail, use umask 022 if you want everyone to be able to see all of the files and directories that you make, and use umask 077 if you don't. You need to put the umask command with the desired mode in one of your startup files to make your new default permissions apply to later sessions (see Chapter 16).

## 1.17.2 Symbolic Links

A *symbolic link* is a file that points to another file or a directory, effectively creating an alias. It is similar to a shortcut in Windows. Symbolic links offer a quick way to provide access to an obscure directory path.

In a long directory listing, these links look like this (notice the l as the file type in the file mode):

```
lrwxrwxrwx 1 ruser  users  11 Feb 27 13:52 funk -> /home/skunk
```

If you try to access funk in this directory, the system gives you /home/skunk instead. Symbolic links are nothing more than names that point to other names.

The names of the symbolic links and the paths to which they point don't actually have to mean anything. In the preceding example, /home/skunk doesn't need to exist. If /home/skunk does not in fact exist, any program that accesses funk just reports that funk doesn't exist (except for ls funk, a command that stupidly informs you that funk is funk). This can be baffling, because you can see something named funk right there in front of you.

This is not the only way that symbolic links can be confusing. Another problem is that you cannot identify the characteristics of a link target just by looking at the name of the link. You must follow the link to find out if it goes to a file or directory. Your system may also have links that point to other links, which are called *chained symbolic links*.

To create a symbolic link from *target* to *linkname*, use this command:

```
ln -s target linkname
```

The linkname argument is the name of the symbolic link, the target argument is the path of the file or directory that the link *points* to, and the -s flag specifies a symbolic link (see the warning on the next page).

When making a symbolic link, check the command twice before you run it, because there are a number of things that can go wrong. For example, if you reverse the order of the arguments (`ln -s linkname target`) you're in for some fun when *linkname* is a directory that already exists. In this case, `ln` creates a link named *target* inside *linkname* (the link points to itself unless *linkname* is a full path). Therefore, if something goes wrong when you create a symbolic link to a directory, check that directory for errant symbolic links and remove them.

Symbolic links can also cause headaches when you're not aware of their presence. For example, you can easily edit what you think is a copy of a file but is actually a symbolic link to the original.

**WARNING** *Don't forget the -s option when creating a symbolic link. Without it, `ln` creates a hard link, giving an additional real filename to a single file. The new filename has all of the status of the old one; it points (links) directly to the file data instead of to another filename, as a symbolic link does. Hard links can be even more confusing than symbolic links. Avoid them.*

With all of these warnings regarding symbolic links, you may wonder why anyone ever bothers with them. The simple reason is that they offer a convenient way to share files and patch up small problems.

## 1.18 Archiving and Compressing Files

Now that you know all about files, permissions, and the errors that you might get, you need to master tar and gzip.

Start with gzip (GNU Zip), the current standard Unix compression program. A file that ends with `.gz` is a GNU Zip archive. Use gunzip *file*.gz to uncompress *file*.gz and remove the suffix; to compress it again, use gzip *file*.

gzip does not perform the additional function of archiving, like the ZIP programs for other operating systems — that is, it does not pack multiple files and directories into one file, thus creating an archive. To create an archive, use tar instead:

```
tar cvf archive.tar file1 file2 ...
```

tar archives have a `.tar` suffix. In the preceding example, *file1*, *file2*, and so on are the names of the files and directories that you wish to place in the archive named *archive*.tar. The c flag denotes create mode. You will learn about the v and f flags later in this section.

You can also unpack a `.tar` file with tar:

```
tar xvf file.tar
```

Study this command. The xvf part specifies the *mode* and *options*; it is the same as -xvf. The meanings are as follows:

- The x flag puts tar into extract (unpack) mode. You can extract individual parts of the archive by placing the names of the parts at the end of the command line, but you must know their exact names. To find out for sure, see the table of contents mode described shortly.

- The v flag activates verbose diagnostic output, causing tar to print the names of the files and directories in the archive when it encounters them. Adding another v causes tar to print details such as file size and permissions.

- The f flag denotes the file option. The next argument on the command line must be the file on which tar is to work (in the preceding example, it is *file*.tar). You *must* use this option and a filename at all times — there is one exception, but it involves tape drives (see Section 13.6). To use standard input or output, use - instead of the filename.

**NOTE**    *When using extract mode, remember that* tar *does not remove the archived* .tar *file after extracting its contents.*

Before unpacking, it's usually a good idea to check the contents of a .tar file with the t (table of contents) mode instead of x. This mode verifies the archive's basic integrity and prints the names of all files inside.

The most important reason for testing an archive is that sometimes unpacking an archive can dump a huge mess of files into the current directory. This is difficult to clean up. When you check an archive with the t mode, verify that everything is in a rational directory structure — that is, all file pathnames in the archive should start with the same directory. If you're not sure, create a temporary directory, change to that, and then extract. You can always use mv * .. if it turned out to be a false alarm.

One last significant option to tar is p, which preserves permissions. Use this in extract mode to override your umask and get the exact permissions specified in the archive. The p option is the default when working as the superuser. If you're having trouble with permissions and ownership when unpacking an archive as the superuser, make sure that you are waiting until the command terminates and you get the shell prompt back. Although you may only want to extract a small part of the archive, tar must run through the whole thing. You must not interrupt the process, because it sets the permissions only *after* checking the entire archive.

You should commit *all* of the tar options and modes in this section to memory; know them cold. If you're having trouble, make some flash cards. This may sound like a grade-school strategy, but it is very important to avoid careless mistakes with this command.

### 1.18.1 Compressed Archives (.tar.gz)

Many beginners find it confusing that archives normally come compressed, where the archive file ends in .tar.gz. To unpack a compressed archive, work from the right side to the left; get rid of the .gz first and then worry about the .tar. For example, these two commands decompress and unpack *file*.tar.gz:

```
gunzip file.tar.gz
tar xvf file.tar
```

When you're starting out, it's fine to do this one step at a time, first running gunzip to decompress and then tar to verify and unpack. When you do it enough, you soon memorize the entire archiving and compression process. However, this is not the fastest or most efficient way to invoke tar on a compressed archive. In particular, it wastes system resources — disk space and kernel I/O time.

You can combine archival and compression functions with a pipeline; for example, this command pipeline unpacks *file*.tar.gz:

```
zcat file.tar.gz | tar xvf -
```

zcat is the same as gunzip -dc. The -d option decompresses and the -c option sends the result to standard output (in this case, to the tar command).

Because this is such a common operation, the version of tar that comes with Linux has a shortcut. You can use z as an option to automatically invoke gzip on the archive. For example, use tar ztvf *file*.tar.gz to verify a compressed archive. However, for the sake of learning, you should make an effort to master the longer form before taking the shortcut.

**NOTE**    *A* .tgz *file is the same as a* .tar.gz *file. The name is meant to fit into FAT (MS-DOS based) filesystems.*

### 1.18.2 Other Compression Utilities

A newer compression program gaining some popularity in Unix is bzip2, where compressed files end with .bz2. Marginally slower than gzip, it often compacts text files a little more, and is therefore increasingly popular in the distribution of source code. The decompressing program is bunzip2, and the options of both components are close enough to those of gzip that you don't need to learn anything new.

Most Linux distributions come with zip and unzip programs compatible with the ZIP archives on Windows systems. They work on the usual .zip files as well as self-extracting archives ending in .exe.

If you encounter a file that ends in .Z, you have found a relic created by the compress program, once the Unix standard. gunzip can unpack these files, but gzip will not create them.

# DEVICES, DISKS, FILESYSTEMS, AND THE KERNEL

This chapter is a guided tour of the infrastructure in a functioning Linux system, including the system directories, devices, and the kernel. A large part of the material in this chapter deals with filesystems. When you master the workings of Linux filesystems, you will find it much easier to deal with system crashes, manage software, and accommodate new hardware.

**NOTE**    *You must do most system configuration and maintenance work as the superuser; this and all remaining chapters assume that you have this capability.*

## 2.1 Directory Hierarchy

As mentioned in Chapter 1, your Linux system has a root directory (/). The root contains several subdirectories and possibly a file or two. Keep this area clean; don't let stray files end up here. But don't fall victim to a syndrome that affects many administrators — removing files in a zealous attempt to keep the system "clean." If you don't know what something does (and can't figure it out), don't remove it.

The names of the directories in / have special meanings that pervade the Linux system in many other subdirectories. For example, there is a /bin directory in the root, but there are also many other bin directories throughout the system, including /usr/bin and /usr/local/bin. All of these bin directories contain executables.

If you want to know the gory details of the many directories on the system, have a look at the Filesystem Hierarchy Standard [Filesystem]. For the most part, the directory names reflect the root and /usr directory patterns described in the next sections.

### 2.1.1 The Essential Root Subdirectories

The most important of the root directory's subdirectories are the following:

- **bin**   Contains binary programs (also known as an *executables*), which are programs that are ready to run. Most of the basic Unix commands such as ls and cp are in /bin. However, some of the files in /bin are not in binary format because shell scripts perform the tasks of binaries in modern systems.

- **dev**   Contains device files. Read more about these special files in Section 2.3.

- **etc**   The core system configuration directory (pronounced EHT-cee). User password, boot, device, networking, and other setup files are here. Many items in /etc are specific to the particular hardware on the machine — for example, the /etc/X11 directory contains the graphics card configuration.

- **home**   Holds personal directories for normal users on the system. Most Unix installations conform to this standard.

- **lib**   An abbreviation for library. In Linux, this directory holds library files containing code that executables can use. There are two types of libraries: *static* and *shared*. The /lib directory should contain only shared libraries, but other lib directories such as /usr/lib contain both varieties, as well as other auxiliary files.

- **proc**   Provides system statistics through a directory-and-file interface that you can browse with standard Unix tools, like those introduced in Chapter 1. Much of the /proc subdirectory structure on Linux is unique, but many other Unix variants have similar features.

- **sbin** The place to find system executables. Programs in sbin directories pertain to system management, so regular users usually do not have sbin components in their command paths. Many of the utilities don't work for normal users.

- **tmp** The place to put smaller temporary files that you don't care much about. Any user may read to and write from /tmp, but they may not have permission to access another user's files there. Some programs use this directory as a workspace. If something is extremely important, don't put it in /tmp. Most distributions clear /tmp when the machine boots, and some even remove its old files periodically. Don't fill /tmp either, because its space is usually shared with something critical (like the rest of /, for example).

- **usr** Pronounced as "user," but this subdirectory does not contain user files (there have been no user files in /usr on Unix systems long before Linux existed). Instead, /usr is a large directory hierarchy that looks a little like the root. The bulk of the Linux system resides in /usr. Many of the directory names in /usr are the same as in the root and hold the same type of files; /usr/bin and /usr/lib are two examples. The primary reason that the root does not contain the complete system is to keep space requirements low. The /usr directory is so important that Section 2.1.3 is dedicated to it.

- **var** The "variable" subdirectory, where programs record runtime information. System logging, user tracking, caches, and other files that system programs create and tend all go into /var. There is a /var/tmp similar to /tmp, but the system doesn't wipe it clean on boot.

### 2.1.2 Other Root Subdirectories

There are a few other interesting subdirectories in the root:

- **boot** Contains kernel boot loader files. These files pertain only to the very first stage of the Linux startup process; you will not find information about how Linux starts up its services in this directory.

- **cdrom** Where most Linux distributions attach a CD drive; the contents of the disc are under this directory. The root may contain similar directories for other removable devices.

- **opt** May contain additional third-party software. Many systems don't use /opt.

### 2.1.3 The /usr Directory

The /usr directory may look relatively clean at first glance, but a quick look at /usr/bin and /usr/lib reveals that there's a lot here. In addition to the subdirectories that you just read about, /usr contains the following:

- **include**  Holds header files used by the C compiler (see Section 8.1.2).

- **info**  Contains GNU info pages (see Section 1.13).

- **local**  Where administrators can install their own software. Its structure should look like that of / and /usr.

- **man**  Contains manual pages. Unformatted pages go in the man* directories here (according to the numbered category described in Section 1.13), and human-readable formatted pages go in cat*.

- **share**  Contains files that should work on other kinds of Unix machines with no loss of functionality. That's the theory, anyway; a true share directory is becoming rare because there are no space issues on modern disks. It is often more of a pain to maintain a share directory than it's worth. In any case, man, info, and some other subdirectories are often found here.

- **X11R6**  Holds the core Linux windowing system software, called XFree86. However, the custom configuration files for your computer are usually in /etc/X11.

- **dict**  An oddball subdirectory containing dictionaries; /usr/dict/words is one such dictionary file.

## 2.2 The Kernel

You now know what the Linux directory structure looks like. Before going on to devices and filesystems, you must learn some higher-level concepts about the kernel.

The *kernel* of an operating system is the very core of a running system. It's a very special program that manages all processes, device drivers, and I/O. When the system boots, the kernel runs first, initializing hardware and internal data structures. After the kernel completes this stage, it loads and starts the init program.

The kernel also has many functions once the system boots. Process and device management are the most important. The idea is that although computers with one CPU run only one program at a time, the kernel can keep several programs in memory at the same time. Process and device management run together in a cycle like this:

1. The kernel has control of the processor. There are several processes in memory.
2. The kernel selects a process and finds out where that process was last running.
3. The kernel relinquishes control of the processor to that process.
4. That process runs for a few microseconds.
5. When the time is up, a clock interrupt stops the process and gives control back to the kernel.

6.  The kernel takes care of any system work that it needs to do, such as reading to and from devices.

7.  Go to step 2.

This description of the kernel's work is somewhat simplified, but as you can see, there is nothing magic about the kernel. It is not a process; it is just a piece of code that runs every now and then *between* processes.

On Linux systems, the kernel is normally in a file called /vmlinuz or /boot/vmlinuz. A *boot loader* loads this file into memory and sets it in motion when the system boots. Details on to how to configure the boot loader and how to create a Linux kernel are in Chapters 3 and 10.

If you are interested in the detailed workings of a kernel, the classic textbook is *Operating System Concepts* [Silberschatz].

## 2.3 Devices

You will find it very easy to manipulate devices on a Unix system because the kernel normally presents the device I/O interface to system and user processes as files. Not only can a programmer use regular file operations to work with a device, but some devices are also accessible to standard programs like cat, so you don't have to be a programmer to use a device. Linux uses the same design of device files as other Unix flavors, but device filenames and functionality vary among flavors.

Linix device files are in the /dev directory, and running ls /dev reveals that there are more than a few files in /dev. So how do you work with devices?

To get started, consider this command:

```
echo blah blah > /dev/null
```

Like any command with redirected output, this sends some stuff on the standard output to a file. However, the file is /dev/null, a device, and the kernel decides what to do with any data written to this device. In the case of /dev/null, the kernel simply ignores the data (making /dev/null a *bitbucket*). Of course, other devices actually do things, such as /dev/dsp, which plays a sound if you send appropriate output there (for example, cat blab.wav > /dev/dsp).

To identify a device, use ls -l to get a long listing and look at the permissions. Here are four examples:

```
brw-rw----  1 root   disk   3,  65 Jul 20  1998 hdb1
crw-rw-rw-  1 root   root   1,   3 Jul 20  1998 null
prw-r--r--  1 root   root        0 Mar  3 19:17 gpmdata
srw-rw-rw-  1 root   root        0 Dec 18 07:43 log
```

Notice the very first character of each line in the listing. If this character is b, c, p, or s, then the file is a device. These letters stand for *block, character, pipe,* and *socket,* respectively:

- **Block device**   Programs access data in a *block device* in fixed chunks. The hdb1 in the preceding example is a disk device. Because disks break down into blocks of data, it is only natural that a disk be a block device. A block device's total size is fixed, and a program has random access to any block in the device.

- **Character device**   *Character devices* work with data streams. You can only read characters from or write characters to these devices, like /dev/null in the previous example. Character devices don't have a size; when you read from or write to a character device, the kernel usually performs a read or write operation on the device, leaving no record of the activity inside the kernel. Printers are character devices, and after the kernel sends data to a printer, the responsibility for that data passes to the printer; the kernel cannot back up and reexamine the data stream.

- **Pipe device**   *Named pipes* are like character devices, but there is another process at the other end of the I/O stream instead of a kernel driver. An example of such a process is gpm, a program that can duplicate mouse events and send them to the named pipe /dev/gpmdata for use by other programs.

- **Socket device**   *Sockets* are special-purpose I/O files offering a type of network interface. For example, the gpm program accepts control commands through the /dev/gpmctl socket. You don't need to worry about sockets if you're not a network programmer.

The numbers before the dates in the first two lines of the previous listing are the *major* and *minor* device numbers that help the kernel identify the device. Similar devices usually have the same major number, such as hda3 and hdb1 (these are both hard disk partitions).

### 2.3.1 dd and Devices

The name dd stands for convert and copy. dd is extremely useful when working with block and character devices. This program's sole function is to read from an input file or stream and write to an output file or stream, possibly doing some encoding conversion on the way. It was originally developed for reblocking.

dd copies data in blocks of a fixed size. Here is an example of using dd with a character device and some common options:

```
dd if=/dev/zero of=new_file bs=1024 count=1
```

As you can see, the dd option format is different than the option formats of most other Unix commands; rather than use the - character to signal an option, you name an option and set its value to something with the = sign. The preceding example copies a single 1024-byte block from /dev/zero (a continuous stream of zero bytes) to the file new_file. These are the important dd options:

- **if=*file*** The input file. The default is the standard input.

- **of=*file*** The output file. The default is the standard output.

- **bs=*size*** The block size; dd reads and writes this many bytes of data at a time. To abbreviate large chunks of data, you may use b and k to signify 512 and 1024 bytes. Therefore, the example above could read bs=1k instead of bs=1024.

- **ibs=*size*, obs=*size*** The input and output block sizes. If you can use the same block size for both input and output, use the bs option, but if this is impossible, then use ibs and obs for input and output, respectively.

- **count=*num*** The total number of blocks to copy. When working with a huge file, or with a device that supplies an endless stream of data (like /dev/zero), you want dd to stop at a fixed point. Otherwise you could waste a lot of disk space, CPU time, or both. count can be used in conjunction with the skip parameter to copy a small piece out of a large file or device.

- **skip=*num*** Skip past the first *num* blocks in the input file or stream; do not copy them to the output.

### 2.3.2 Device Name Summary

Sometimes it is difficult to find the name of a device (for example, when partitioning a disk). Here are two tactics for finding out:

- Guess the name from the output of the dmesg command (which prints out the last few kernel messages) or the kernel system log file (see Section 4.1); this output might contain a description of the devices on your system.

- Run cat /proc/devices to see the block and character devices for which your system currently has drivers. Each line consists of a number and name. The number is the major number of the device described in Section 2.3. If you can guess the device from the name, look in /dev for the character or block devices with the corresponding major number, and you've found the device files.

Neither method is terribly reliable, especially because the kernel does not load certain device drivers until you try to use them. (Section 10.8 has information on the driver-loading mechanism.)

The following sections list the most common Linux devices and their naming conventions.

### Hard Disks: /dev/hd*

These are the ATA (IDE) disks and partitions. All are block devices.

Two example names are /dev/hda1 and /dev/hdb. The letter after hd identifies the disk, and the number represents the partition. A device without a number is a device for an entire disk. (Information on how to partition disks is in Section 2.3.4. To connect disks to your current systems, start at Section 2.4.3.)

### SCSI Disks: /dev/sd*

SCSI disks carry the names /dev/sda, /dev/sdb, and so on, and the disks work much like their ATA counterparts, although the SCSI disk names do not directly correspond to a SCSI host controller and target. Linux assigns the devices in the order that it encounters the disks.

For example, if you have two SCSI controllers, scsi0 and scsi1, with disks at scsi0 targets 0, 3, and scsi1 target 1, the device assignments are as shown in Table 2-1.

**Table 2-1:** Sample Device Assignments

| Controller | Target | Device Assignment |
|------------|--------|-------------------|
| scsi0      | 0      | /dev/sda          |
| scsi0      | 3      | /dev/sdb          |
| scsi1      | 1      | /dev/sdc          |

This naming scheme can cause problems when reconfiguring hardware. Let's say that scsi0 target 3 explodes and you must remove the disk so that the machine can work again. When you do so, scsi1 target 1 moves to /dev/sdb from /dev/sdc, and you have to change the fstab file (described later in this chapter).

### Terminals: /dev/tty*, /dev/pts/*, /dev/tty

Terminals are devices for moving characters between the system and an I/O device, usually for text output to a terminal screen. The terminal device interface goes back a long way, to the days when terminals were typewriter-based devices.

*Pseudo-terminal* devices are emulated terminals that understand the I/O features of real terminals, but rather than talk to a real piece of hardware, the kernel presents the I/O interface to a piece of software, such as a shell window.

Two common terminal devices are /dev/tty1 (the first virtual console) and /dev/pts/0 (the first pseudo-terminal device).

The /dev/tty device is the controlling terminal of the current process. If a program is currently reading from and writing to a terminal, this device is a synonym for that terminal. A process does not need to be attached to a terminal.

### Serial Ports: /dev/ttyS*

Serial ports are special terminal devices. You can't do much on the command line with serial port devices because there are too many settings to worry about, such as baud rate and flow control.

The port known as COM1 on Windows is /dev/ttyS0, COM2 is /dev/ttyS1, and so on. For add-in modem cards, check the output of the dmesg command for the port assignment.

### Floppy Disks: /dev/fd*

Section 11.1.1 covers operations on these block devices. The 3.5-inch floppy on most modern systems is /dev/fd0.

### Parallel Ports: /dev/lp0, /dev/lp1

These unidirectional port devices correspond to LPT1 and LPT2 in Windows. You can send files (such as a file to be printed) directly to a parallel port with the cat command, but you might need to give the printer an extra form feed or reset afterward.

The bidirectional parallel ports are /dev/parport0 and /dev/parport1.

### Audio Devices: /dev/dsp, /dev/audio, /dev/mixer, /dev/snd/*, etc.

Linux has two different sets of audio devices. There are separate devices for the OSS (Open Sound System) and the newer ALSA (Advanced Linux Sound Architecture) system interface. Linux systems that use ALSA usually contain OSS compatibility devices, because most applications still use OSS. Some rudimentary operations are possible with the dsp and audio devices that belong to OSS. As mentioned earlier, the computer plays any WAV file that you send to /dev/dsp. However, it may not sound right due to frequency mismatches. The ALSA devices are in the /dev/snd directory, but you can't do much by redirecting standard I/O to them.

**NOTE**    *The* play *and* aplay *programs can play samples from the command line. To adjust the volume and mixer settings,* aumix *and* alsamixer *are available on most systems.*

## 2.3.3 Creating Device Files

To create one individual device file, use mknod. You must know the device name as well as its major and minor numbers. For example, if you remove /dev/hda2 by accident, you can create it again with this command:

```
mknod /dev/hda2 b 3 2
```

The b 3 2 specifies a block device with a major number 3 and a minor number 2. For character or named pipe devices, use c or p instead of b.

The mknod command is useful only for creating the occasional missing device or named pipe. As you upgrade your system and add device drivers, you may need to create entirely new groups of devices. Because there are so many devices, it's better to use the MAKEDEV program (found in /dev) to create groups of devices. Device groups can be named after the common part of several device names, such as hda, or they can have a completely separate name, such as std-hd. For example, to create all devices beginning with hda, run this command:

```
/dev/MAKEDEV hda
```

**NOTE**    *The* MAKEDEV *command is harmless if the devices already exist on your system.*

### devfs

Before you go to the trouble of making any device files, you should see whether you're running devfs, an automatic device-file generation system. The easiest way to check for devfs is to run mount and look for devfs in the output.

If your system runs devfs, you should not have to create missing device files because the kernel maintains the directory of available device files. Linux kernels typically configure devfs at boot time, starting a special auxiliary system program called devfsd that gives the administrator the ability to customize the device system.

**NOTE**    devfs *was an experimental feature in older Linux kernels, but is classified as obsolete in the latest Linux kernels.*

## 2.3.4 Partitioning Disk Devices

Before you can use a new disk on your system, you need to know how to partition disks with their device files. If you've never worked with partitions before, don't worry. A disk *partition* is just a piece of the disk dedicated to one purpose, such as a specific directory tree. On PCs, partitions have numbers starting at 1.

To get started, identify the disk device that you want to partition. Most PCs have two ATA interfaces, called primary and secondary interfaces, and each interface can have a master and slave disk, for a total of four disk devices. The standard ATA disk assignments are as follows:

- **/dev/hda**   Master disk, primary interface
- **/dev/hdb**   Slave disk, primary interface
- **/dev/hdc**   Master disk, secondary interface
- **/dev/hdd**   Slave disk, secondary interface

There are several partitioning utilities, but the most simple and direct is fdisk. To get started, run fdisk *dev* (where *dev* is one of the devices listed above), then print the current partition list with p.

Here is sample from fdisk output for a device with three partitions, two containing filesystems and one with swap (see Section 2.5 for more information on swap partitions).

```
Disk /dev/hda: 240 heads, 63 sectors, 2584 cylinders
Units = cylinders of 15120 * 512 bytes

Device Boot      Start       End    Blocks   Id  System
/dev/hda1            1       136  1028128+   83  Linux
/dev/hda2          137       204   514080   82  Linux swap
/dev/hda3          205      2584 17992800   83  Linux
```

Partition dimensions are usually in units of *cylinders*. Each partition has a start and end cylinder, determining its size, but the amount of space per cylinder varies depending on the disk. The second line in the preceding output shows you the cylinder size, but you don't need to do any weird computations to create partitions.

When creating a new partition, you only need to know the starting cylinder. Cylinders do not overlap in PC partitions, so if you're partitioning a disk, pick the first available cylinder in the fdisk partition list output. In the preceding example, you would choose 2585 as the starting cylinder.

Each partition also has a *system ID*, a number that represents an operating system. Linux uses 83 for partitions containing files and 82 for Linux swap.

When you partition a new disk, there is usually one partition on the disk already, containing some sort of variant on the FAT filesystem for Microsoft systems. If you want only a single partition on the disk, just change the system ID to Linux with the t command inside fdisk. However, if you want to customize the partitions, use d to delete any old partitions and n to add new ones.

fdisk is easy to use because each command steps you through the partition number and size. In addition, there is an important safety feature: fdisk does not actually change the partition table until you tell it to with the w command. If you're uneasy about your changes, or you were just testing something, use q to exit without altering the disk.

Here is an example of fdisk in action on a very small disk. Command input is in boldface:

```
# fdisk /dev/hdc

Command (m for help): p

Disk /dev/hdc: 2 heads, 16 sectors, 247 cylinders
Units = cylinders of 32 * 512 bytes

   Device Boot      Start       End    Blocks   Id  System
/dev/hdc1    *           1       494     7891+   1   FAT12

Command (m for help): d
Partition number (1-4): 1

Command (m for help): n
```

```
Command action
   e   extended
   p   primary partition (1-4)
p
Partition number (1-4): 1
Last cylinder or +size or +sizeM or +sizeK (1-247, default 247): 120

Command (m for help): t
Partition number (1-4): 1
Hex code (type L to list codes): 83

Command (m for help): p

Disk /dev/hdc: 2 heads, 16 sectors, 247 cylinders
Units = cylinders of 32 * 512 bytes

   Device Boot    Start      End    Blocks   Id  System
/dev/hdc1              1      120      1912   83  Linux

Command (m for help): w
The partition table has been altered!

Calling ioctl() to re-read partition table.

WARNING: If you have created or modified any DOS 6.x
partitions, please see the fdisk manual page for additional
information.
Syncing disks.
```

When you write the partition table to the disk with the w command, fdisk tells the kernel to re-read the partition table from the disk and update the system's in-memory partition list (fdisk does not relay the new partition list directly to the kernel). Therefore, you should never write the partition table to a disk that already has a mounted (attached) filesystem; doing so risks damage to the filesystem.

**NOTE**    *The ioctl operation that causes the kernel to re-read the partition table can fail on rare occasions. If such a failure occurs, you need to reboot the system to get the kernel to see the changes.*

After writing the partition table, a new list of partition tables should appear on the console. If you don't see this list, run dmesg to see the kernel messages and look at the end of the output. For the fdisk session earlier in this section, here is what you would see:

```
hdc: hdc1
```

The hda indicates the disk that you repartitioned. The new partition list appears after the colon. For example, if you create three partitions on the disk, the output might appear as hdc: hdc1 hdc2 hdc3.

*Looking at the* fdisk *session in this section, you may be wondering what the difference between a primary and an extended partition is. The standard PC disk-partitioning scheme originally only allowed a maximum of four partitions, 1–4. These are the primary partitions. If you want more partitions,* fdisk *can designate one of these primary partitions as an extended partition, allowing you to place subpartitions in the extended partition. Each of these subpartitions is called a* logical partition.

After partitioning a disk, you're not quite ready to attach it to your system because you must put a filesystem on your partition(s) first.

## 2.4 Filesystems

A *filesystem* is a database of files and directories that you can attach to a Unix system at the root (/) or some other directory (like /usr) in a currently attached filesystem. At one time, filesystems resided on disks and other physical media used exclusively for data storage. However, the tree-like directory structure and I/O interface of filesystems is quite versatile, so filesystems now perform a variety of tasks.

### 2.4.1 Filesystem Types

Linux supports an extraordinarily large number of filesystems, including native designs optimized for Linux, foreign types such as the Windows FAT family, universal filesystems like ISO9660, and others. The following list includes the most common types of filesystems for data storage; the type names as recognized by Linux are in parentheses next to the boldfaced filesystem names.

- The **Second Extended** filesystem (ext2) is native to Linux. It is fairly quick, and it defragments itself. Nearly every Linux system uses ext2 or its newer, journaled version, ext3.

- **Third Extended** filesystems (ext3) are ext2 filesystems augmented with journal support. This can make recovery from an abrupt system reboot or failure quicker and less painful.

- **ISO9660** (iso9660) is a CD-ROM standard. Most CD-ROMs use some variety of ISO9660 extension; Linux supports them.

- **FAT** filesystems (msdos, vfat, umsdos) pertain to Microsoft systems. The simple msdos type supports the very primitive monocase variety in MS-DOS systems. For Windows filesystems, use vfat. The umsdos filesystem is peculiar to Linux; it supports Unix features such as symbolic links on top of an MS-DOS filesystem. It is also not very common.

- The **Reiser** filesystem (reiserfs) is relatively new. It supports a journal and is optimized for fairly small files, a condition that often occurs in Unix systems.

## 2.4.2 Creating a Filesystem

You cannot mount and store files on a partition that does not contain a filesystem. The partitioning process described in Section 2.3.4 does not create any filesystems; you must place the filesystems on the partitions in a separate step. To create a Second Extended (ext2) filesystem, use the mke2fs program on the target device, as in this example for /dev/hdc3:

```
mke2fs /dev/hdc3
```

The mke2fs program automatically determines the number of blocks in a device and sets some reasonable defaults. Unless you really know what you're doing and feel like reading the mke2fs(8) manual page in detail, you shouldn't change these.

When you create a filesystem, you initialize its database, including the *superblock* and the *inode tables*. The superblock is at the top level of the database, and it's so important that mke2fs creates a number of backups in case the original is destroyed. You may wish to record a few of the superblock backup numbers when mke2fs runs, in case you need to recover it later in the event of a disk failure (see Section 2.4.8).

**WARNING** *Filesystem creation is a rare task that you should only need to perform after adding a new disk or repartitioning an old disk. You should create a filesystem just once for each new partition that has no preexisting data (or data that you want to remove). Creating a new filesystem on top of an existing filesystem will effectively destroy the old data.*

### Creating ext3 Filesystems

The only substantial difference between ext2 and ext3 filesystems is that ext3 filesystems have a *journal file* containing changes not yet written to the regular filesystem database. To create an ext3 filesystem, use the -j option to mke2fs:

```
mke2fs -j /dev/disk_device
```

Don't worry if you forget the -j option when creating a filesystem. You can add a journal file to an existing filesystem with the utility. Here's an example:

```
tune2fs -j /dev/hda1
```

When upgrading a filesystem to ext3, don't forget to change the ext2 to ext3 in the /etc/fstab file.

## 2.4.3 Mounting a Filesystem

On Unix, the process of attaching a filesystem is called *mounting*. When the system boots, the kernel reads some configuration data and mounts / based on that data. To mount a filesystem, you must know the following:

- The filesystem's device (such as a disk partition; where the actual filesystem data resides).

- The filesystem type, or design. Operating system developers use different types to adapt to their particular system for backward compatibility or for other reasons that aren't necessarily that good. For example, the ext2-/ext3-based filesystems common on Linux are quite different than the FAT-based types found on many Windows machines.

- The *mount point*; that is, the place in the current system's directory hierarchy where the filesystem will be attached. The mount point is always a normal directory. For instance, Linux uses /cdrom as a mount point for CD-ROM devices. The mount point need not be directly below /; it may be anywhere on the system.

When mounting a filesystem, the common terminology is "mount a device *on* a mount point." To learn the current filesystem status of your system, run mount. The output looks like this:

```
/dev/hda1 on / type ext2 (rw,errors=remount-ro)
proc on /proc type proc (rw)
/dev/hda3 on /usr type ext2 (rw)
tmpfs on /dev/shm type tmpfs (rw)
none on /proc/bus/usb type usbdevfs (rw)
```

Each line corresponds to one currently mounted filesystem, with items in this order:

- The device, such as /dev/hda3. Notice that some of these aren't real devices (proc, for example); these are stand-ins for real device names, because these special-purpose filesystems do not need devices.

- The word on.

- The mount point.

- The word type.

- The filesystem type, usually in the form of a short identifier.

- Mount options (in parentheses) — see Section 2.4.5 for more details.

To mount a filesystem, use the mount command as follows with the filesystem type, device, and desired mount point:

```
mount -t type device mountpoint
```

For example, to mount the Second Extended filesystem /dev/hdb3 on /home/extra, use this command:

```
mount -t ext2 /dev/hdb3 /home/extra
```

To unmount (detach) a filesystem, use the umount command:

---

umount *mountpoint*

---

See Section 2.4.6 for a few more long options.

## 2.4.4 Filesystem Buffering

Linux, like other versions of Unix, buffers (caches) all requested changes to filesystems in memory before actually writing the changes to the disk. This cache system is transparent to the user and improves performance because the kernel can perform a large collection of file writes at once instead of performing the changes on demand.

When you unmount a filesystem with umount, the kernel automatically synchronizes with the disk. At any other time, you can force the kernel to write the changes in its buffer to the disk by running the sync command. If (for whatever reason) you can't unmount a filesystem before you turn off the system, make sure that you run sync first.

## 2.4.5 Filesystem Mount Options

There are many ways to change the mount command behavior. This is often necessary with removable media or when performing system maintenance.

The total number of mount options is staggering. The very extensive mount(8) manual page is a good reference, but it's hard to know where to start and what you can safely ignore.

Options fall into two rough categories: general options and filesystem-specific options. General options include -t for specifying the filesystem type, which was mentioned earlier. By contrast, a filesystem-specific option pertains only to certain filesystem types. To activate a filesystem option, use the -o switch followed by the option. For example, -o norock turns off Rock Ridge extensions on an ISO9660 filesystem, but it has no meaning for any other kind of filesystem.

### Short Options

The most important general options are the following:

-r   The -r option mounts the filesystem in read-only mode. This has a number of uses, from write protection to bootstrapping. You don't need to specify this option when accessing a read-only device such as a CD-ROM; the system will do it for you (and will also tell you about the read-only status).

-n   The -n option ensures that mount does not try to update the system mount database, /etc/mtab. The mount operation fails when it cannot write to this file. This is important at boot time, because the root partition (and therefore, the system mount database) are read-only at first. You will also find this option handy if you are trying to fix a system problem in single-user mode (see Section 3.2.4), because the system mount database may not be available at the time.

**-t**   The -t *type* option specifies the filesystem type.

## Long Options

Short options like -r are too limited for the ever-increasing number of mount options; there are too few letters in the alphabet to accommodate all possible options. Short options are also troublesome because it is difficult to determine an option's meaning based on a single letter. Many general options and all filesystem-specific options use a longer, more flexible option format.

To use long options with mount on the command line, start with -o and supply some keywords. Here is a complete example with the long options in boldface:

```
mount -t vfat /dev/hda1 /dos -o ro,conv=auto
```

There are two long options here, ro and conv=auto. The ro option specifies read-only mode, and it is the same as the -r short option. The conv=auto option is a filesystem option telling the kernel to automatically convert certain text files from the DOS newline format to the Unix style (which will be explained shortly).

The most useful long options are the following:

**exec, noexec**   Enables or disables execution of programs on the filesystem.

**suid, nosuid**   Enables or disables setuid programs (see Section 1.17).

**ro, rw**   Mounts the filesystem as read-only or read-write.

**remount**   Reattaches a currently mounted filesystem at the same mount point. The only real reason to do this is to change mount options, and the most frequent case is making a read-only filesystem writable. An example of why you might use this is when the system leaves the root in read-only mode during crash recovery. The following command remounts the root in read-write mode (you need the -n option because the mount command cannot write to the system mount database when the root is read-only):

```
mount -n -o remount /
```

The preceding command assumes that the correct device listing for / is in /etc/fstab (explained in the next section). If it is not, you must specify the device.

**norock, nojoliet**   (ISO9660 filesystem) Disables Rock Ridge (Unix) or Joliet (Microsoft) extensions. Be warned that plain, raw ISO9660 is really ugly.

**conv=*rule*** (FAT-based filesystems) Converts the newline characters in files based on *rule*, which can be binary, text, or auto. The default is binary, which disables any character translation. To treat all files as text, use text. The auto setting converts files based on their extension. For example, a .jpg file gets no special treatment, but a .txt file does. Be careful with this option, because it can damage files. You may want to use it in read-only mode.

### 2.4.6 The /etc/fstab Filesystem Table

To mount filesystems at boot time and take the drudgery out of the mount command, Linux systems keep a permanent list of filesystems and options in /etc/fstab. This is a plain text file in a very simple format, as this example shows:

```
/dev/hda1   /       ext2      defaults,errors=remount-ro   0 1
/dev/hda2   none    swap      sw                           0 0
/dev/hda3   /usr    ext2      defaults                     0 2
proc        /proc   proc      defaults                     0 0
/dev/hdc    /cdrom  iso9660   ro,user,nosuid,noauto        0 0
```

Each line corresponds to one filesystem, broken into six fields:

- The device. Notice that the /proc entry has a stand-in device.
- The mount point.
- The filesystem type. You may not recognize swap, for /dev/hda2. This is a swap partition (see Section 2.5).
- Options.
- Backup information for the dump command; dump does not see common use, but you should always specify this field with a 0.
- The filesystem integrity test order (see the fsck command in Section 2.4.8). To ensure that fsck always runs on the root first, you should always set this to 1 for the root filesystem and 2 for any other filesystems on a hard disk. Use 0 to disable the bootup check for everything else, including CD-ROM drives, swap, and the /proc filesystem.

When using mount, you can take some shortcuts if the filesystem you want to work with is in /etc/fstab. For the example fstab above, to mount a CD-ROM, you need only run

```
mount /cdrom
```

You can also try to mount all entries in /etc/fstab that do not contain the noauto option at once, with this command:

```
mount -a
```

You may have noticed some new options in the preceding fstab listing, namely defaults, errors, noauto, and user. These aren't covered in Section 2.4.5 because they don't make any sense outside of the /etc/fstab file. The meanings are as follows:

**defaults** This uses the mount defaults — read-write mode, enable device files, executables, the setuid bit, and so on. You should use this when you don't want to give the filesystem any special options, but you do want to fill all fields in /etc/fstab.

**errors** This ext2-specific parameter sets the system behavior if there is trouble mounting a filesystem. The default is normally errors=continue, meaning that the kernel should return an error code and keep running. To get the kernel to try again in read-only mode, use errors=remount-ro. The errors=panic setting tells the kernel (and your system) to halt when there is a problem.

**noauto** This option tells a mount -a command to ignore the entry. Use this to prevent a boot-time mount of a removable-media device, such as a CD-ROM or floppy drive.

**user** This option allows normal users to run mount on this entry. This can be handy for enabling access to CD-ROM drives. Because users can put a setuid-root file on removable media with another system, this option also sets nosuid, noexec, and nodev (to bar special device files). The fstab example in this section explicitly sets nosuid.

### 2.4.7 Filesystem Capacity

To view the size and utilization of your currently mounted filesystems, use the df command. The output looks like this:

| Filesystem | 1024-blocks | Used | Available | Capacity | Mounted on |
|---|---|---|---|---|---|
| /dev/hda1 | 1011928 | 71400 | 889124 | 7% | / |
| /dev/hda3 | 17710044 | 9485296 | 7325108 | 56% | /usr |

The listing has the following fields:

**Filesystem** The filesystem device

**1024-blocks** The total capacity of the filesystem in blocks of 1024 bytes

**Used** The number of occupied blocks

**Available** The number of free blocks

**Capacity** The percentage of blocks in use

**Mounted on** The mount point

It is relatively easy to see that the two filesystems here are roughly 1GB and 17.5GB in size. However, the capacity numbers may look a little strange because 71400 + 889124 does not equal 1011928, and 9485296 does not constitute 56 percent of 17710044. In both cases, 5 percent of the total capacity is unaccounted for. Nevertheless, the space is there. These hidden blocks are called the *reserved* blocks, and only the superuser may use the space if the rest of the partition fills up. This keeps system servers from immediately failing when they run out of disk space.

If your disk fills up and you need to know where all of those space-hogging, illegal MP3s are, use the du command. With no arguments, du prints the disk usage of every directory in the directory hierarchy, starting at the current working directory. (That's kind of a mouthful, so just run cd /; du to get the idea. Press CONTROL-C when you get bored.) The du -s command turns on summary mode to print only the grand total. If you want to evaluate a particular directory, change to that directory and run du -s *.

The following pipeline is a handy way to create a searchable output file (du_out) and see the results on the terminal at the same time.

```
du | tee du_out
```

## 2.4.8 Checking and Repairing Filesystems

The optimizations that Unix filesystems offer are made possible by a sophisticated database-like mechanism. For filesystems to work seamlessly, the kernel has to trust that there are no errors in a mounted filesystem. Otherwise, serious errors such as data loss and system crashes can happen.

The most frequent cause of a filesystem error is shutting down the system in a rude way (for example, with the power switch on the computer). The system's filesystem cache in memory may not match the data on the disk, and the system also may be in the process of altering the filesystem when you decide to give the computer a kick. Even though a new generation of filesystems supports journals to make filesystem corruption far less common, you should always shut the system down properly (see Section 3.1.5). Furthermore, filesystem checks are still necessary every now and then as sanity checks.

You need to remember one command name to check a filesystem: fsck. However, there is a different version of this tool for each filesystem type that Linux supports. The information presented here is specific to second and third extended (ext2/ext3) filesystems and the e2fsck utility. You generally don't need to type e2fsck, though, unless fsck can't figure out the filesystem type, or you're looking for the e2fsck manual page.

To run fsck in interactive manual mode, use the device or the mount point (in /etc/fstab) as the argument. For example:

```
fsck /dev/hdd1
```

*Never use* fsck *on a mounted filesystem. The kernel may alter the disk data as you run the check, causing mismatches that can crash your system and corrupt files. There is only one exception. If you mount the root as read-only in single user mode, you may use* fsck *on the root filesystem.*

In manual mode, fsck prints verbose status reports on its passes, which should look something like this when there are no problems:

```
Pass 1: Checking inodes, blocks, and sizes
Pass 2: Checking directory structure
Pass 3: Checking directory connectivity
Pass 4: Checking reference counts
Pass 5: Checking group summary information
/dev/hdd1: 11/1976 files (0.0% non-contiguous), 265/7891 blocks
```

If fsck finds a problem in manual mode, it stops and asks you a question relevant to fixing the problem. These questions deal with the internal structure of the filesystem, such as reconnecting loose inodes and clearing blocks. The reconnection business means that fsck found a file that doesn't appear to have a name; reconnecting places the file in the lost+found directory filesystem as a number. You need to guess the name based on the content of the file.

In general, it's pointless to sit through the fsck process if you just made the mistake of an impolite shutdown. e2fsck has a -p option to automatically fix silly problems without asking you, aborting if there is a serious error. This is so common that Linux distributions run some variant of fsck -p at boot time (fsck -a is also common).

However, if you suspect that there is some major disaster, such as a hardware failure or device misconfiguration, you need to decide on a course of action, because fsck can really mess up a filesystem with larger problems. A telltale sign of a serious problem is a *lot* of questions in manual mode.

If you think that something really bad happened, try running fsck -n to check over the filesystem without modifying anything. If there's some sort of problem with the device configuration (an incorrect number of blocks in the partition table, loose cables, whatever) that you think you can fix, then fix it before running fsck for real. You're likely to lose a lot of data otherwise.

If you suspect that only the *superblock*, a key filesystem database component, is corrupt (for example, someone wrote to the beginning of the disk partition), you might be able to recover the filesystem with one of the superblock backups that mke2fs creates. Use fsck -b *num* to replace the corrupted superblock with an alternate at block *num*.

You may not know where to find a backup superblock, because you didn't write the numbers down when mke2fs ran. If the filesystem was created with the default values, you can try mke2fs -n on the device to view a list of superblock backup numbers without destroying your data (again, *make dead sure* that you're using -n, because you'll *really* tear up the filesystem otherwise).

If the device still appears to function properly except for a few small parts, you can run `fsck -c` before a manual `fsck` to search for bad blocks. Such a failure is somewhat rare.

### Checking ext3 Filesystems

You normally do not need to check ext3 filesystems because the journal ensures data integrity. However, you may wish to mount an ext3 filesystem in ext2 mode. The kernel will not mount an ext3 filesystem that contains a non-empty journal (if you don't shut your system down cleanly, you can expect that the journal contains some data). To flush the journal in an ext3 filesystem to the regular filesystem database, run `e2fsck` as follows:

```
e2fsck -fy /dev/disk_device
```

### The Worst Case

Disk problems that are worse in severity leave you with few choices:

- You can try to pull the entire filesystem from the disk with `dd` and transfer it to a partition on another disk that's the same size.
- You could try to patch up the filesystem as well as you can, mount it in read-only mode, and salvage what you can.

In both cases, you still need to repair the filesystem before you mount it (unless you feel like picking through the raw data by hand). To answer y to all of the `fsck` questions, use `fsck -y`, but do this as a last resort.

**NOTE**    *There is an advanced utility called* debugfs *for users with in-depth knowledge of filesystems, or for those who feel like experimenting on a filesystem that isn't important.*

If you're really desperate, such as in the event of a catastrophic disk failure without backups, there isn't a lot you can do other than try to get a professional service to "scrape the platters."

## 2.4.9 Special-Purpose Filesystems

Not all filesystems represent storage on physical media. Most versions of Unix have filesystems that serve as system interfaces. This idea goes back a long way; the /dev mechanism is an early model of using files for I/O interfaces. The /proc idea came from the eighth edition of research Unix [Killian]. Things really got rolling when the people at Bell Labs (including many of the original Unix designers) created Plan 9 [Bell Labs], a research operating system that took filesystem abstraction to a whole new level.

The special filesystem types in common use on Linux include the following:

**proc**, mounted on /proc. The name "proc" is actually an abbreviation of "process." Each *numbered* directory inside /proc is actually the process ID of a current process on the system, and the files in those directories represent various aspects of the processes. /proc/self represents the current process. The Linux proc filesystem includes a great deal of additional kernel and hardware information, such as /proc/cpuinfo. Purists shudder and say that this additional information does not belong in /proc, but rather in /dev or some other directory, but it's probably too late to change it in Linux now.

**usbdevfs**, mounted on /proc/bus/usb. Programs that interact with the USB interface and its devices often need the files here. The files in a usbdevfs filesystem provide interesting information on the bus status.

**tmpfs**, mounted on /dev/shm. You can employ your physical memory and swap space as temporary storage with tmpfs. You can mount tmpfs wherever you like, using the size and nr_blocks long options to control the maximum size. However, you must be careful not to pour things into a tmpfs, because your system will eventually run out of memory, and programs will start to crash. For years, Sun systems used a version of tmpfs for /tmp, and this is a frequent problem on long-running systems.

## 2.5 Swap and Virtual Memory

If you run out of real memory, Linux has a virtual memory system that automatically moves memory pages (chunks) to and from a hard disk. This is called *swapping*, because the pages of idle programs are swapped to the disk in exchange for active pages residing on the disk. The disk area used to store memory pages is called *swap space*.

The free command's output includes the current swap usage in kilobytes as follows:

|       | total  | used   | free   |
|-------|--------|--------|--------|
| ...   | ...    | ...    | ...    |
| Swap: | 514072 | 189804 | 324268 |

### 2.5.1 Using a Disk Partition as Swap Space

To use an entire disk partition as swap, follow these steps:

1.  Make certain that the partition is empty.
2.  Run mkswap *dev*, where *dev* is the partition's device. This command puts a swap signature on the partition.
3.  Execute swapon *dev* to register the space with the kernel.

After creating a swap partition, you can put a new swap entry in your /etc/fstab to make the system use the swap space as soon as the machine boots. This entry is from the fstab example in Section 2.4.6:

```
/dev/hda2   none   swap   sw                      0 0
```

## 2.5.2 Using a File as Swap Space

You can also use a regular file as swap space. It's not quite as fast as a swap partition, but if you're in a pinch where you would be forced to repartition the disk to use a swap partition, using a file as swap space works fine.

Use these commands to create an empty file, initialize it as swap, and add it to the swap pool:

```
dd if=/dev/zero of=swap_file bs=1024k count=num_mb
mkswap swap_file
swapon swap_file
```

Here, *swap_file* is the name of the new swap file, and *num_mb* is the desired size, in megabytes.

To remove a swap partition or file from the kernel's active pool, use the swapoff command.

## 2.5.3 How Much Swap Do You Need?

At one time, the Unix conventional wisdom said that you should always reserve at least twice as much swap as you have real memory. The enormous disk and memory capacities now available cloud the issue. On one hand, disk space is so plentiful that double the memory size may seem inadequate, given the amount of disk space available. On the other hand, you may never even dip into your swap space because you have so much real memory.

Some things never change, though. Reserve two to five times as much disk space as you have real memory for swap. It doesn't make sense to go any lower, because you may actually risk running out of memory. If you go higher and actually intend to use all of this swap space, you will likely suffer serious performance problems because the system will spend all of its time swapping (a condition known as *thrashing*).

# HOW LINUX BOOTS

You now know the physical structure of a Linux system, what the kernel is, and how to work with processes. This chapter teaches you how the system starts *(boots)* — that is, how the kernel gets into memory and how the regular system processes get started.

As it turns out, there isn't much to the boot process:

1. A boot loader finds the kernel image on the disk, loads it into memory, and starts it.
2. The kernel initializes the devices and its drivers.
3. The kernel mounts the root filesystem.
4. The kernel starts a program called init.
5. init sets the rest of the processes in motion.
6. The last processes that init starts as part of the boot sequence allow you to log in.

Identifying each stage of the boot process is invaluable in fixing boot problems and understanding the system as a whole. To start, zero in on the boot loader, which is the initial screen or prompt you get after the computer does its power-on self-test, asking which operating system to run. After you make a choice, the boot loader runs the Linux kernel, handing control of the system to the kernel.

There is a detailed discussion of the kernel elsewhere in this book (Section 2.2 explains the role of the kernel, and Chapter 10 tells you how to build one yourself), but this chapter covers the kernel initialization stage, the stage when the kernel prints a bunch of messages about the hardware present on the system. The kernel starts init just after it displays a message proclaiming that the kernel has mounted the root filesystem:

```
VFS: Mounted root (ext2 filesystem) readonly.
```

Soon after, you will see a message about init starting, followed by system service startup messages, and finally you get a login prompt of some sort.

**NOTE**  *On Red Hat Linux, the* init *note is especially obvious, because it "welcomes" you to "Red Hat Linux." All messages thereafter show success or failure in brackets at the right-hand side of the screen.*

Most of this chapter deals with init, because it is the part of the boot sequence where you have the most control. Section 3.2 deals with the boot loaders.

# 3.1 init

There is nothing special about init. It is a program just like any other on the Linux system, and you'll find it in /sbin along with other system binaries. The main purpose of init is to start and stop other programs in a particular sequence. All you have to know is how this sequence works.

There are a few different variations, but most Linux distributions use the System V style discussed here. Some distributions use a simpler version that resembles the BSD init, but you are unlikely to encounter this.

## 3.1.1 Runlevels

At any given time on a Linux system, a certain base set of processes are running. This state of the machine is called its *runlevel*, and it is denoted with a number from 0 through 6. The system spends most of its time in a single runlevel. However, when you shut the machine down, init switches to a different runlevel in order to terminate the system services in an orderly fashion and to tell the kernel to stop. Yet another runlevel is for *single-user mode*, discussed in Section 3.2.4.

The easiest way to get a handle on runlevels is to examine the init configuration file, /etc/inittab. Look for a line like the following:

```
id:5:initdefault:
```

This line means that the default runlevel on the system is 5. All lines in the inittab file take this form, with four fields separated by colons occuring in the following order:

- A unique identifier (a short string, such as id in the preceding example)
- The applicable runlevel number(s)
- The action that init should take (in the preceding example, the action is to set the default runlevel to 5)
- A command to execute (optional)

There is no command to execute in the preceding initdefault example because a command doesn't make sense in the context of setting the default runlevel. Look a little further down in inittab, until you see a line like this:

```
l5:5:wait:/etc/rc.d/rc 5
```

This particular line is important because it triggers most of the system configuration and services through the rc*.d and init.d directories (see Section 3.1.2). You can see that init is set to execute a command called /etc/rc.d/rc 5 when in runlevel 5. The wait action tells when and how init runs the command: run rc 5 once when entering runlevel 5, and then wait for this command to finish before doing anything else.

There are several different actions in addition to initdefault and wait, especially pertaining to power management, and the inittab(5) manual page tells you all about them. The ones that you're most likely to encounter are explained in the following sections.

### respawn

The respawn action causes init to run the command that follows, and if the command finishes executing, to run it again. You're likely to see something similar to this line in your inittab file:

```
1:2345:respawn:/sbin/mingetty tty1
```

The getty programs provide login prompts. The preceding line is for the first virtual console (/dev/tty1), the one you see when you press ALT-F1 or CONTROL-ALT-F1 (see Section 3.3). The respawn action brings the login prompt back after you log out.

### ctrlaltdel

The ctrlaltdel action controls what the system does when you press CONTROL-ALT-DELETE on a virtual console. On most systems, this is some sort of reboot command, using the shutdown command, which is covered in Section 3.1.5.

**sysinit**

The sysinit action is the very first thing that init should run when it starts up, before entering any runlevels.

### 3.1.2 How Processes in Runlevels Start

You are now ready to learn how init starts the system services, just before it lets you log in. Recall this inittab line from earlier:

```
l5:5:wait:/etc/rc.d/rc 5
```

This small line triggers many other programs. rc stands for *run commands*, and you will hear people refer to the commands as scripts, programs, or services. So, where are these commands, anyway?

For runlevel 5, in this example, the commands are probably either in /etc/rc.d/rc5.d or /etc/rc5.d. Runlevel 1 uses rc1.d, runlevel 2 uses rc2.d, and so on. You might find the following items in the rc5.d directory:

| | | |
|---|---|---|
| S10sysklogd | S20ppp | S99gpm |
| S12kerneld | S25netstd_nfs | S99httpd |
| S15netstd_init | S30netstd_misc | S99rmnologin |
| S18netbase | S45pcmcia | S99sshd |
| S20acct | S89atd | |
| S20logoutd | S89cron | |

The rc 5 command starts programs in this runlevel directory by running the following commands:

```
S10sysklogd start
S12kerneld start
S15netstd_init start
S18netbase start
  ...
  ...
S99sshd start
```

Notice the start argument in each command. The S in a command name means that the command should run in start mode, and the number (00 through 99) determines where in the sequence rc starts the command.

The rc*.d commands are usually shell scripts that start programs in /sbin or /usr/sbin. Normally, you can figure out what one of the commands actually does by looking at the script with less or another pager program.

You can start one of these services by hand. For example, if you want to start the httpd Web server program manually, run S99httpd start. Similarly, if you ever need to kill one of the services when the machine is on, you can run the command in the rc*.d directory with the stop argument (S99httpd stop, for instance).

Some rc*.d directories contain commands that start with ~~with~~ K (for "kill," or stop mode). In this case, rc runs the command with the stop argument instead of start. You are most likely to encounter K commands in runlevels that shut the system down.

### 3.1.3 Adding and Removing Services

If you want to add, delete, or modify services in the rc*.d directories, you need to take a closer look at the files inside. A long listing reveals a structure like this:

```
lrwxrwxrwx . . . S10sysklogd -> ../init.d/sysklogd
lrwxrwxrwx . . . S12kerneld -> ../init.d/kerneld
lrwxrwxrwx . . . S15netstd_init -> ../init.d/netstd_init
lrwxrwxrwx . . . S18netbase -> ../init.d/netbase
  ...
```

The commands in an rc*.d directory are actually symbolic links to files in an init.d directory, usually in /etc or /etc/rc.d. Linux distributions contain these links so that they can use the same startup scripts for all runlevels. This convention is by no means a requirement, but it often makes organization a little easier.

To prevent one of the commands in the init.d directory from running in a particular runlevel, you might think of removing the symbolic link in the appropriate rc*.d directory. This does work, but if you make a mistake and ever need to put the link back in place, you might have trouble remembering the exact name of the link. Therefore, you shouldn't remove links in the rc*.d directories, but rather, add an underscore (_) to the beginning of the link name like this:

```
mv S99httpd _S99httpd
```

At boot time, rc ignores _S99httpd because it doesn't start with S or K. Furthermore, the original name is still obvious, and you have quick access to the command if you're in a pinch and need to start it by hand.

To add a service, you must create a script like the others in the init.d directory and then make a symbolic link in the correct rc*.d directory. You may need to read Chapter 7 first if you aren't familiar with shell scripts. However, the easiest way to write a script is to examine the scripts already in init.d, make a copy of one that you understand, and modify the copy.

When adding a service, make sure that you choose an appropriate place in the boot sequence to start the service. If the service starts too soon, it may not work, due to a dependency on some other service. For non-essential services, most systems administrators prefer numbers in the 90s, after most of the services that came with the system.

Linux distributions usually come with a command to enable and disable services in the rc*.d directories. For example, in Debian, the command is update-rc.d, and in Red Hat Linux, the command is chkconfig. Graphical user interfaces are also available. Using these programs helps keep the startup directories consistent and helps with upgrades.

**HINT** *One of the most common Linux installation problems is an improperly configured XFree86 server that flicks on and off, making the system unusable on console. To stop this behavior, boot into single-user mode and alter your runlevel or runlevel services. Look for something containing* xdm, gdm *or* kdm *in your* rc*.d *directories, or your* /etc/inittab.

### 3.1.4 Controlling init

Occasionally, you need to give init a little kick to tell it to switch runlevels, to re-read the inittab file, or just to shut down the system. Because init is always the first process on a system, its process ID is always 1.

You can control init with telinit. For example, if you want to switch to runlevel 3, use this command:

```
telinit 3
```

When switching runlevels, init tries to kill off any processes that aren't in the inittab file for the new runlevel. Therefore, you should be careful about changing runlevels.

When you need to add or remove respawning jobs or make any other change to the inittab file, you must tell init about the change and cause it to re-read the file. Some people use kill -HUP 1 to tell init to do this. This traditional method works on most versions of Unix, as long as you type it correctly. However, you can also run this telinit command:

```
telinit q
```

You can also use telinit s to switch to single-user mode (see Section 3.2.4).

### 3.1.5 Shutting Down

init also controls how the system shuts down and reboots. The proper way to shut down a Linux machine is to use the shutdown command.

There are two basic ways to use shutdown. If you *halt* the system, it shuts the machine down and keeps it down. To make the machine halt immediately, use this command:

```
shutdown -h now
```

On most modern machines with reasonably recent versions of Linux, a halt cuts the power to the machine. You can also *reboot* the machine. For a reboot, use -r instead of -h.

The shutdown process takes several seconds. You should never reset or power off a machine during this stage. In the preceding example, now is the time to shut down. This argument is mandatory, but there are many ways of specifying it. If you want the machine to go down sometime in the future, one way is to use +*n*, where *n* is the number of minutes shutdown should wait before doing its work. For other options, look at the shutdown(8) manual page.

To make the system reboot in ten minutes, run this command:

```
shutdown -r +10
```

On Linux, shutdown notifies anyone logged on that the machine is going down, but it does little real work. If you specify a time other than now, shutdown creates a file called /etc/nologin. When this file is present, the system prohibits logins by anyone except the superuser.

When system shutdown time finally arrives, shutdown tells init to switch to runlevel 0 for a halt and runlevel 6 for a reboot. When init enters runlevel 0 or 6, all of the following takes place, which you can verify by looking at the scripts inside rc0.d and rc6.d:

1. init kills every process that it can (as it would when switching to any other runlevel).
2. The initial rc0.d/rc6.d commands run, locking system files into place and making other preparations for shutdown.
3. The next rc0.d/rc6.d commands unmount all filesystems other than the root.
4. Further rc0.d/rc6.d commands remount the root filesystem read-only.
5. Still more rc0.d/rc6.d commands write all buffered data out to the filesystem with the sync program (see Section 2.4.4).
6. The final rc0.d/rc6.d commands tell the kernel to reboot or stop with the reboot, halt, or poweroff program.

The reboot and halt programs behave differently for each runlevel, potentially causing confusion. By default, these programs call shutdown with the -r or -h options. but if the system is already at the halt or reboot runlevel, the programs tell the kernel to shut itself off immediately. If you really want to shut your machine down in a hurry (disregarding any possible damage from a disorderly shutdown), use the -f option.

## 3.2 Boot Loaders

Before the kernel runs init, a boot loader starts the kernel. On occasion, you need to tell the boot loader to load different kernels or operating systems, and to start in different modes. This is especially important when trying to fix a system that has a problem that prevents a full boot. To fix such a problem, you may need single-user mode or an alternate kernel.

The boot loader loads a kernel image into memory and hands control of the CPU to the new image, possibly supplying it with some parameters. These parameters are simple text strings like -s for booting in single-user mode and root=*partition* for using *partition* as the root filesystem instead of the default. You can specify a runlevel number as a parameter to make the system boot into a runlevel other than the default.

To type in a kernel name and parameters, however, you first need to know how to get to a boot prompt. Unfortunately, there are several different boot loaders out there, and because you can control a boot loader's behavior, Linux distributions customize to their hearts' content.

The next sections tell you how to get to a boot prompt in order to enter a kernel name and parameters. If you need to know how to install a boot loader or change its configuration, see Section 10.5.

## 3.2.1 LILO

LILO (Linux Loader) has been around for almost as long as the Linux kernel. The LILO boot prompt usually ends with boot:. If your system boots with LILO, it's likely that you get a fancy screen of graphics at boot time, because this is the default for many distributions, including Red Hat Linux. If you see a screen like this, look for a part that reads "Press Control-x for text mode." If you see that message, type CONTROL-X to get to the boot prompt.

If the system defaults to text mode, look at the prompt as soon as it appears. If the prompt says LILO with nothing else, press the SHIFT key to get the rest of the boot prompt to appear. On the other hand, if you get a boot prompt immediately, you need to watch out, because the system likely will boot if you don't type anything in a certain amount of time.

Once you're at a LILO boot prompt, press the TAB key to show a list of kernel and operating system options. The default kernel name is probably something like linux. To boot this kernel with no options, enter linux. To use options, specify them after the kernel name:

```
linux option1 option2 ...
```

For example, to boot the system in single-user mode, type this:

```
linux -s
```

Or, to boot linux in single-user mode with the root filesystem as /dev/hda3 instead of your normal default, type this:

```
linux root=/dev/hda3 -s
```

## 3.2.2 GRUB

GRUB stands for Grand Unified Bootloader, a system that is slowly replacing LILO. GRUB has plenty of whiz-bang features, but most important is its ability to navigate filesystems, so you can read files without loading a kernel.

Wiseguy Solaris and BSD administrators like to say that they have enjoyed this capability for some time.

GRUB has a menu interface that's easy enough to navigate, but if you need to boot from a different kernel, change the root partition, or supply extra kernel parameters, you should get into the mini-shell. Press c at the menu to get this prompt:

```
grub>
```

Let's say that you want to boot the kernel at /boot/vmlinuz with a root of /dev/hda3. Furthermore, your system is messed up, so you need single-user mode with the -s kernel option. Type the following at the GRUB prompt:

```
root (hd0,2)
kernel /boot/vmlinuz root=/dev/hda3 -s
boot
```

The root (hd0,2) line sets GRUB's idea of the current root partition — that is, the filesystem where GRUB expects to find the kernel. hd0 is the first hard drive (that is, the first disk that GRUB finds; for example, the Linux device /dev/hda if this is your first hard disk). However, 2 specifies the *third* partition (/dev/hda3) because GRUB partition numbers start at 0.

The word kernel sets a kernel image and its parameters. /boot/vmlinuz refers to a kernel image file on (hd0,2). Unfortunately, GRUB does not normally pass the information from the preceding root() line on to the kernel, so you should always specify root=*partition* as a kernel parameter.

**NOTE**    *You can combine the* root *and* kernel *lines by preceding the kernel image with the GRUB root partition. Therefore, the preceding two lines could be written as the single line* kernel (hd0,2)/boot/vmlinuz root=/dev/hda3 -s.

The last line, boot, tells GRUB to load and execute the kernel image.

**NOTE**    *On certain systems (especially those with SCSI disks and stock kernels), you may need an initial RAM disk:*

```
initrd /boot/initrd
```

*See Section 10.5.4 for information on why you may need an initial RAM disk.*

In case you're trying to boot a partition with another boot loader (such as a Windows partition) by hand with GRUB, try the following, where *partition* uses the GRUB device syntax explained earlier (e.g., hd(0,1)):

```
rootnoverify partition
makeactive
chainloader +1
boot
```

### 3.2.3 Other Boot Loaders

There are many other ways to boot a kernel, including from DOS via LOADLIN or SYSLINUX, over the network, or even directly from the PC BIOS with LinuxBIOS! Most other boot loaders work like LILO, although some do not support the TAB key to list options. You may need to pay attention to boot diagnostics for this information. However, the way you enter parameters is usually identical to LILO and GRUB.

### 3.2.4 Single-User Mode and Emergency Booting

When something goes wrong with the system, an administrator's first recourse for booting quickly to a usable state is *single-user mode.* The idea is that the system quickly boots to a root shell instead of going through the whole mess of services. On Linux, single-user mode is usually runlevel 1. You may need to type the root password to enter single-user mode.

Common tasks in single-user mode include the following:

- Checking filesystems after a system crash
- Fixing problems in critical files, such as /etc/fstab, /etc/passwd, and /etc/inittab
- Restoring from backups after a system crash

Don't expect too many amenities in single-user mode. You may need to set the terminal type (enter TERM=linux) to get full-screen editors to work, and the network may not be available. You can configure the network and other systems by hand if necessary, but it's a pain.

When you finish with single-user mode, you can exit the shell to see if the system starts normally. However, it's usually a good idea to reboot the system, because the transition from single-user mode to regular multi-user mode is not always perfect.

If you have a real mess on your hands, and even single-user mode doesn't work, you can try the -b kernel parameter for an emergency boot shell instead of any kind of orderly startup. This does not mount the root filesystem as read-write or give you much of anything else, so you'll probably need to do some remounting, and possibly mount the /proc filesystem before getting anything useful done. However, if things are really this broken, you might consider using a rescue CD-ROM instead of this rudimentary emergency boot shell mode. You may also be able to get an emergency boot shell by using the init=/bin/sh kernel parameter.

Finally, if you break your kernel or boot loader, you won't be able to get to single-user mode without extra help. You can often boot your system with a kernel from a bootable CD-ROM by passing the root parameter to the CD-ROM's kernel boot loader. Your system might look somewhat strange without your regular kernel, but you should still be able to move files around or perhaps even compile a new kernel to get yourself out of the jam.

## 3.3 Virtual Consoles

The final stage of the boot process starts one or more programs that allow you to log in to the system console. Linux has two primary display modes: console (text) mode, and an X Window System server (graphics mode, usually via a display manager). The kernel boots in console mode, but on most distributions the system switches over to graphics mode near when the rc*.d commands complete.

Linux has several *virtual consoles*. Each virtual console may run in graphics or text mode. When in text mode, you can switch between consoles with an ALT-Function key combination — for example, ALT-F1 takes you to /dev/tty1, ALT-F2 goes to /dev/tty2, and so on.

A virtual console used by XFree86 in graphics mode is slightly different. Rather than getting a virtual console assignment directly from /etc/inittab, an XFree86 server takes over a free virtual console. For example, if you have getty processes running on tty1 and tty2, a new XFree86 server takes over tty3. In addition, after XFree86 puts a virtual console into graphics mode, you must normally press a CONTROL-ALT-Function key combination to switch to another virtual console instead of the simpler ALT-Function key combination.

The upshot of all of this is that if you want to see your text console after your system boots, press CONTROL-ALT-F1. To get back to the X11 session, press ALT-F2, ALT-F3, and so on, until you get to the X session.

# 4

# ESSENTIAL SYSTEM FILES, SERVERS, AND UTILITIES

When you first look in the /etc directory or do a process listing, you may feel overwhelmed. Fortunately, very few of these files are terribly critical to the system's operation. This chapter shows you what is important.

The subject material in this chapter covers the parts of the system that make the infrastructure covered in Chapter 2 available to the user-level tools covered in Chapter 1. In particular, you will see the following:

- Configuration files that the system libraries access to get server and user information
- Server programs (sometimes called *daemons*) that run when the system boots
- Configuration utilities that can be used to tweak the server programs and configuration files

As in the previous chapters, there is virtually no networking material here. The network is separate from the elementary parts of the system. In Chapter 5 you'll see where the network fits in.

## 4.1 System Logging

Most system programs write their diagnostic output to the *syslog* service. The syslogd daemon waits for messages, and depending on the type of message received, funnels the output to a file, the screen, users, some combination of these, or just ignores it. The system logger is one of the most important parts of the system. When something goes wrong and you don't know where to start, you should check the system log files first. Here is a sample log file message:

```
Aug 19 17:59:48 duplex sshd[484]: Server listening on 0.0.0.0 port 22.
```

Most Linux distributions use the /var/log directory to store log files, but you can find out for sure by looking at /etc/syslog.conf, the syslogd configuration file. It contains lines like this:

```
kern.*                  /dev/console
*.info;authpriv.none    /var/log/messages
authpriv.*              /var/log/secure,root
mail.*                  /var/log/maillog
cron.*                  /var/log/cron
*.emerg                 *
local7.*                /var/log/boot.log
```

The type of information to be logged is on the left, and the place where it is logged to is on the right. Most of the log targets in this example are normal files, but there are some exceptions: /dev/console is a special device for the system console, root means to send a message to the superuser if that user is logged in, and * means to send a message to all users currently on the system. You can also send messages to another host with @*host*.

Log messages carry a *facility* and a *priority*. The facility is a general category of message (Check the syslog.conf(5) manual page for a current list of all facilities). Most are fairly obvious from their name (mail, for example). The preceding syslog.conf sample catches messages carrying the authpriv, mail, cron, and local7 facilities. In line 6, * is a wildcard that catches output related to all facilities.

In the syslog.conf file, the priority follows the dot (.) after the facility. The priority may be one of debug, info, notice, warning, err, crit, alert, or emerg. This is also the order of the priorities, with emerg being the highest.

**NOTE**    *You can exclude log messages from a facility in* syslog.conf *by specifying a priority of* none, *as shown on line 2 of the preceding example.*

It is important to understand that when you put a specific priority in a syslog.conf line, syslogd sends messages with that priority *and all higher priorities* to the destination on that line. Therefore, in the preceding example file, the *.info actually catches most syslog messages and puts them into /var/log/messages because info is a relatively low priority. You can catch all priorities by using * as a wildcard.

An extra daemon called klogd traps kernel messages and (usually) sends them to syslogd. You may wish to direct kernel messages into a separate file with a line like this in your syslog.conf:

```
kern.*                    /var/log/kern.log
```

If you want to send a log message to the syslog service manually (for example, when writing a script), use the logger command, as in this example:

```
logger -p daemon.info something bad just happened
```

Very little can go wrong with syslogd. The most common problem is where syslog.conf doesn't catch a certain facility or priority. Another problem is that log files have a tendency to fill their disk partitions after some time. However, most distributions automatically trim the files in /var/log with automatic invocations of logrotate or some other utility.

The Linux syslogd has a few more features than its counterparts in other Unix variants. The discussion here only covers the basics that apply to most Unix systems. If you're really interested in it, or if there's some character in your configuration file that you can't figure out, take a look at the syslog.conf(5) manual page.

## 4.2 A Glance at /etc

Most configuration files on a Linux system are in /etc, and because there are so many packages on a Unix system, /etc accumulates files quickly. This makes it hard to see what actually matters to a running system.

In previous chapters, you saw files like inittab and fstab for booting the system. Table 4-1 identifies those and other critical configuration files and where they are discussed in the book.

**Table 4-1:** Essential Configuration Files

| File | Function | Section |
|------|----------|---------|
| fstab | Filesystems | 2.4.6 |
| group | User management | 4.3.2 |
| init.d | Boot sequence | 3.1.3 |
| inittab | Boot sequence | 3.1.1 |
| ld.so.cache | Shared libraries | 8.1.4 |
| ld.so.conf | Shared libraries | 8.1.4 |

**Table 4-1:** Essential Configuration Files (continued)

| File | Function | Section |
|------|----------|---------|
| passwd | User management | 4.3 |
| rc*.d | Boot sequence | 3.1.2 |
| shadow | User management | 4.3 |

# 4.3 User Management Files

The user system in Unix allows different people to log in to the same machine without interfering with one another. At the lowest level, users are nothing more than numbers *(user IDs),* but *login names* help to avert confusion and boredom.

The plain-text file /etc/passwd maps login names to user IDs, and it looks something like this:

```
root:x:0:0:Superuser:/root:/bin/sh
daemon:*:1:1:daemon:/usr/sbin:/bin/sh
bin:*:2:2:bin:/bin:/bin/sh
sys:*:3:3:sys:/dev:/bin/sh
nobody:*:65534:65534:nobody:/home:/bin/false
juser:x:3119:1000:J. Random User:/home/juser:/bin/bash
beazley:x:143:1000:David Beazley:/home/beazley:/bin/bash
```

The format is straightforward. Each line represents one user, with seven fields separated by colons:

- The user (login) name.

- The user's encrypted password. On most Linux systems, the password is not actually stored in the passwd file, but in the shadow file. shadow is similar to passwd, but normal users do not have read permission on shadow. The second field in passwd or shadow is the encrypted password, and it looks like a bunch of garbage, such as d1CVEWiB/oppc (in Unix, passwords are never stored in clear text). The rest of the fields in shadow deal with matters such as password expiration dates.

  An x in the second field in the passwd file indicates that the encrypted password is stored in shadow. An * indicates that the user cannot log in, and if the field is blank (that is, appears as ::), no password is required to log in. Watch out for blank passwords. You should never have a user without a password.

- The *user ID* (UID), the user's representation to the kernel. It should be unique. You can have two entries with the same user ID, but it will confuse you and some of your software.

- The *group ID* (GID). It should be one of the numbered entries in the /etc/group file. Groups determine file permissions and little else. This group is also called the user's *primary group.*

- The user's real name (often called the *GECOS* field). Sometimes there are commas in this field, denoting room and telephone numbers.
- The user's home directory.
- The user's shell (the program that runs when the user logs in).

Figure 4-1 identifies the various fields in one of the entries in the preceding example.

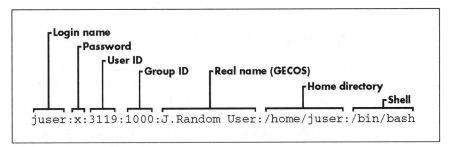

*Figure 4-1: An entry in the password file.*

**NOTE**   *A user and home directory are collectively known as an* account.

There are a few special users in /etc/passwd. The superuser (root) always has UID 0 and GID 0, as in the preceding example. There are other users with no login privileges, such as daemon. These generally vary from system to system, and you should leave them alone. "nobody" is a special under-privileged user that some processes run as, because the nobody user cannot write to anything on the system.

   These special users are called *pseudo-users.* They can't log in to the system, but the system can start processes with their user IDs for security reasons.

**NOTE**   *The* /etc/passwd *file syntax is special and fairly strict, allowing for no comments or blank lines.*

## 4.3.1 Manipulating Users and Passwords

Regular users interact with /etc/passwd with the passwd command. By default, the passwd command changes the user's password, but you can also use -f to change the user's real name, or -s to change the user's shell to one listed in /etc/shells. (Two other commands for changing the real name and shell are chfn and chsh.) passwd is an suid-root program, running as the superuser when changing the /etc/passwd file.

### Changing /etc/passwd as the Superuser

Because the passwd file is in plain text, the superuser may use any text editor to make changes. To add a user, you need to do nothing more than add an appropriate line and create a home directory for the user; deleting is the opposite. There is a special program called `vipw` that allows you to lock the passwd file and edit it as the superuser. To set another user's password, use `passwd` *user* as the superuser.

However, most distributions frown on editing `passwd` directly because it is easy to make a mistake. For example, Red Hat Linux has the commands `adduser` and `userdel` to add and remove users. Even if you use these commands or `vipw`, though, you should still know about the password file format, because you may need to edit it in a pinch.

## 4.3.2 Working with Groups

*Groups* in Unix offer a way to share files with certain other users on the system, but deny access to all other users. The idea is that you can set read or write permission bits (described in Section 1.17) for the group, but not the world (everyone else). This was once important because many users shared one machine, but this has become less significant in recent years as workstations have become more personal.

As mentioned earlier, `/etc/passwd` has a group field. The `/etc/group` file defines the group IDs, as shown in this example:

```
root:*:0:juser
daemon:*:1:
bin:*:2:
sys:*:3:
adm:*:4:
disk:*:6:juser,beazley
nogroup:*:65534:
user:*:1000:
```

The fields in `/etc/group` are as follows:

- The group name. (This is what shows up when you run a command like `ls -l`.)

- The group password. This is hardly ever used; you can use * or any other default value.

- The group ID (a number). The GID must be unique within the group file. This number goes into a user's group field in their `/etc/passwd` entry.

- An optional list of users that belong to the group. In addition to the users listed here, users with the corresponding group ID in their `passwd` file entries also belong to the group.

Figure 4-2 identifies the fields in a group file entry.

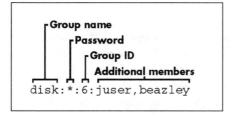

Figure 4-2: An entry in the group file.

To see the groups you belong to, run the groups command.

## 4.4 getty and login

Section 3.1.1 mentioned getty, a program that attaches to terminals and displays a login prompt. On most Linux systems, getty is uncomplicated because the system only uses it for logins on virtual terminals, with lines in /etc/inittab like this one for /dev/tty1:

```
1:2345:respawn:/sbin/getty 38400 tty1
```

In this example, 38400 is the baud rate. Virtual terminals ignore the baud rate; it's only there for backward compatibility with terminals connected to real serial lines. Some getty programs (like the mingetty that Red Hat Linux uses for virtual terminals) don't need the baud rate setting.

You are probably most interested in the name of the file that getty prints as the login greeting: /etc/issue. This is a quick and satisfying way to deface your system without doing any real damage.

After you type your login name, getty replaces itself with the login program, which then asks for your password. If you type the correct password, login replaces itself with your shell. Otherwise, you get a "Login incorrect" message.

You now know what getty and login do, but it's unlikely that you'll ever need to configure or change them, because terminals on serial ports have been largely confined to the dustbin of history. The login program has an excessive number of options and configuration files, but they are mostly useless because they deal with security for network login methods, such as telnet, that are insecure in the first place. You will learn in Chapter 6 that you should not use them.

**NOTE** *If you want to send and receive faxes or dial up to your machine through your own modem, you may need to work with* mgetty, *an advanced* getty *that can work with fax and voice modems.*

## 4.5 Setting the Time

A well-functioning Unix machine depends on accurate timekeeping. The kernel is responsible for maintaining the *system clock*, the clock consulted when you run commands such as date. You can also set the system clock with the date command, but this is usually a bad idea, because you'll never get the time exactly right. You want your system clock to be very close to the correct time.

PC hardware has a battery-backed "real-time" clock. It's not the greatest clock in the world, but it's better than nothing. The kernel usually sets its time based on this clock at boot time, and you can reset the system clock to the current hardware time with hwclock. If your hardware clock is in UTC (Universal Coordinated Time, or Greenwich Mean Time), run this command:

```
hwclock --hctosys --utc
```

You should try to keep your hardware clock in UTC to avoid any trouble with time zone or daylight savings time corrections. However, if you insist on keeping the hardware clock set to the local time, run this command instead:

```
hwclock --hctosys --localtime
```

Unfortunately, the kernel isn't terribly good at keeping time, and because Unix machines often stay up for months and years at a time, they tend to develop a *drift*. In addition, it's fairly rude to make the system clock jump ahead or back by running hwclock on a frequent basis; time-based system events can get lost or munged. If you want to gradually change the system clock based on the hardware clock, run this command:

```
adjtimex --adjust
```

However, this is only good for updating the clock manually when it has already drifted. To keep the time up to date, you need to run a network time daemon (see Section 4.5.2).

### 4.5.1 Time Zones

The system clock runs in UTC. System libraries convert this into local time and compensate for daylight savings time and any other strange circumstances (such as living in Indiana).

To set your system's time zone, make a symbolic link to the appropriate time zone file in /usr/share/zoneinfo from /etc/localtime. For example, here is the command to configure a United States Pacific Time Zone setting:

```
ln -sf /usr/share/zoneinfo/US/Pacific /etc/localtime
```

A long listing of the link should contain this output:

```
/etc/localtime -> /usr/share/zoneinfo/US/Pacific
```

If you want to use a different time zone than the system default, you can do so by setting the TZ environment variable like this:

```
$ export TZ=US/Central
$ date
```

### 4.5.2 Network Time

If your machine is permanently connected to the Internet, you can run an NTP (Network Time Protocol) daemon and get the time from a remote server. The main NTP Web page is http://www.ntp.org/, but if you don't really feel like reading through the mounds of documentation there, do this:

1. Ask your ISP for the closest NTP time server.
2. Put that time server in /etc/ntpd.conf.
3. Run ntpdate *server* at boot time.
4. Run ntpd at boot time.

If your machine does not have a permanent Internet connection, you can use a daemon such as chronyd to maintain the time during disconnections.

HINT     *You can also set your hardware clock based on the network time. First, set your system time from the network with* ntpdate *(or* ntpd*). Then run this command:*

```
hwclock --systohc –utc
```

# 4.6 Scheduling Recurring Tasks with cron

Unix provides a service called cron that runs programs repeatedly on a fixed schedule. Most experienced administrators consider cron to be vital to the system because it can perform automatic system maintenance. For example, cron runs log file rotation utilities. You should know about cron not only in the interest of knowing about everything that runs on your system, but also because it is just plain useful.

You can run any program you like with cron, choosing the times that suit you. A program running through cron is called a *cron job*. To install a cron job, you need to create an entry line in your *crontab file*, usually with the crontab command. Here is a typical crontab file entry that runs a command daily at 9:15 AM:

```
15 09 * * * /home/juser/bin/spmake
```

The five whitespace-delimited fields at the beginning specify the schedule time (see also Figure 4-3):

- Minute (0–59)
- Hour (0–23)
- Day of month (1–31)
- Month (1–12)
- Day of week (0–7; 0 and 7 are Sunday)

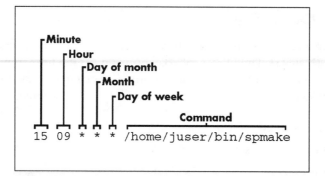

*Figure 4-3: An entry in the crontab file.*

The preceding example says to run spmake daily, because the day of month, month, and day of week fields are all * (the * character matches all possible values, meaning every day of the month, every month, or every day of the week). If you want to run the job only on the 14th of each month, use this crontab line:

```
15 09 14 * * /home/juser/bin/spmake
```

You may select more than one time for each field. For example, if you would like the program to run on the 5th as well as the 14th, use 5,14 in the third field:

```
15 09 5,14 * * /home/juser/bin/spmake
```

The remainder of the line is the command to run. When cron runs the job, the command may generate standard output or error or exit abnormally. If that happens, cron mails this information to you. You may want to redirect the output to /dev/null or some log file if you find this annoying.

The crontab(5) manual page is a full reference for the cron file format. However, there is also a crontab(1) manual page for the installation utility, so you'll need to use man 5 crontab to get to the right one.

### 4.6.1 Installing Crontab Files

Each user can have their own crontab file. The system usually stores all crontabs in /var/spool/cron/crontabs. Normal users can't write to this directory. Instead, the crontab command installs, lists, edits, and removes a user's crontab.

The easiest way to install a crontab is to put your crontab entries into a file, then use crontab *file* to install *file* as your current crontab. The crontab command checks the file format to make sure that you haven't screwed anything up. If you want to list your cron jobs, run crontab -l. To remove the crontab, use crontab -r.

Using temporary files to create and manipulate your crontab can be a little messy, so if you want to edit and install your crontab in one motion, run crontab -e. If you make a mistake, crontab tells you where the mistake is and asks if you would like to try editing again.

### 4.6.2 System Crontab Files

Rather than use the superuser's crontab for scheduling recurring system tasks, Linux distributions normally have an /etc/crontab file. Do not use the crontab command to edit this file; it has a slightly different format with one more field — the user that should run the job. Here is an example for a job to run at 6:42 AM, running as the superuser (root):

```
42 6 * * * root /usr/local/bin/cleansystem > /dev/null 2>&1
```

Some distributions also use the /etc/cron.d directory to store system crontab files. These files may have any name, but they have the same format as /etc/crontab.

## 4.7 Scheduling One-Time Tasks with at

If you want to run a job in the future but don't want to use cron because the command should only run once, you can do it with the at service. For example, if you want to run myjob at 10:30 PM, enter this command:

```
at 22:30
myjob
```

End the input with a CONTROL-D (at reads the commands from the standard input).

To check that the job has been scheduled, use atq, or to remove it, use atrm. You also can schedule jobs days into the future by adding the date (in DD.MM.YY format; for example, at 22:30 30.09.03).

There isn't too much else to the at command. at actually does not see much use in common practice. However, it can be handy for the odd time that you need to shut the system down in the future.

## 4.8 Tracking Individual Processes

You saw how to use ps in Section 1.16 for listing process characteristics at any given time. ps is good for getting a snapshot of the current processes, but it does little to tell you how processes change over time. Using ps alone, it's not terribly easy to pick out processes that are using too much CPU time or memory.

The top program displays the current system status and many of the fields that you might see in a ps listing, but it also updates the display every second. By default, top shows the most active processes (that is, those currently taking up the most CPU time).

You can send commands to top with keystrokes. These are some of the most important commands:

SPACEBAR    Updates the display immediately

M    Sorts by current resident memory usage

T    Sorts by total (cumulative) CPU usage

P    Sorts by current CPU usage (the default)

u    Displays only one user's processes

?    Displays a usage summary for all top commands

If you want to know how much CPU time a process uses during its entire lifetime, use time. (If your shell has a built-in time command, you may need to run /usr/bin/time to get the full output shown below.) For example, to measure the CPU time used by ls, run this command:

```
time ls
```

After ls terminates, you should get some output like this:

```
0.05user 0.09system 0:00.44elapsed 31%CPU (0avgtext+0avgdata 0maxresident)k
0inputs+0outputs (125major+51minor)pagefaults 0swaps
```

- *User time* is the number of seconds that the CPU has spent running the program's *own* code. On modern processors, some commands run so quickly that you may get a zero value here because the actual CPU time is so low that time rounds down to zero.

- *System time* is how long the kernel spends doing the process's work (for example, reading files and directories).

- *Elapsed time* is the total time it took to run the process from start to finish, including the time that the CPU spent doing other tasks. This number is not very useful for performance measurements.

See Section 4.10 for a description of the other fields.

### 4.8.1 Finding Open Files with lsof

The lsof command lists open files and the processes that are using these open files. Because Unix places such a great emphasis on files, lsof is among the most useful tools for finding trouble spots. lsof does not stop at regular files — it can list network sockets, dynamic libraries, pipes, and more.

Running lsof on the command line usually produces a tremendous amount of output. Here is a fragment of what you might see:

| COMMAND | PID | USER | FD | TYPE | DEVICE | SIZE | NODE | NAME |
|---------|-----|------|------|------|--------|------|------|------|
| init | 1 | root | cwd | DIR | 3,1 | 4096 | 2 | / |
| init | 1 | root | rtd | DIR | 3,1 | 4096 | 2 | / |
| init | 1 | root | txt | REG | 3,1 | 24480 | 16212 | /sbin/init |
| init | 1 | root | mem | REG | 3,1 | 999542 | 32329 | /lib/ld-2.3.2.so |
| init | 1 | root | mem | REG | 3,1 | 1251176 | 32208 | /lib/libc-2.3.2.so |
| init | 1 | root | 10u | FIFO | 3,1 | | 97634 | /dev/initctl |
| ... | | | | | | | | |
| ... | | | | | | | | |
| vi | 3511 | juser | cwd | DIR | 3,4 | 4096 | 163866 | /home/juser/w |
| vi | 3511 | juser | rtd | DIR | 3,1 | 4096 | 2 | / |
| vi | 3511 | juser | txt | REG | 3,3 | 327048 | 561520 | /usr/bin/vi |
| ... | | | | | | | | |
| vi | 3511 | juser | 3rW | REG | 3,4 | 18993 | 163867 | /home/juser/w/c |

The fields in this output are as follows:

**COMMAND**   The command name for the process that holds the file descriptor.

**PID**   The process ID.

**USER**   The user running the process.

**FD**   The *file descriptor* or the purpose of the open file. A file descriptor is a number that a process uses in conjunction with the system libraries to identify and manipulate a file.

**TYPE**   The file type (regular file, directory, socket, etc.).

**DEVICE**   The major and minor number of the device that holds the file.

**SIZE**   The file's size.

**NODE**   The file's inode number.

**NAME**   The filename.

The lsof(1) manual page contains a full list of what you might see for each field, but you should be able to guess just by looking at the output. For example, look at the entries with cwd in the FD field. These lines indicate current working directories of the processes. Another example is the very last line, showing a file that the user is currently editing with vi.

There are two basic approaches to running lsof:

- List everything and pipe the output to a command like less, and then run a search to find what you're looking for.
- Narrow down the list that lsof provides with command-line options.

If you use command-line options, you can provide a filename as an argument, and lsof will list only the entries that match the argument. For example, the following command displays entries for open files in /usr:

```
lsof /usr
```

To list the open files for a particular process ID, run this command:

```
lsof -p pid
```

lsof has dozens of other options; lsof -h provides a short summary. Most options pertain to the output format. Make sure that you look at Section 6.5.1 for lsof network features.

**NOTE** *lsof is highly dependent on kernel information. If you upgrade your kernel, you may need to upgrade lsof.*

### 4.8.2 Tracing Program Execution with strace and ltrace

With the exception of time, the tools you have seen so far examine active processes. However, if you have no idea why a program dies almost immediately after starting up, even lsof won't help you. You would have a difficult time even running lsof concurrently with a failed command.

The strace (system call trace) and ltrace (library trace) commands can help you discover what a program attempts to do. These tools produce extraordinarily large amounts of output, but once you know what to look for, you will be in a good position for tracking down problems.

A *system call* is a privileged operation that the kernel must perform for a process, such as opening and reading data from a file. strace prints all of the system calls that a process makes. To get the idea, run this command:

```
strace cat /dev/null
```

The first part of the output deals primarily with loading shared libraries. You can ignore this stuff:

```
execve("/bin/cat", ["cat", "/dev/null"], [/* 52 vars */]) = 0
brk(0)                                    = 0x804b348
open("/etc/ld.so.preload", O_RDONLY)     = -1 ENOENT (No such file or directory)
open("/etc/ld.so.cache", O_RDONLY)       = 3
fstat64(3, {st_mode=S_IFREG|0644, st_size=14834, ...}) = 0
old_mmap(NULL, 14834, PROT_READ, MAP_PRIVATE, 3, 0) = 0x40015000
```

```
close(3)                              = 0
open("/lib/libc.so.6", O_RDONLY)      = 3
read(3, "\177ELF\1\1\1\0\0\0\0\0\0\0\0\0\3\0\3\0\1\0\0\0\200^\1"..., 1024) = 1024
```

In addition, you can skip by all of the mmap output until you get to the lines
that look like this:

```
fstat64(1, {st_mode=S_IFCHR|0666, st_rdev=makedev(1, 3), ...}) = 0
open("/dev/null", O_RDONLY|O_LARGEFILE) = 3
fstat64(3, {st_mode=S_IFCHR|0666, st_rdev=makedev(1, 3), ...}) = 0
brk(0)                                = 0x804b348
brk(0x804c348)                        = 0x804c348
brk(0)                                = 0x804c348
brk(0x804d000)                        = 0x804d000
read(3, "", 4096)                     = 0
close(3)                              = 0
close(1)                              = 0
_exit(0)                              = ?
```

Now you see some interesting things. First, look at the open() call, which
opens a file. The 3 as a result means success (3 is a file descriptor). Then,
near the end, you see where cat reads from /dev/null (the read() call —
notice that the file descriptor is 3). Then there is nothing more to read, so
the program closes the file descriptor and exits.

So what happens when there's a problem? Try strace cat not_a_file
instead and examine the open() call:

```
open("not_a_file", O_RDONLY|O_LARGEFILE) = -1 ENOENT (No such file or
directory)
```

Here, strace not only reports the error at the system-call level, but it also gives
you a small description of the error.

Missing files are the most common problems with Unix programs, so
if the syslog and other log information isn't very helpful, and you have
nowhere else to turn, strace can be of great use. You can even use strace
on daemons that detach themselves. Here's an example:

```
strace -o crummyd_strace -ff crummyd
```

In this example, the -o option to strace logs the action of any child process
that crummyd spawns into crummyd_strace.*pid*, where *pid* is the process ID of the
child process.

The ltrace command tracks shared library calls. The output is similar to
strace, but be warned, there are usually *many* more shared library calls than
system calls. See Section 8.1.4 for more information on shared libraries
(ltrace doesn't work on statically linked binaries).

## 4.9 Adjusting Process Priorities

It is possible to change the way the kernel schedules a process so that the process gets more or less CPU time than other processes. The kernel runs each process according to its scheduling *priority*, which is a number between −20 and 19, with −20 being the foremost priority (yes, this can be confusing).

The ps -l command lists the current priority of a process, but it's a little easier to see how it works with the top command, as shown here:

```
Tasks:  79 total,   1 running,  77 sleeping,   0 stopped,   1 zombie
Cpu(s):  9.4% us,  1.0% sy,  0.4% ni, 88.4% id,  0.6% wa,  0.0% hi,  0.1% si
Mem:    320364k total,   301420k used,   18944k free,   17320k buffers
Swap:   514072k total,    13260k used,  500812k free,   68260k cached
```

| PID | USER | PR | NI | VIRT | RES | SHR | S | %CPU | %MEM | TIME+ | COMMAND |
|---|---|---|---|---|---|---|---|---|---|---|---|
| 23066 | bri | 16 | 0 | 1868 | 896 | 1732 | R | 5.6 | 0.3 | 0:00.06 | top |
| 10382 | bri | 15 | 0 | 93288 | 74m | 28m | S | 1.9 | 23.7 | 200:04.75 | MozillaFirebird |
| 1 | root | 16 | 0 | 1348 | 480 | 1316 | S | 0.0 | 0.1 | 0:04.28 | init |
| 2 | root | 34 | 19 | 0 | 0 | 0 | S | 0.0 | 0.0 | 0:00.00 | ksoftirqd/0 |
| 3 | root | 5 | -10 | 0 | 0 | 0 | S | 0.0 | 0.0 | 0:06.36 | events/0 |
| 4 | root | 5 | -10 | 0 | 0 | 0 | S | 0.0 | 0.0 | 0:08.89 | kblockd/0 |
| 5 | root | 15 | 0 | 0 | 0 | 0 | S | 0.0 | 0.0 | 0:00.02 | khubd |
| 6 | root | 25 | 0 | 0 | 0 | 0 | S | 0.0 | 0.0 | 0:00.00 | pdflush |
| 7 | root | 15 | 0 | 0 | 0 | 0 | S | 0.0 | 0.0 | 1:29.48 | pdflush |
| 8 | root | 15 | 0 | 0 | 0 | 0 | S | 0.0 | 0.0 | 1:01.23 | kswapd0 |
| 9 | root | 10 | -10 | 0 | 0 | 0 | S | 0.0 | 0.0 | 0:00.00 | aio/0 |
| 10 | root | 19 | 0 | 0 | 0 | 0 | S | 0.0 | 0.0 | 0:00.00 | scsi_eh_0 |
| 11 | root | 15 | 0 | 0 | 0 | 0 | S | 0.0 | 0.0 | 0:00.00 | kseriod |
| 127 | root | 16 | 0 | 1412 | 572 | 1360 | S | 0.0 | 0.2 | 0:03.24 | syslogd |
| 129 | root | 16 | 0 | 1344 | 464 | 1312 | S | 0.0 | 0.1 | 0:00.02 | klogd |
| 134 | daemon | 19 | 0 | 1436 | 404 | 1388 | S | 0.0 | 0.1 | 0:00.00 | portmap |
| 136 | root | 16 | 0 | 1380 | 516 | 1352 | S | 0.0 | 0.2 | 0:00.03 | inetd |

In the top output, the PR column lists the kernel's current schedule priority for the process. The higher the number, the less likely the kernel is to schedule the process if others need CPU time. The schedule priority changes frequently during program execution according to the amount of CPU time that the process consumes.

The schedule priority alone does not determine the kernel's decision to give CPU time to a process. Next to the priority column is the *nice value* (the NI column), a hint for the kernel's scheduler. This is what you care about when trying to influence the kernel's decision. The kernel adds the nice value to the current priority to determine the next time slot for the process. By default, the nice value is 0. If you want a certain process to take a backseat to other processes, running only when the other tasks have nothing to do, you can change the nice value to 19 with the renice command (where *pid* is the process ID of the process that you want to change):

```
renice 19 pid
```

This comes in handy when you're running some big computation in the background and don't want it to bog down your interactive session.

If you're the superuser, you can set the nice value to a negative number, but this is almost always a bad idea because system processes may not get enough CPU time. In fact, you likely won't need to alter nice values much because most Linux systems have only a single user, and that user does not perform much real computation. The nice value was much more important in the days when there were many users on a single machine.

## 4.10 Monitoring System Performance

Most Linux systems behave well under a distribution's default settings, and you can spend hours and days trying to tune your machine's performance without attaining any meaningful results. Sometimes performance can be improved, though, and this section concentrates primarily on memory and processor performance, and looks at how you can find out if a hardware upgrade might be worthwhile.

The two most important things that you should know about performance on your system are the load average and the system's swap/page fault behavior. The *load average* is the average number of processes currently ready to run. The uptime command tells you three load averages in addition to how long the kernel has been running:

```
... up 91 days, ... load average: 0.08, 0.03, 0.01
```

The three numbers here are the load averages for the past minute, 5 minutes, and 15 minutes. As you can see, this system isn't very busy, because the processor has been running at 1 percent capacity for the past quarter hour (because the last number is 0.01). Most systems exhibit a load average of 0 when you're doing anything *except* compiling a program or playing a game. A load average of 0 is usually a good sign, because it means that your processor isn't even being challenged, and you're saving power by not running a silly screensaver.

If the load average is around 1, it's not necessarily a bad thing; it simply means that the processor has something to do all of the time — you can find the process currently using most of the CPU time with the top command. If the load average goes up near 2 or above, multiple processes are probably starting to interfere with each other, and the kernel is trying to divide the CPU resources evenly. (Unless, of course, you have two processors, in which case, a load average of 2 means that both processors have just enough to do all of the time.)

A high load average does not necessarily mean that your system is having trouble. A system with enough memory and I/O resources can easily handle many running processes. Don't panic if your load average is high and your system still responds well. The system is just running a lot of processes. The processes have to compete with each other for the CPU, and therefore, they will take longer to do their computation than they would if there were one CPU for each process, but there's nothing to worry about.

However, if you sense that the system is slow and the load average is high, you're probably running into memory problems. A high load average can result from the kernel *thrashing*, or rapidly swapping processes to and from swap space on the disk. Check the free command or /proc/meminfo to see how much of the real memory is being used for buffers. If there isn't much buffer memory (and the rest of the real memory is taken), then you need more memory.

A situation where the kernel does not have a piece of memory ready when a program wants to use it is called a *page fault* (the kernel breaks memory into small chunks called *pages*). When you get a lot of page faults, it bogs the system down because the kernel has to work to provide the pages, robbing normal processes of their chance to run.

The vmstat command tells you how much the kernel is swapping pages in and out, how busy the CPU is, and a number of other things. It is probably the single most powerful memory-performance monitoring tool out there, but you have to know what the output means. Here is some output from vmstat 2, which reports statistics every two seconds:

| procs | | | memory | | | swap | | io | | system | | cpu | | |
|---|---|---|---|---|---|---|---|---|---|---|---|---|---|---|
| r | b | w | swpd | free | buff | cache | si | so | bi | bo | in | cs | us | sy | id |
| 2 | 0 | 0 | 145680 | 3336 | 5812 | 89496 | 1 | 1 | 2 | 2 | 2 | 2 | 2 | 0 | 0 |
| 0 | 0 | 0 | 145680 | 3328 | 5812 | 89496 | 0 | 0 | 0 | 0 | 102 | 38 | 0 | 0 | 99 |
| 0 | 0 | 0 | 145680 | 3328 | 5812 | 89496 | 0 | 0 | 0 | 42 | 111 | 44 | 1 | 0 | 99 |
| 0 | 0 | 0 | 145680 | 3328 | 5812 | 89496 | 0 | 0 | 0 | 0 | 101 | 35 | 0 | 1 | 99 |

...

The output falls into categories: procs for processes, memory for memory usage, swap for the pages pulled in and out of swap, io for disk usage, system for the number of times the kernel switches into kernel code, and cpu for the time used by different parts of the system.

The preceding output is typical for a system that isn't doing much. You need to ignore the first line of numbers because it's incomplete and doesn't make sense. Here, the system has 145680KB of memory swapped out to the disk (swpd) and 3328KB of real memory free, but it doesn't seem to matter, because the si and so columns report that the kernel is not swapping anything in or out from the disk. (In this example, Mozilla is taking up extensive residence on the swap partition. Mozilla has a habit of loading a lot of stuff into memory when it is started, never bothering to actually use it.) The buff column indicates the amount of memory that the kernel is using for disk buffers.

On the far right, you see the distribution of CPU time, under us, sy, and id. These are the percentages of time that the CPU is spending on user tasks, system (kernel) tasks, and idle time. In the preceding example, there aren't too many user processes running (using a maximum of 1 percent of the

CPU), the kernel doing practically nothing, while the CPU is sitting around doing nothing 99 percent of the time.

Now, watch what happens when a big, nasty program starts up sometime later (the first two lines are right before the program runs):

| procs | | | memory | | | | swap | | io | | system | | cpu | | |
|---|---|---|---|---|---|---|---|---|---|---|---|---|---|---|---|
| r | b | w | swpd | free | buff | cache | si | so | bi | bo | in | cs | us | sy | id |
| 1 | 0 | 0 | 140988 | 4668 | 7312 | 58980 | 0 | 0 | 0 | 0 | 118 | 148 | 0 | 0 | 100 |
| 0 | 0 | 0 | 140988 | 4668 | 7312 | 58980 | 0 | 0 | 0 | 0 | 101 | 31 | 0 | 0 | 99 |
| 1 | 0 | 0 | 140988 | 3056 | 6780 | 58496 | 6 | 14 | 1506 | 14 | 174 | 2159 | 23 | 5 | 72 |
| 1 | 1 | 0 | 140988 | 3304 | 5900 | 58364 | 32 | 268 | 100 | 268 | 195 | 2215 | 41 | 5 | 53 |
| 0 | 0 | 0 | 140988 | 3496 | 5648 | 58160 | 88 | 0 | 250 | 0 | 186 | 573 | 4 | 6 | 89 |
| 1 | 0 | 0 | 140988 | 3300 | 5648 | 58248 | 0 | 0 | 38 | 0 | 188 | 1792 | 11 | 6 | 83 |
| 2 | 3 | 0 | 140988 | 3056 | 4208 | 59588 | 42 | 14 | 2062 | 14 | 249 | 1395 | 20 | 6 | 74 |
| 2 | 1 | 0 | 140464 | 3100 | 2608 | 65416 | 16 | 96 | 2398 | 176 | 437 | 713 | 3 | 11 | 85 |
| 4 | 0 | 0 | 140392 | 3180 | 2416 | 69780 | 0 | 14 | 4490 | 14 | 481 | 704 | 1 | 5 | 94 |
| 2 | 2 | 0 | 140392 | 3056 | 2428 | 73076 | 106 | 0 | 7184 | 68 | 549 | 1173 | 0 | 9 | 90 |
| 2 | 1 | 0 | 141176 | 4072 | 2112 | 81544 | 28 | 220 | 7314 | 252 | 514 | 1748 | 20 | 19 | 61 |
| 1 | 2 | 0 | 141636 | 3056 | 1892 | 87012 | 0 | 1960 | 3532 | 1974 | 504 | 1054 | 2 | 7 | 91 |
| 3 | 0 | 0 | 145960 | 3056 | 1876 | 89864 | 0 | 3044 | 1458 | 3056 | 490 | 876 | 1 | 6 | 92 |

...

The CPU starts to see some usage for an extended period, especially from user processes. The amount of buffer space starts to deplete as the new program requires new pages, and the kernel starts to kick pages out into swap space (the so column) to make space. Unfortunately, as the kernel does this, it has to wait for the disk to do its work, and the CPU sits idle while processes *block* (the b column), because they also have to wait for the memory pages that they need. You can see the effects of swapping all over the output here; more memory would have fixed this particular problem.

This section hasn't explained all of the vmstat output columns. You can check on them in the vmstat(8) manual page, but you may have to learn more about operating systems first from a class or a book like *Operating System Concepts* [Silberschatz]. However, try to avoid getting really obsessed with performance. If you're trying to squeak 3 percent more speed out of something and you're not working on a huge computation, you're probably wasting your time.

# 4.11 Running Commands as the Superuser

Before you see any more system commands, you should learn more about how to run commands as the superuser. You probably already know that you can run the su command and enter the root password to start a root shell. This practice works, but it has these disadvantages:

- You have no record of system-altering commands.
- You have no record of the users who performed system-altering commands.

- You don't have access to your normal familiar shell environment.
- You have to type the root password.

Most larger workstation installations employ a package named sudo to allow administrators to run commands as root when they are logged in as themselves. For example, if you want to use vipw to edit the /etc/passwd file, you could do it like this:

```
sudo vipw
```

When you run this command, sudo logs this action with the syslog service under the local2 facility, so that you have a record of what you did.

Of course, the system doesn't let just *any* user run commands as the superuser; you must configure the privileged users in the /etc/sudoers file. As it turns out, sudo has a great many options (that you'll probably never use), and the side effect of this is that the /etc/sudoers file has a somewhat complicated syntax. Here is an example file that gives *user1* and *user2* the power to run any command as root without having to enter a password:

```
User_Alias ADMINS = user1, user2

ADMINS  ALL = NOPASSWD: ALL

root    ALL=(ALL) ALL
```

The first line defines an ADMINS user alias with the two users, and the second line grants the privileges. The ALL = NOPASSWD: ALL part means that the users in the ADMINS alias can use sudo to execute commands as root. The second ALL means "any command." The first ALL means "any host" (if you have more than one machine, you can set different kinds of access for each machine or for groups of machines, but this book will not explain that feature).

The root ALL=(ALL) ALL simply means that the superuser may also use sudo to run any command on any host. The extra (ALL) means that the superuser may also run commands as any other user. You can extend this privilege to the ADMINS users by changing the /etc/sudoers line shown earlier to this:

```
ADMINS  ALL = (ALL) NOPASSWD: ALL
```

**NOTE**    *Use the* visudo *command to edit* /etc/sudoers. *This command checks for file syntax errors after you save the file.*

That's all you need to know about sudo for now. If you need its more advanced features, consult the sudoers(5) and sudo(8) manual pages.

### 4.11.1 Real UID and Effective UID

When changing user IDs with programs like sudo, keep in mind that there is more than one active user ID in a running program. The ID that controls your access rights is the *effective* user ID. When you run a setuid program, Linux sets the effective user ID to the program's owner during execution, but it keeps your original user ID in what is called a *real* user ID.

There is an additional *saved* user ID that is set to the program's owner when you run a setuid program. The idea is that a process can switch its effective user ID to the real or saved user ID during execution to perform different tasks as different user IDs.

The reason that you might see different user IDs is that, by default, sudo changes the real user ID along with the effective and saved user IDs. Some programs don't like to have a real user ID of root. If you do not want sudo to change the real user ID, add this line to your /etc/sudoers file:

```
Defaults     stay_setuid
```

# 5

# CONFIGURING YOUR NETWORK

Networking is the practice of sending data from one computer to another computer. For a simple connection to the Internet, you need to do the following:

- Connect a network interface on your machine to a network
- Define a gateway to the rest of the Internet
- Show your machine how to resolve hostnames

Unfortunately, there are so many different kinds of networks that there is no one simple formula to get your system talking to the rest of the world. For Ethernet connections with a static (fixed) IP address, a separate command or file performs each of the preceding steps. However, DHCP (Dynamic Host Configuration Protocol) configurations and PPP (Point-to-Point Protocol) connections use different configuration schemes. This chapter begins with setting up static Ethernet interfaces because they are easy to understand, and then it moves on to DHCP and PPP, including DSL (Digital Subscriber Line) and PPPoE (PPP over Ethernet) connections.

After you know how to connect your machine to a network, you're ready to move on to more advanced topics, such as building your own networks and configuring firewalls, described later in this chapter.

# 5.1 Network Layers

If you really want to understand Linux network configuration, you must be able to distinguish each *layer* in the network. Here are the layers in the Internet, from the top level to the bottom level:

**Application Layer**   Contains the "language" that applications and servers use to communicate; usually a protocol of some sort. Common application layer protocols include Hypertext Transfer Protocol (HTTP, used for the World Wide Web), Secure Shell (SSH), and the File Transfer Protocol (FTP).

**Transport Layer**   Defines the data transmission characteristics of the application layer. This is host-specific information, and it includes data-integrity checking, source and destination ports, and specifications for breaking application data into packets. TCP (Transmission Control Protocol) is the most common transport layer protocol.

**Internet Layer**   Defines how to move packets from the source host to the destination host. The particular packet-transit rule set for the Internet is known as IP (Internet Protocol). This is sometimes called the network layer.

**Host-to-Network Layer**   Defines how to send packets from the Internet layer across the physical medium, such as Ethernet or a modem. This is sometimes called the physical layer.

This may sound overly complicated, but it's important that you understand it, because your data must travel through these layers twice before it reaches its destination. Your bytes leave the application layer on the source host, then go down to the physical medium, across the medium, and then up again to the application layer on the destination host.

Unfortunately, the layers sometimes bleed in strange ways, and terms like TCP/IP reflect the integration. The distinction is only getting more vague — in particular, devices that once only dealt with the Internet layer now sometimes look at the transport layer data to determine where to send data.

To connect your Linux machine to the network, you need to concentrate on the Internet and host-to-network layers, so let's get straight to them. If you want to know a *lot* more about layers (and networks in general), look at *Computer Networks* [Tanenbaum].

**NOTE**   *You have heard of another set of layers known as the ISO OSI (Open Systems Interconnection) Reference Model. This is a seven-layer network model often used in teaching and designing networks, but this book does not cover the OSI model because it is of little practical use for understanding how Linux Internet networking works.*

## 5.2 The Internet Layer

The Internet as we know it is based on the Internet Protocol, version 4 (IPv4). The basic idea is that each computer on the Internet has a numeric *IP address* in the form of *a.b.c.d,* where *a* and *d* are one-byte numbers from 1 to 254, and *b* and *c* are one-byte numbers from 0 to 255. Technically, an IP address is just a four-byte (32-bit) number, but it's usually easiest to deal with the address as a *dotted-quad* sequence of decimal numbers, like 10.23.2.37, instead of something ugly like the hexadecimal 0x0A170225.

A *subnet* is a group of IP addresses in some (hopefully) regular order. For example, the hosts between 10.23.2.1 and 10.23.2.254 could comprise a subnet, or all of the hosts between 10.23.1.1 and 10.23.255.254 could also be a subnet.

Subnets are important because they determine how your packets move between different machines. To communicate with another computer, your machine must know that other computer's IP address. If the destination is on your local area network's subnet, your system can send the data directly to that host, but if not, your machine probably has to send it to a *gateway* (or *router*) that transmits your data across another network on its way to the final destination.

### 5.2.1 More on Subnets

A *subnet mask* defines a subnet; for example, the subnet mask for 10.23.2.1–10.23.2.254 is 255.255.255.0. In pure binary form, the mask "covers" the bits in an address that are common to the subnet. For example, here are the binary forms of 10.23.2.0 and 255.255.255.0:

| | |
|---|---|
| `10.23.2.0:` | `00001010 00010111 00000010 00000000` |
| `255.255.255.0:` | `11111111 11111111 11111111 00000000` |

Now, let's "cover" the bits in 10.23.2.0 with the 1s in 255.255.255.0 by marking these bits in bold:

| | |
|---|---|
| `10.23.2.0:` | **`00001010 00010111 00000010`** `00000000` |

Look at the bits that aren't in bold. You can set any number of these bits to 1 to get a valid IP address in this particular subnet (with two exceptions: all 0s and all 1s).

Putting it all together, you can see that a host computer with an IP address of 10.23.2.1 and a subnet mask of 255.255.255.0 can directly communicate with other computers that have IP addresses beginning with 10.23.2 (to talk to the rest of the Internet, your computer needs to use a gateway). You can denote this entire subnet as 10.23.2.0/255.255.255.0.

If you're lucky, you will deal only with easy subnet masks like 255.255.255.0 or 255.255.0.0, but you may be unfortunate and encounter stuff like 255.255.255.192, where it isn't quite so simple to determine the set of addresses that belong to the subnet. It helps to know that 192 is 0xC0 in hexadecimal, from which you should be able to figure out what addresses belong to such a subnet. If you aren't familiar with conversion between decimal, binary, and hexadecimal formats, you should probably learn now. The dc (desk calculator) program has excellent facilities for converting between different radix representations.

A common shorthand for subnet masks is to identify the number of bits at the start of the subnet mask that have a value of 1. For example, 255.255.255.0 contains 24 1-bits to start the 32-bit sequence, so you can write the earlier example of 10.23.2.0/255.255.255.0 as 10.23.2.0/24. Table 5-1 shows several example subnet masks.

**Table 5-1:** Subnet Masks

| Long Form | Short Form |
|---|---|
| 255.0.0.0 | 8 |
| 255.255.0.0 | 16 |
| 255.240.0.0 | 12 |
| 255.255.255.0 | 24 |
| 255.255.255.192 | 26 |

Therefore, to specify 10.0.0.0/255.0.0.0, you can use 10.0.0.0/8.

## 5.3 Basic ICMP Tools

Before you configure your network devices, you should learn how to use some ICMP (Internet Control Message Protocol) tools. ICMP packets help you root out problems with connectivity and routing.

ping (see http://ftp.arl.mil/~mike/ping.html) is one of the most basic network debugging tools. It sends ICMP echo request packets to a host. If the host gets the packet and feels nice enough, it sends an ICMP echo response packet in return.

Let's say that you run ping 10.1.2.21 and you get this output:

```
PING 10.1.2.21 (10.1.2.21): 56 data bytes
64 bytes from 10.1.2.21: icmp_seq=0 ttl=255 time=8.0 ms
64 bytes from 10.1.2.21: icmp_seq=1 ttl=255 time=3.2 ms
64 bytes from 10.1.2.21: icmp_seq=2 ttl=255 time=3.4 ms
64 bytes from 10.1.2.21: icmp_seq=4 ttl=255 time=3.4 ms
64 bytes from 10.1.2.21: icmp_seq=5 ttl=255 time=3.2 ms
```

The most important parts of the output are the icmp_seq number and the round-trip time. ping sends a sequence of echo request packets, one every second.

Notice that there's a gap between 2 and 4 in this example. This usually means that there's some kind of connectivity problem. It is possible to get packets out of order, but if this happens, there's still some kind of problem because ping sends only one packet a second. If a response takes more than a second to arrive, the connection is extremely slow.

The round-trip time is the total elapsed time between the moment that the request packet was transmitted and moment that the response packet arrived. If there are incomplete routes between the request source and the destination, ping immediately reports the ICMP "host unreachable" packets that come back as a result of the disconnection.

On a wired LAN, you should expect absolutely no packet loss and very low numbers for the round-trip time (the preceding example output is from a wireless network). You should also expect no packet loss from your network to and from your ISP, as well as reasonable, steady round-trip times.

Sadly, not all hosts on the Internet respond to ICMP echo request packets as they once did. Therefore, you may come across situations where you can connect to a Web site on a host, but not get a ping response.

Another useful ICMP-based program is traceroute; it will come in handy when you reach the material on routing later in the chapter. Use traceroute *host* to see the exact path your packets take to a remote host. One of the best things about traceroute is its reporting of return-trip times at each step in the route, as demonstrated in this output fragment:

```
 4  206.220.243.106  1.163 ms  0.997 ms  1.182 ms
 5  4.24.203.65  1.312 ms  1.12 ms  1.463 ms
 6  64.159.1.225  1.421 ms  1.37 ms  1.347 ms
 7  64.159.1.38  55.642 ms  55.625 ms  55.663 ms
 8  209.247.10.230  55.89 ms  55.617 ms  55.964 ms
 9  209.244.14.226  55.851 ms  55.726 ms  55.832 ms
10  209.246.29.174  56.419 ms  56.44 ms  56.423 ms
```

Because this output shows a big latency jump between hop 6 and hop 7, that part of the route is probably some sort of long-distance link.

You can put these ICMP tools to use when setting up a working network interface, as the next few sections will show you how to do.

## 5.4 Configuring Interfaces and the Host-to-Network Layer

On a Linux system, you connect the Internet layer to the physical medium, such as an Ethernet network or a modem-based connection, with a *network interface*. Common network interface names are eth0 (the first Ethernet card in the computer) and ppp0 (a PPP interface).

The most important command for viewing or manually configuring the network interface settings is ifconfig. To see your current interface's settings, run this command:

```
ifconfig -a
```

You do not need the -a in Linux, but other Unix variants require this option. The output should look something like this:

```
eth0      Link encap:Ethernet  HWaddr 00:40:05:A0:7F:96
          inet addr:10.1.2.2  Bcast:10.1.2.255  Mask:255.255.255.0
          UP BROADCAST RUNNING MULTICAST  MTU:1500  Metric:1
          RX packets:806961 errors:1 dropped:0 overruns:0 frame:0
          TX packets:811658 errors:0 dropped:0 overruns:0 carrier:0
          collisions:0
          RX bytes:726765161 (693.0 Mb)  TX bytes:110229902 (105.1 Mb)

lo        Link encap:Local Loopback
          inet addr:127.0.0.1  Mask:255.0.0.0
          UP LOOPBACK RUNNING  MTU:16436  Metric:1
          RX packets:44 errors:0 dropped:0 overruns:0 frame:0
          TX packets:44 errors:0 dropped:0 overruns:0 carrier:0
          collisions:0
          RX bytes:3569 (3.4 Kb)  TX bytes:3569 (3.4 Kb)
```

The left side contains interface names, and the right side contains the settings for each interface. You can see that each interface has an IP address (inet addr) and a subnet mask (Mask), but you should also take careful note of the lines containing UP and RUNNING, because these tell you that the interface is working.

The lo interface is a virtual network interface that is called the *loopback* because it "loops back" to itself. 127.0.0.1 is the IP address of *localhost*, so connecting to this address is the same as connecting to the machine that you're currently using.

Your system calls ifconfig from one of its init.d scripts at boot time to configure the lo loopback interface. It's the only part of the network that is actually the same on any Linux machine, so it's a great place to start when you're trying to figure out how your particular distribution sets up networks. For example, in Red Hat Linux, each network interface has a script in /etc/sysconfig/network-scripts. You should be able to find the loopback device configuration by digging around in /etc with grep ifconfig.

If you have a static IP address on an Ethernet interface, your system's boot sequence should set up the interface in a manner very similar to the loopback. However, you can manually configure an IP address and netmask for an Ethernet network interface named eth0 with this command:

```
ifconfig eth0 address netmask mask
```

The preceding command allows your machine to talk to every other host in the subnet defined by *address* and *mask*, but it does not let you go beyond the subnet, because you have not supplied a default gateway (gateways will be explained in the next section).

If you do not connect your system to the network with a static IP address on an Ethernet network, but rather, have a link such as a PPP or PPP-over-Ethernet (PPPoE) DSL connection, or if you use DHCP to get host information, you do not configure your interface with ifconfig (see Sections 5.7, 5.8, and 5.9 for those cases). However, even with those other types of connections, ifconfig -a is very useful for debugging.

## 5.5 Configuring a Default Gateway

In the previous section, you saw how to manually configure an Ethernet network interface with a particular address and mask. You can connect to networks outside your subnet by adding a default gateway to your kernel's IP routing table with this command:

```
route add default gw gw-address
```

The *gw-address* parameter is the IP address of your default gateway; it *must* be an address in a locally connected subnet defined by the *address* and *mask* settings of your network interface (as described in the previous section). If you have a static IP address, a default route setting usually goes along with an ifconfig command in your boot sequence. For other kinds of connections, other programs usually set the default route.

To view the current default route, run this command:

```
route -n
```

The output should look something like this:

```
Kernel IP routing table
Destination     Gateway         Genmask         Flags Metric Ref    Use Iface
10.1.2.0        0.0.0.0         255.255.255.0   U     0      0        0 eth0
0.0.0.0         10.1.2.1        0.0.0.0         UG    0      0        0 eth0
```

The ifconfig command that configured the eth0 network interface in this example added the first route line. However, the last line is the default gateway, because it has a netmask of 0.0.0.0, which allows the host to reach all other hosts on the Internet. The gateway's IP address is 10.1.2.1, and you can see that you reach that gateway through the eth0 network interface.

If you mistype a gateway address when adding a route, you cannot attach another gateway until you delete the erroneous entry. To remove the current default gateway, run this command:

```
route del -net default
```

Figure 5-1 on the next page shows a typical local area network with a gateway, or router. The subnet is 10.1.2.0/255.255.255.0 with a default gateway of 10.1.2.1. Each IP address represents a network interface, as does the uplink

IP on the gateway. If you do not run the gateway, you do not need to worry about its uplink — for example, if you are configuring a host with an IP address of 10.1.2.4, you need only know that 10.1.2.1 is the local IP address on the gateway.

**NOTE**    *If your netmask is 255.255.255.0, your router is probably at node 1 of the subnet (for example, 10.1.2.1 in 10.1.2.0/255.255.255.0). This is convention, not necessarily reality.*

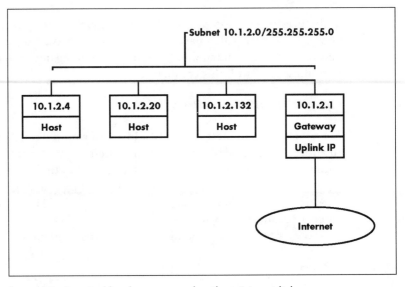

*Figure 5-1: A typical local area network with an Internet link.*

A properly configured default gateway allows you to connect to the rest of the world. However, you still need to know how to convert common names, or hostnames, to IP addresses.

## 5.6 Resolving Hostnames

The last bit of configuration for a simple network connection is hostname resolution. Simply put, your computer needs to know how to translate a name such as www.example.com to an IP address. Without this capability, your Internet connection is practically worthless — no one in their right mind advertises IP addresses for Web sites and email addresses, partly because a host's IP address is subject to change, but also because it's not easy to remember a bunch of numbers.

The most basic way to do this mapping is with the /etc/hosts file, which looks like this:

```
127.0.0.1       localhost
10.1.1.3        atlantic.aem7.net       atlantic
10.1.1.4        pacific.aem7.net        pacific
```

In the bad old days, there was one central hosts file that everyone repeatedly copied to their own machine to stay up to date. This might have worked for a handful of machines, but as the ARPANET/Internet grew, this quickly got out of hand. The Domain Name System (DNS) decentralized hostname resolution. The idea is that your machine's resolver (in the C library) asks a *nameserver* for the IP address corresponding to a hostname. If the nameserver does not know, it can find out who is responsible for that name and ask for the IP address from the responsible party's nameserver. If you do not already know the DNS server addresses that your ISP uses, ask your provider for them.

Let's say that your ISP's nameserver addresses are 10.32.45.23 and 10.3.2.3. Put the servers in your system's /etc/resolv.conf file like this:

```
search mydomain.example.com example.com
nameserver 10.32.45.23
nameserver 10.3.2.3
```

The search line in the preceding example asks the resolver to look for the IP address of *host*.mydomain.example.com, and for *host*.example.com if you ask for an incomplete domain name *host* that does not resolve on the first attempt.

For a simple network configuration where you do not have control of your own nameserver, there is little else to know about DNS except how to make sure that your machine's hostname resolution works. To verify this, type host *known_name* where *known_name* is some Internet name that you know exists (such as www.example.com). The output should be something like this:

```
known_name has address 10.218.44.5
```

You should also be able to look up a name based on its IP address with host *address*. If the address owner is doing their part, you should get the hostname corresponding to *address*, but DNS administrators often do not configure their servers to return these hostnames. Furthermore, the mapping of hostname to address is not one-to-one; you can have many hostnames for a single address.

Before moving on, take a look at /etc/nsswitch.conf. It should have a line like this:

```
hosts:          files dns
```

Putting files ahead of dns here ensures that your system checks the /etc/hosts file for the hostname of your requested IP address before asking the DNS server. This is usually a good idea (especially for looking up localhost), but your /etc/hosts file should be as *short* as possible. Don't put anything in there because you want to boost performance; it will burn you later. You can put all the hosts within a small private LAN in /etc/hosts, but the general rule of thumb is that if a particular host has a DNS entry, it has no place in /etc/hosts.

**NOTE** *The /etc/hosts file is also useful for resolving hostnames in the early stages of booting, when the network may not be available.*

DNS is a fairly broad topic, and if you have any responsibility for domain names, have a look at *DNS and BIND* [Albitz].

## 5.7 Using DHCP Clients

The Dynamic Host Configuration Protocol (DHCP) allows a host to get its IP address, subnet mask, default gateway, DNS servers, and other information from the network, so that you don't have to type these parameters by hand. Network administrators like DHCP because users don't have to nag them for IP addresses when they want to connect to the network.

Like ifconfig, DHCP works on a network interface name. All Linux distributions have a network interface setup option for DHCP, so if you don't feel like digging around to try to find out what file controls the interface settings, it's all right to let your distribution's setup program do the work.

When your machine asks a DHCP server for an IP address, it is really asking for a *lease* on an address for a certain amount of time. When the lease is up, your machine can ask to renew the lease.

Most distributions use the ISC (Internet Software Consortium) dhclient program to request and retrieve IP address information from a DHCP server. To get a lease, you can run dhclient by hand on the command line, but before doing so you *must* remove any default gateway route. Once you have done that, you can request an IP lease by running the following command:

```
dhclient eth0
```

dhclient stores its process ID in /var/run/dhclient.pid and its lease information in /var/state/dhclient.leases.

Red Hat Linux versions 7 and earlier use a program called pump instead of dhclient. You can run it with pump -i *interface*, but you may want to consider getting dhclient from ISC or as an RPM.

## 5.8 PPP Connections

So far, you have seen Internet connections based on a local area network (LAN) and a default gateway on that network. However, if you have a modem and telephone line to connect to the Internet, you cannot use the same host-to-network layer interfaces described in previous sections because your connection does not run over the Ethernet physical medium.

The most popular standard for single-machine Internet connectivity with a modem is PPP (Point-to-Point Protocol). Although PPP is a very flexible protocol, its main use is to connect one machine without a direct IP connection to second machine (a PPP server) that has one, with the second machine possibly asking the first for a username and password along the way.

When you dial up and register with a PPP server, the server gives you your own IP address and tells you about its IP address. After the connection initiates, the PPP software on your machine knows how to reach the server's IP address, and the server knows how to reach your machine's IP address. To reach the rest of the Internet, you set the default gateway to the server's IP address and let the server do the rest. Figure 5-2 shows the link between your local IP address and the server's IP address. As with the routers in LANs, you do not need to worry about the server's uplink IP address.

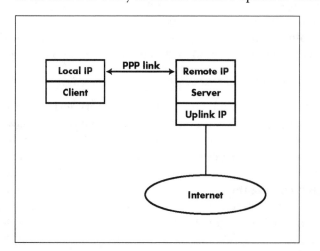

Figure 5-2: A typical PPP link.

Although it's nice to know how this process works, you are probably more interested in actually getting a connection to work. Specifically, you want to know the answers to these questions:

- How do I get my modem to dial the server's number?
- Where do I put my username and password?
- How do I start and stop a network interface like ppp0?

The key to the whole mess is a pppd, a system daemon that acts as an intermediary between a serial port on your machine and a PPP network interface such as ppp0. To set up everything, you need to do four things:

1. Verify that your serial port, modem, and login (username and password) work.
2. Create an options file in /etc/ppp/peers containing configuration options.

3. Create a chat script to make your modem dial out (and possibly log in).
4. Set up Password Authentication Protocol (PAP) or Challenge Handshake Authentication Protocol (CHAP) user authentication if necessary.

These four steps are explained in the following sections. If your distribution's dial-up configuration tool works for you, it may not be worth your while to read through these sections. However, if you don't read through them, at least run ifconfig when you're connected to see what the PPP interface name is, because you may need it later in the chapter for Network Address Translation (NAT) or firewalling.

### 5.8.1 Testing Your Serial Port and Modem

Before you start with the full pppd setup, you should use minicom to make sure that your modem works and that you can initiate a PPP connection. Modems talk to your computer through serial port devices, so the first thing you need to do is determine the serial port that your modem is connected to.

**NOTE**    *Don't try to use a Winmodem with Linux. See Section 17.2.4.*

As mentioned in Section 2.3.2, Linux serial port devices are at /dev/ttyS*. If you're having problems, it's best to check your boot messages as described in Section 4.1 to see if the modem setup looks right and to verify that you're using the correct serial port device. In addition, you can run cat /proc/ioports for more port statistics. Most modern hardware and kernels actually recognize the hardware configuration correctly, but if you have extra serial ports on different hardware interrupt numbers (IRQs), you may need to run setserial to specify the hardware parameters that the serial port uses. For example:

```
setserial /dev/ttyS3 irq 5
```

See the setserial(8) manual page for more options and a good overall explanation of serial ports.

Now you can get down to the business of checking the connection to the dial-up server with these steps:

1. Configure the baud rate, serial port, and other minicom settings with this command:

```
minicom -s
```

2. After choosing your settings, exit the configuration menu. minicom then attempts to connect to the serial port.
3. Upon success, you should be able to enter AT commands. Test it by typing AT and then pressing ENTER. You should get OK as a response. If you're having trouble, skip to step 7 and then back to step 1.

4. Reset your modem (that is, clear its volatile data) and dial your ISP's number by typing these two modem commands:

```
atz
atdtnumber
```

5. Your modem should connect with a CONNECT message. Wait five or ten seconds after you see the CONNECT message. You're looking for "garbage" like this:

```
~ÿ}#À!}!}!} }.}%}&} }
```

If you get this junk immediately after you see the CONNECT message, you've got a PPP connection, and furthermore, you probably need to use the PAP or CHAP authentication system when dialing up. Make a note of this and skip to the last step.

6. If you get something like Username: instead, type in your username (and password, if necessary). After logging in, keep going (you might need to type ppp or something similar) until you get the "garbage" mentioned in the previous step. In this case, you probably do *not* need to use PAP or CHAP.

7. Exit minicom by pressing CONTROL-A, then x. If minicom hangs when you're trying to exit, you can wait a little while to see if it times out, or you can be impatient, open another window, and use kill -KILL on the minicom process.

When interacting with the modem and remote server, take careful notes of all the settings you used, what you had to type, and the responses you got back. You'll need this information to write a chat script.

## 5.8.2 Starting pppd with Options Files

Now that you know how to log in to your ISP's server manually, you can create a configuration file containing the same connection settings you used with minicom -s. This allows you to make pppd dial the telephone number automatically.

Pick a name for the ISP and create an options file called /etc/ppp/peers/name, with the following lines:

```
ttyS1 115200 crtscts
connect '/usr/sbin/chat -v -f /etc/ppp/chat-name'
noauth
defaultroute
mru 1500
```

The first line specifies the modem device, the CPU-to-modem speed, and the hardware flow control. You will read about these options in Section 5.8.5. Don't bother to tweak anything yet; for now, just make sure that your pppd can start properly.

Now make a chat file named /etc/ppp/chat-*name*. This chat file determines the connection commands sent through the serial line and the responses that you expect from your ISP. For now, just fill it with the following lines, where *number* is your ISP's telephone number:

```
ABORT "NO CARRIER"
ABORT BUSY
"" ATZ OK
ATDTnumber CONNECT
```

Try to establish a connection by starting pppd with this command:

```
pppd call name
```

Monitor the progress by looking at your system log. The pppd syslog facility name is daemon, so the log information is probably in /var/log/daemon.log or something similar. However, the chat program used for initializing the modem connection may use a different facility, such as local2.

You should get messages like this in your log file:

```
Jul 29 18:40:46 mikado pppd[634]: pppd 2.4.1 started by root, uid 0
Jul 29 18:40:47 mikado chat[635]: [chat messages]
Jul 29 18:40:47 mikado pppd[634]: Connect script failed
Jul 29 18:40:48 mikado pppd[634]: Exit.
```

Take a careful look at the chat messages. They should tell you if the modem is dialing up, and if it gets an answer and connection from the remote server.

Even if the preceding connection settings work so far, expect the configuration to fail because you haven't supplied a username and password. Watch the failure in the log carefully, because it tells you how to proceed. For example, if the log file says Connect script failed as in the preceding example, then you have a problem with the dial-up portion (in addition to not having supplied a username and password).

In particular, look out for these types of failures:

- I/O errors happen when your serial port and modem are not set up correctly. Double-check the first line of the options file to make sure it matches the settings that you verified earlier with minicom.

- If the remote system uses PAP or CHAP, expect an authentication error. Skip to Section 5.8.4 to see how to configure PAP and CHAP.

- Timeouts generally go along with incomplete chat scripts. Proceed to the next section to see how to finish your script.

- Bad chat output, such as NO CARRIER and BUSY, are signs of telephone line problems. Double-check the ISP's telephone number.

To stop a PPP daemon after it finishes its chat sequence, use the following command, substituting the appropriate network interface name if yours is not ppp0:

```
kill `cat /var/run/ppp0.pid`
```

### 5.8.3 Chat Scripts

A chat script is a file containing commands that go out through the serial line and responses that you expect to receive from the serial line (the responses come from the modem or ISP, depending on the current stage of the dial-up process). Recall this chat script line from the previous section:

```
ATDTnumber CONNECT
```

This means that the chat program should dial with the ATDT*number* modem command and expect a response of CONNECT. After receiving a CONNECT response, chat moves to the next thing in the chat file. After stepping through the entire file, and assuming that everything goes as anticipated, chat returns success and pppd proceeds with a PPP connection.

The details of your chat script depend on your ISP, and you should be armed with the information you got in Section 5.8.1 before trying to complete your script. However, here is a script that works for most service providers that use Cisco equipment (where *username* is your username and *password* is your password):

```
ABORT "NO CARRIER"
ABORT BUSY
"" ATZ OK
ATDTnumber CONNECT
"" ername:
username ssword:
\qpassword >
ppp
```

The ABORT keywords and strings at the top of the script cause chat to exit with an error if it encounters one of those strings. In addition, \q*string* tells chat not to send *string* to syslogd. In this case, it tells chat not to send *password* to syslogd when making a record of the connection.

Remember that if you use PAP or CHAP, your chat script likely should not contain any username or password information. However, if your chat script does contain username and password details (like the preceding script), you should be mostly done after you finish the script — try to verify the connection with `ifconfig -a`, and try to access the Internet. If everything works, skip to Section 5.8.5 for information on how to tweak your options file.

**NOTE** *For more information on* `chat`, *see the* chat(8) *manual page.*

## 5.8.4 PAP and CHAP

Many dial-up ISPs require that logins use PAP (Password Authentication Protocol) or CHAP (Challenge Handshake Authentication Protocol). If your ISP has such a requirement, get started by adding the following entry for your username to the end of the /etc/ppp/peers/*name* options file from Section 5.8.2:

```
name username
```

**WARNING** *Don't put* require-pap *in your options file. This option is primarily for running a PPP gateway; it requires the remote system to authenticate with your system.*

### PAP

If your ISP uses a PAP server, edit /etc/ppp/pap-secrets. The lines in that file have this format:

```
your_hostname    remote_hostname    password    ip_address
```

The references to hostnames are primarily for use by PPP servers. For a simple client machine, you can put this in pap-secrets:

```
username          *                 password    *
```

The * means to accept any remote hostname. Don't bother with the IP address, either, because the server should give you one.

The preceding instructions will work if you have only one ISP. However, if you have multiple ISPs, do the following for each:

1. Pick a name for the ISP (*isp_name*).

2. Add the following line to the ISP's options file in /etc/ppp/peers:

```
remotename isp_name
```

3. Add the following to your `pap-secrets` file:

| username | isp_name | password | * |

### CHAP

If you run into a CHAP server, proceed as you would with a PAP server and multiple ISPs, but enter the username and password into /etc/ppp/chap-secrets in the two-line format that follows:

| username | isp_name | your_password |
| isp_name | username | their_password |

## 5.8.5 Options Files

The options files in /etc/ppp/peers contain valid pppd command-line options. Therefore, you could run pppd at the shell prompt with these options as command-line arguments, and indeed, some distributions (like Red Hat Linux) use scripts to set up big pppd invocations, completely bypassing /etc/ppp/peers. However, it's far more convenient to use options files because they enable you to invoke pppd call *file* to activate the connection.

**NOTE**   *In addition to the per-connection file in* /etc/ppp/peers, *you need a* /etc/ppp/options *file for global settings that apply to all* pppd *processes. This file must exist, even if it's empty.*

As mentioned earlier, the first two options in the options file are the serial device (with or without /dev/ at the front) and the serial port speed. For most serial ports and modems, 115200 is an appropriate speed, but you may wish to lower it to 57600 or lower for really slow systems. Recall that the following was the first options line in Section 5.8.2:

```
ttyS1 115200 crtscts
```

All other pppd options follow the serial port and baud rate. Here are some of the most important pppd options:

**crtscts**   Enables RTS/CTS hardware flow control (popular with PC hardware).

**defaultroute**   Sets the kernel's default route to the machine on the other side of the PPP connection. Don't forget this option; otherwise, you won't be able to reach anything on the Internet beyond the host on the other end of the PPP connection, which usually isn't very useful. If you happen to forget this when testing, you can manually add a route with the route command (see Section 5.11).

**noauth**   Specifies that the remote machine should not send *you* a user-name and password; this is another option that you don't want to forget.

**connect** *command*   Initializes the serial port with the specified *command*, usually a chat invocation like this:

```
connect '/usr/sbin/chat -v -f /etc/ppp/chat-name'
```

**nodetach**   Run pppd in non-daemon mode; this prevents the shell prompt from returning immediately after you run pppd from the command line. This is handy for debugging, because you can press CONTROL-C to interrupt a connection.

**mru** *size*   The maximum receive unit option tells the remote server not to send any chunks of data larger than *size*. The default is 1500 bytes; 3000 works for faster connections. Do not set this (or mtu) to a number lower than 1300, because many applications prefer that their data be sent in larger chunks.

**mtu** *size*   The maximum transmission unit option requests that your machine not send (transmit) any chunks of data larger than *size* to the remote server. The default is 1500 bytes. The quality of your telephone line or switch often determines how high you may set *size*.

**name** *name*   Forces pppd to use *name* as the username (or local system name) for PAP or CHAP authentication.

**remotename** *name*   Forces pppd to use *name* as the remote system name for PAP or CHAP authentication.

**debug**   Activates verbose syslog debugging.

**NOTE**   *If your connection frequently hangs or drops, and the ARQ light on your modem blinks often, you probably have a poor switch or telephone line. If you hear any "static" when you pick up your telephone (especially before making a call), your telephone company may be overloading your local phone switch. See if they will put you on a better switch. It's also possible that there's a problem between your phone jack and the phone network box in your building.*

The pppd(8) manual page has many more options. Keep in mind that most options are only relevant when you're running a PPP server, not a client. To be entirely truthful, there is no technical difference between a PPP server and a PPP client. They are simply peers that know how to contact each other. However, when one of the peers acts as a gateway to the rest of the Internet, you often say that this peer is the server.

### 5.8.6 PPP Directory Permissions

The /etc/ppp directory should be mode 700; that is, the superuser should have read-write-execute access, and no other users should have access.

However, any user can run `pppd call` *name* if that user has read access to the chat script and `pppd` is setuid root. Some distributions do not trust `pppd` and do not have the setuid bit set by default. As with any program, the setuid bit is a certainly a matter of concern if you don't trust your own users, but it's not so critical if you're the only user on the system.

There is no standard for which user should start PPP (or even how to set up the connection). PPP has always been somewhat clumsy to operate because the Internet grew up around networks that were always active. Broadband connections solve this problem, though not everyone has access to them (or wants them).

## 5.9 Broadband Connections

The term *broadband* vaguely refers to connections faster than a conventional modem link. For most users, this means a DSL or cable modem connection. One of the most frustrating things about broadband providers is that they don't tend to tell you what kind of technology they use.

Most DSL or cable modems have an Ethernet port, requiring you to have an Ethernet interface on your computer, and as you saw in Section 5.4, it's not hard to set up an Ethernet interface (in theory, at least). Unfortunately, not all providers send straight IP from the Ethernet port, so things can get more complicated.

For the most part, your setup depends on the kind of broadband connection you have. These rules generally apply:

**Cable modem**   These devices usually speak straight IP, and you can do the network configuration with DHCP. Plug your Linux machine into the cable modem and look at Section 5.7. If you have a static (fixed) IP address, you should be able to set up the connection by hand as described in Section 5.4. You may need to perform some configuration on the cable modem before it will connect to the outside world, but that's usually done with a Web browser.

**DSL with a dynamic IP address**   DSL providers usually send PPP over Ethernet (PPPoE) through their devices. This is the most common kind of DSL connection, and as luck would have it, it's the most complicated. See Section 5.9.2 for more information on PPPoE.

**DSL with a static IP address**   Some DSL providers talk straight IP over Ethernet if you have a fixed IP address. In this case, you can use the manual configuration described in Section 5.4.

The preceding rules are based on the hardware available to service providers, but your provider may be different. Telephone companies prefer PPPoE because it's easier for them to monitor and authenticate, but cable companies tend not to care. You can probably determine the type of connection the ISP provides by looking at the setup instructions for Windows. If you see anything in the Windows screenshots with "pppoe" in the name, it's probably a PPP-over-Ethernet connection.

**NOTE** *If a broadband service forces you to use a modem or another device that doesn't have an Ethernet port, you will probably have a very difficult time getting it to work under Linux. Evaluate alternative ISPs.*

Don't expect your ISP's technical support to be very helpful to anyone running Unix. It doesn't matter that they're using technology that came straight from Unix machines — you're a fringe user, meaning that you have to figure it out yourself.

### 5.9.1 Routers

Before you connect your Linux machine directly to a broadband connection, you need to ask yourself this very important question: *Is it really worth it?*

The alternative is to purchase a small router. These very inexpensive devices not only speak straight IP and PPPoE, but often include a multi-port 10/100Base-T Ethernet switch and a wireless access point. They can do network address translation, route packets from the outside world to ports on their internal networks, and more. (Sometimes they even have pretty lights that serve as eye candy when you have nothing else to do.)

Routers are especially attractive for Linux users with PPPoE connections. PPPoE is a hassle, because you have to worry about several configuration files and daemons, not to mention possible trouble when upgrading. If you put a router between a DSL connection and your Linux machine, you can configure your machine's IP address statically or with DHCP.

You can also build a network with a router. Their built-in switches not only share the broadband connection with all of the machines on the network, but also link those machines with each other.

Of course, a Linux machine with two Ethernet cards and a hub or switch can do anything that a router can do. In fact, you have much finer control over a full-blown Linux machine acting as a router. However, very few people actually have a use for the fancy tricks you get with Linux, and the cost of a router is not much more than the cost of a switch.

If you decide to purchase a router, skip to Section 5.10 for Ethernet networking details. Otherwise, if you are using PPPoE to connect to your ISP and you want to do everything on your Linux machine, continue reading.

### 5.9.2 PPP Over Ethernet (PPPoE)

PPPoE support in Linux is still in a somewhat experimental stage. To use it, get the rp-pppoe package from http://www.roaringpenguin.com/ to extend pppd to full Asymmetric Digital Subscriber Line (ADSL) support. You also need a reasonably recent version of pppd, such as 2.4.1. All of this might come with your distribution, but as with most new software, it's a good idea to compile your own set from source code (see Chapter 9).

The easiest way to set up rp-pppoe is to run adsl-setup as root. This creates appropriate /etc/ppp/pppoe.conf and /etc/ppp/pap-secrets files for your machine. If you read through pppoe.conf, you'll find only two critical settings:

---

ETH=*interface*

USER=username

---

Most computers have only one Ethernet card, so you'll probably use eth0 as the ETH setting. USER is your username at your ISP. This must match the settings in pap-secrets (see Section 5.8.4 for information on PAP).

To manually start the connection, run this command:

---

adsl-start

---

After you verify that everything works correctly, you can put adsl-start in an init.d script to activate the connection at boot time. adsl-start is a shell script that processes pppoe.conf and then runs asdl-connect, which in turn runs a big, ugly pppd command line. In principle, you could put all of this into an options file, but it is almost certainly not worth the hassle.

To stop the connection, use adsl-stop.

**WARNING** *Back up your* /etc/resolv.conf *if you put any kind of work into it, because* adsl-connect *may replace your DNS settings.*

## 5.10 Ethernet Networks

Ethernet is by far and away the most popular physical medium for local area networks. Although there have been several kinds of cables, cable topologies, connectors, and speeds in Ethernet history, the basic hardware, protocol specification, and programming techniques have proved remarkably robust. Figure 5-3 on the next page shows the physical appearance of an Ethernet network.

Ethernet networks have always been cheap, but the unshielded twisted-pair (UTP) devices that gained popularity in the 1990s are now inexpensive almost to the point of absurdity. Many new computers (and devices such as video game consoles) have built-in Ethernet interfaces. Old twisted-pair networks operate at 10 megabits per second and are called 10Base-T networks. The current standard is 100Base-T (running at 100 Mb/s); it's sometimes called *Fast* Ethernet. 100Base-T requires category 5 cable, and 10Base-T devices work with most 100Base-T switches and hubs. If you need something a little bit faster, you can go to *Gigabit* Ethernet; 1000Base-T uses twisted-pair like its predecessors, and 1000Base-SX is the fiber-optic version. If you don't run a supercomputer center, it's unlikely that you'll need anything like this — you'll be hard-pressed to saturate a 100Base-T network.

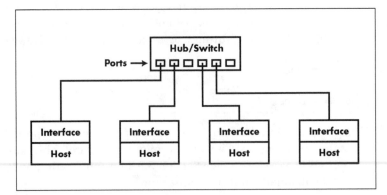

Figure 5-3: A twisted-pair Ethernet local area network.

To build a network, you need a network interface card (NIC) for each of your computers, a hub or switch, and some cables to connect the computers to the hub or switch. If you run out of network ports, it's easy to add another hub or switch.

Each node on an Ethernet network has a hardware address, also called the MAC (Media Access Control) address. Running `ifconfig -a` shows yours; in the example in Section 5.4, the hardware address was 00:40:05:A0:7F:96.

The first three bytes of a MAC address make up a vendor code, or OUI (Organizationally Unique Identifier). For example, Sun Microsystems' OUI is 08-00-20. You can look up an OUI at http://standards.ieee.org/regauth/oui/index.shtml. You do not need to bother with the MAC address except when debugging.

NOTE   *Each node on your network should have a different MAC address even if two Ethernet cards are of the same model, and most Ethernet devices carry a label with the MAC address. Unfortunately, you may come across a batch of NIC cards with a duplicate address or two. You could try to return the duplicates, but many modern cards also allow you to change the MAC address with an extra utility.*

### 5.10.1 Ethernet and IP

IP over Ethernet is very straightforward. When you want to send a packet to some other host on your local area network, your machine must know that host's MAC address. Using a series of ARP (Address Resolution Protocol) broadcasts, your host maps the IP address of the target to the target's MAC address and then sends the IP packet out on the wire to that MAC address.

Your host also caches the destination MAC address inside the kernel. To view your system's current ARP cache, run the following command:

```
arp -a
```

If you don't have DNS working yet, use arp -na instead, to disable hostname resolution. Linux arp with no arguments gives a slightly more formatted list than either of the above options, but this format is not standard across all versions of Unix.

**NOTE**    *Remember that ARP only applies to machines on local subnets. To reach destinations outside your subnet, your host sends the packet to the router, and it's someone else's problem after that.*

The only real problem you can have with ARP is that your system's cache can get out of date if you're moving an IP address from one network interface card to another, because the cards have different MAC addresses (for example, this can happen when testing a machine). Unix systems invalidate the ARP cache entry if there is no response after a while, so there shouldn't be any trouble other than a small delay for invalidated data. However, if you want to delete an ARP cache entry immediately, use this command:

```
arp -d host
```

You can also view the ARP cache for a single network interface like this:

```
arp -i interface
```

The arp(8) manual page explains how to manually set ARP cache entries, but you should not need to do this.

**NOTE**    *Don't confuse ARP with RARP (Reverse Address Resolution Protocol). RARP transforms a MAC address back to a hostname or IP address. Before DHCP became popular, some diskless workstations and other devices used RARP to get their configuration, but RARP is rare today.*

### 5.10.2 Private Networks

Let's say that you decide to build your own network at home or at the office. You have your Ethernet cards, hub or switch, and cables ready. Your next question is, "What IP subnet should I use?"

You can pay your ISP for a block of Internet addresses if you need real Internet routing to a number of individual hosts inside your local network. However, this costs a lot of money and isn't useful for anything but a highly decentralized site, such as a university. As a much less expensive alternative, you can pick a subnet from the addresses in the RFC 1918 Internet standards document, shown in Table 5-2 on the next page.

**Table 5-2:** Private Networks Defined by RFC 1918

| Network | Subnet Mask | Short Form |
|---|---|---|
| 10.0.0.0 | 255.0.0.0 | 10.0.0.0/8 |
| 192.168.0.0 | 255.255.0.0 | 192.168.0.0/16 |
| 172.16.0.0 | 255.240.0.0 | 172.16.0.0/12 |

Unless you plan to have more than 254 hosts on a single network, pick a small subnet such as 10.0.0.0/255.255.255.0, which uses the addresses 10.0.0.1 through 10.0.0.254. (Networks with this netmask are sometimes called *class C* subnets. This term is technically somewhat obsolete but still useful in practice.) You can carve up private subnets in any way that you please, experimenting to your heart's content.

So what's the catch, you say? It's very simple — hosts on the real Internet know nothing about these private subnets and will not route to them. With no extra help, your hosts cannot talk to the outside world. Therefore, if you have a single Internet connection, you need to have some way to fill in the gap between that connection and the rest of the hosts on your private network. Network Address Translation (NAT) does exactly this; see Section 5.14. Refer back to Figure 5-1 on page 94 for an illustration of a typical network. The gateway can be a regular Linux machine or one of the devices described in Section 5.9.1.

## 5.11 Configuring Routes

Routing is the act of transferring packets from one host or subnet to another. Let's say that you have two LAN subnets, 10.0.0.0/24 and 10.0.1.0/24, and a Linux router machine with two Ethernet cards, one connected to each subnet. The router has two IP addresses: 10.0.0.1 for eth0 and 10.0.1.1 for eth1. Figure 5-4 shows the two networks; the router's routing table looks like this (obtained by running route -n):

```
Destination   Gateway      Genmask         Flags Metric Ref    Use Iface
10.0.0.0      0.0.0.0      255.255.255.0   U     0      0        0 eth0
10.0.1.0      0.0.0.0      255.255.255.0   U     0      0        0 eth1
```

Furthermore, let's say that the hosts on each subnet have the router as their default gateway (10.0.0.1 for 10.0.0.0/24 and 10.0.1.1 for 10.0.0.0/24). Therefore, if 10.0.0.37 wanted to send a packet to anything outside of 10.0.0.0/24, it would pass the packet to 10.0.0.1. Now let's say that you want to send a packet from 10.0.0.37 to 10.0.1.23. The packet goes to 10.0.0.1 (the router) via its eth0 interface, and now you want it to go back out through the router's eth1 interface. To make the Linux kernel perform this basic routing function, the only thing you need to do is enable *IP forwarding* on the router with the following command:

```
echo 1 > /proc/sys/net/ipv4/ip_forward
```

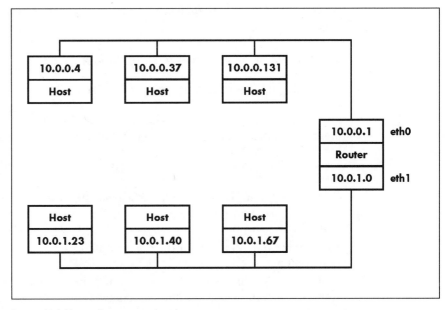

Figure 5-4: Two subnets joined with a router.

This is easy enough, but what if you have another subnet, 10.0.2.0/24, connected to the host at 10.0.0.37 on that host's second network interface, as shown in Figure 5-5? After configuring 10.0.0.37's second Ethernet interface to 10.0.2.1, you now need to figure out how everything else in 10.0.0.0/24 and 10.0.1.0/24 can talk to 10.0.2.0/24. Let's start with the router that connects 10.0.0.0/24 and 10.0.1.0/24.

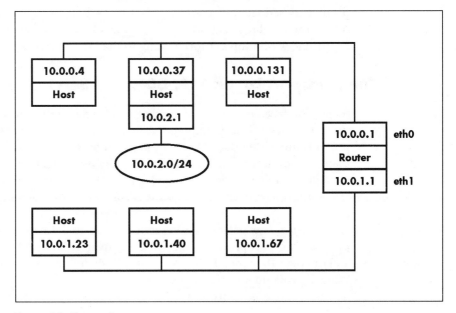

Figure 5-5: Three subnets.

You can tell the router that 10.0.0.37 handles 10.0.2.0/24 with this command:

```
route add -net 10.0.2.0 netmask 255.255.255.0 gw 10.0.0.37
```

The routing table on the router now looks like this:

| Destination | Gateway | Genmask | Flags | Metric | Ref | Use | Iface |
|---|---|---|---|---|---|---|---|
| 10.0.2.0 | 10.1.2.37 | 255.255.255.0 | UG | 0 | 0 | 0 | eth0 |
| 10.0.0.0 | 0.0.0.0 | 255.255.255.0 | U | 0 | 0 | 0 | eth0 |
| 10.0.1.0 | 0.0.0.0 | 255.255.255.0 | U | 0 | 0 | 0 | eth1 |

As an added bonus, recall that all traffic from 10.0.1.0/24 initially goes to the router, because 10.0.1.1 is the default router on that subnet. Therefore, anything on 10.0.1.0/24 can now talk to 10.0.2.0/24, and vice versa (as long as you set the default route for the hosts on 10.0.2.0/24 to 10.0.2.1). But what about 10.0.0.0/24?

Technically, this also works now, because the packets go to 10.0.0.1 (eth0 on the router), then back out the same network interface to 10.0.0.37. This is inefficient and a bit slower, of course, because the packets *to* 10.0.2.0/24 must go across the same wire twice, with the router handling the packet between the transmissions. If you want to "fix" this, you must run a route command similar to the one above for each host on 10.0.0.0/24.

Say that the router has a connection to the Internet, and that this is the router's default gateway. Theoretically, there's no problem in sending packets *out* of your network to the rest of the Internet. Unfortunately, if your IP addresses are in private networks (as in this section) you run into the same problem described in Section 5.10.2 — you will never get anything back. Again, you need to run NAT (see Section 5.14) or do some other trick to get everything within the network talking to the outside world.

## 5.12 The Transport Layer: TCP, UDP, and Services

So far, you have only seen how packets move from host to host on the Internet. That's clear enough, but it says nothing about how your computer presents the packet data it receives to its running processes. You want more than one application to be able to talk to the network at the same time (for example, you might have email and several Web clients running), and you also want to receive the data in some form that's easier to handle than packets.

*Transport layer* protocols and services perform these tasks. The two most popular transport protocols are the Transmission Control Protocol (TCP) and the User Datagram Protocol (UDP). Both define *ports* on network nodes. When a program on your machine wants to talk to a service on a remote machine, it opens a port on the local machine and requests a connection to a port on the remote machine (a connection is defined by the two hosts, the ports on each side, and a special packet sequence). After the transport layer services on both sides establish the connection, the hosts can exchange data.

Transport layer services have complex implementations because they must convert a series of packets (not necessarily arriving in the correct order) into a data stream for programs. Luckily, you need to know next to nothing about this mess.

In TCP and UDP, a port is a number. If a program accepts connections on a port, it is said to *listen* on that port. There are well-known ports for various services; for example, email servers listen on TCP port 25, and most Web servers listen on TCP port 80. Only the superuser may use ports 1 through 1023. All users may listen on and create connections from ports 1024 on up.

On a Unix system, the /etc/services file maps service names to port numbers and transport layer protocols. This plain-text file consists of lines like these:

```
ssh             22/tcp                          # SSH Remote Login Protocol
smtp            25/tcp
domain          53/udp
```

The first column holds the service names. The second column in the /etc/services file defines the port number and a transport layer protocol. Take a look at /etc/services on your machine. Notice that the services file does not define the *programs* that listen on ports on your computer.

You will learn more about how programs listen and connect to the application layer in the next chapter. The rest of this chapter is devoted to three advanced networking topics: firewalls, NAT (IP masquerading), and wireless networking.

## 5.13 Firewalls

A *firewall* is a machine that sits between a network and the rest of the Internet, attempting to ensure that nothing "bad" from the Internet harms the network. You can also set up firewall features for each machine, where the machine screens all of its incoming and outgoing data at the packet level (as opposed to the application layer, where server programs usually try to perform some access control of their own). Firewalling on individual machines is sometimes called *IP filtering*.

To understand how firewalls work, consider that there are three times when a system can filter packets:

- When the system receives a packet
- When the system sends a packet
- When the system forwards (routes) a packet to another host or gateway

With no firewalling in place, a system just processes packets and sends them on their way.

Firewalls put checkpoints for packets at the points of data transfer identified above. The checkpoint drops, rejects, or accepts packets, usually based on some of these criteria:

- The source or destination IP address or subnet
- The source or destination port (in the transport layer information)
- The firewall's network interface

In Linux, you create firewall rules in a series known as a *chain* that is part of a networking *table* (for the most part, you will only work with one table named filter that controls basic packet flow). The iptables command, available since kernel version 2.4.0, manipulates these rules and chains. To use iptables, your kernel configuration must have packet filtering (in the networking options) and IP tables support (in the netfilter configuration submenu). You will learn more about kernel configuration in Chapter 10.

There are three basic chains: INPUT for incoming packets, OUTPUT for outgoing packets, and FORWARD for routed packets. To view the current configuration, run this command:

```
iptables -L
```

The iptables command should list an empty set of chains, as follows:

```
Chain INPUT (policy ACCEPT)
target     prot opt source               destination

Chain FORWARD (policy ACCEPT)
target     prot opt source               destination

Chain OUTPUT (policy ACCEPT)
target     prot opt source               destination
```

Each chain has a default *policy* that specifies what to do with a packet if no rule matches the packet. The policy for all three chains in this example is ACCEPT, meaning that the kernel allows the packet to successfully pass through the packet-filtering system. For the purposes of this book, the only other value that makes any sense is DROP, which means that the kernel will discard the packet. To set the policy on a chain, use iptables -P as in this example:

```
iptables -P FORWARD DROP
```

**WARNING**   *Don't do anything rash with the policies on your machine until you've read through the rest of this section.*

Let's say that someone at 192.168.34.63 is annoying you, so you'd like to prevent them from talking to your machine. Run this command:

```
iptables -A INPUT -s 192.168.34.63 -j DROP
```

The -A INPUT parameter appends a rule to the INPUT chain. The -s 192.168.34.63 part specifies the source IP address in the rule, and -j DROP tells the kernel to discard any packet matching the rule. Therefore, your machine will throw out any packet coming from 192.168.34.63.

To see the rule in place, run iptables -L:

```
Chain INPUT (policy ACCEPT)
target     prot opt source          destination
DROP       all  --  192.168.34.63   anywhere
```

As luck would have it, though, your good buddy at 192.168.34.63 has told everyone on his subnet to open connections to your SMTP port (TCP port 25), so now you want to get rid of that traffic as well:

```
iptables -A INPUT -s 192.168.34.0/24 -p tcp --destination-port 25 -j DROP
```

This example adds a netmask qualifier to the source address, as well as -p tcp to specify TCP packets only. A further restriction, --destination-port 25 says that the rule should only apply to traffic to port 25. The IP table list for INPUT now looks like this:

```
Chain INPUT (policy ACCEPT)
target     prot opt source           destination
DROP       all  --  192.168.34.63    anywhere
DROP       tcp  --  192.168.34.0/24  anywhere           tcp dpt:smtp
```

All is well until you hear from someone you know at 192.168.34.37, saying that they can't send you email because you blocked their machine. Thinking that this is a quick fix, you run this command:

```
iptables -A INPUT -s 192.168.34.37 -j ACCEPT
```

However, it doesn't work. For the reason, look at the new chain:

```
Chain INPUT (policy ACCEPT)
target     prot opt source           destination
DROP       all  --  192.168.34.63    anywhere
DROP       tcp  --  192.168.34.0/24  anywhere           tcp dpt:smtp
ACCEPT     all  --  192.168.34.37    anywhere
```

The kernel reads the chain from top to bottom, using the first rule that matches. The first rule does not match 192.168.34.37, but the second does, because it applies to all hosts from 192.168.34.1 to 192.168.34.254, and this second rule says to drop packets. Once a rule matches, the kernel carries out the action and does not look further down in the chain. (You might remark that 192.168.34.37 can send packets to any port on your machine *except* port 25, because the second rule *only* applies for port 25.)

Therefore, you have to move the third rule to the top. The easiest way to do this is to first delete the third rule with this command:

```
iptables -D INPUT 3
```

Then, *insert* that rule at the top of the chain with `iptables -I`:

```
iptables -I INPUT -s 192.168.34.37 -j ACCEPT
```

If you want to insert a rule at some other place than the top of a chain, put the rule number after the chain name (for example, `iptables -I INPUT 4 ...`).

Although this little tutorial may show you how to insert rules and how the kernel processes IP chains, it doesn't even come close to illustrating firewall strategies that actually work. Let's talk about that now.

### 5.13.1 Firewall Strategies

There are two basic kinds of firewall scenarios: one for protecting individual machines (where you set rules in each machine's INPUT chain), and one for protecting a network of machines (where you set rules in the router's FORWARD chain). In both cases, you cannot expect to have serious security by using a default policy of ACCEPT, continuously inserting rules to drop packets from sources that start to send bad stuff to you. Instead, you must adopt the strategy of allowing only the packets that you trust and denying everything else.

For example, let's say that your machine has an email server on TCP port 25 and an SSH server on TCP port 22. There is no reason for any random host to talk to any other port on your machine, and you shouldn't give any such host a chance. Here's how to set it up.

First, set the INPUT chain policy to DROP:

```
iptables -P INPUT DROP
```

If you want to enable ICMP traffic (for `ping` and other utilities), use this line:

```
iptables -A INPUT -p icmp -j ACCEPT
```

Let's say that your host's IP address is *my_addr*. Make sure that you can receive packets sent from yourself to both your own network IP address and 127.0.0.1 (localhost):

```
iptables -A INPUT -s 127.0.0.1 -j ACCEPT
iptables -A INPUT -s my_addr -j ACCEPT
```

If you have control of your entire subnet (and trust everything on that subnet), you can replace *my_addr* with your subnet address and subnet mask; for example, 10.43.201.0/24.

Now, although you need to make sure that your host can make TCP connections to the outside world, you still want to deny all incoming TCP connections. Because all TCP connections start with a SYN (connection request) packet, if you let all TCP packets through that aren't SYN packets, you are still okay:

```
iptables -A INPUT -p tcp '!' --syn -j ACCEPT
```

Next, you must accept traffic from your nameserver so that your machine can look up names with DNS. Do this for *all* DNS servers in /etc/resolv.conf. Assuming that the nameserver's address is *ns_addr*, you can do this with this command:

```
iptables -A INPUT -p udp --source-port 53 -s ns_addr -j ACCEPT
```

As mentioned before, you want to allow SSH and SMTP connections from anywhere:

```
iptables -A INPUT -p tcp --destination-port 22 -j ACCEPT     # ssh
iptables -A INPUT -p tcp --destination-port 25 -j ACCEPT     # smtp
```

Finally, you need the following command to enable outgoing passive FTP connections, though it's not terribly critical:

```
iptables -A INPUT -p tcp --source-port 20 --destination-port 1024: -j ACCEPT
```

The preceding IP table settings work for many situations. For example, they work for any direct connection, especially broadband, where an intruder is much more likely to port-scan your machine. They work for university environments, which are very similar to regular broadband connections. And you could also adapt these settings for a firewalling router, using the FORWARD chain instead of INPUT, and using source and destination subnets where appropriate. However, if you are using a firewalling router, you might find the discussion of NAT in Section 5.14 more applicable to your situation.

Remember that the key idea is permitting only the things that you find acceptable, not trying to find stuff that is unacceptable. Furthermore, IP firewalling is only one piece of the security picture. See Section 6.7 for more information.

### 5.13.2 IP Tables Reference

This section is a quick reference for the most common iptables options.

All `iptables` invocations must have a command option, as listed in Table 5-3.

**Table 5-3:** iptables Command Options

| Command Option | Description |
| --- | --- |
| -L *chain* | Lists rules (*chain* is optional). |
| -A *chain* | Appends a rule to *chain*. |
| -I *chain rulenum* | Inserts a rule in *chain* (*rulenum* is optional; the default location is the beginning of the chain). |
| -D *chain rulenum* | Deletes *rulenum* from *chain*. You can omit the rule number if you specify a matching parameter (shown in Table 5-4). |
| -F *chain rulenum* | Deletes all rules in *chain*, leaving only the policy. |
| -P *chain newpolicy* | Sets the policy (default rule) of *chain* to *newpolicy*. |

When using -A and -I (and -D without a rule number), you must specify the rule to add or delete as a combination of the packet specification options in Table 5-4. In addition, you can insert a literal ! after the option flag to negate its meaning.

**Table 5-4:** iptables Packet Specification Options

| Parameter Option | Meaning |
| --- | --- |
| -s *addr/mask* | Selects source IP address *addr* with optional netmask *mask* (for an entire subnet). |
| -d *addr/mask* | Selects destination IP address *addr* with optional netmask *mask* (for an entire subnet). |
| -i *interface* | Selects input *interface* (e.g., eth0, ppp0). |
| -o *interface* | Selects output *interface* (e.g., eth0, ppp0). |
| -p *protocol* | Selects *protocol* (e.g., tcp, udp, icmp). |
| --source-port *port* | Selects source *port*. You may specify a range with *port1:port2*. This works in conjunction with -p tcp or -p udp. |
| --destination-port *port* | Selects destination *port*. You may specify a range with *port1:port2*. This works in conjunction with -p tcp or -p udp. |
| --syn | When using -p tcp, selects SYN (connection request) packets. |

To finish off your rule, use -j *target* to decide what to do if a packet matches the rule (the most common types of *target* are ACCEPT and DROP).

This section has only described the basics of `iptables`. There are many advanced features, such as the ability to send a packet to an entirely different destination, to intercept packets at different parts of the routing process, and to create your own subchains. You can read about them in the iptables(8) manual page.

# 5.14 Network Address Translation (IP Masquerading)

Network Address Translation (NAT) permits sharing a single IP address (for example, from a PPP or broadband connection) with an entire internal network. NAT is very popular with home and small office networks. IPv4 addresses are in short supply, and furthermore, ISPs do not really want to bother with more routing than they can handle. As mentioned in Section 5.9.1, many small routers support NAT. In Linux, the variant of NAT that most people use is known as *IP masquerading*.

The basic idea behind NAT is that the machine with the Internet connection acts as a proxy between the internal network and the rest of the Internet. Consider a network like the one back in Figure 5-1 on page 94, and assume that the router (gateway) has an eth0 interface to an internal private network and a ppp0 interface for the uplink to the Internet.

Every host on the Internet knows how to connect to the router, but they know nothing about the internal private network behind the router. Under NAT, each of the internal hosts has the router as its default gateway. The system works roughly as follows:

1. A host on the internal private network wishes to make a connection to the outside world, so it sends its connection request packets through the router as normal.

2. The router intercepts the connection request packet rather than passing it out to the Internet (where it would get lost, because the public Internet knows nothing about private networks such as 10.1.2.0/24).

3. The router determines the destination of the connection request packet and opens its own connection to the destination.

4. When the router obtains the connection, it fakes a "connection established" message back to the original internal host.

5. The router is now the middleman between the internal host and the destination. The destination knows nothing about the internal host; the connection on the remote host looks like it came from the router.

This doesn't sound too bad until you think about how it works. Plain old IP routing knows only source and destination IP addresses in the Internet layer. However, if the router dealt only with the Internet layer, each host on the internal network could establish only one connection to a single destination at one time (among other limitations), because there is no information in the Internet layer part of a packet that could distinguish multiple requests from the same host to the same destination.

Therefore, NAT must dissect packets to pull out more identifying information. The only suitable stuff is in the transport layer — in particular, the TCP and UDP port numbers. The transport layer is very complex, so you can imagine that there are *lots* of things that can go wrong when a router goes mucking about inside transport layer information that comes from two hosts (the internal one and the external one) that it knows nothing about.

That said, NAT works better in practice than this brief description might suggest. To set up a Linux machine to perform as a NAT router, you must activate all of the following inside the kernel configuration: network packet filtering ("firewall support"), connection tracking, IP tables support, full NAT, and MASQUERADE target support.

**NOTE**    *See Chapter 10 for information on the kernel.*

Then you need to run `iptables` commands like the following to make the router perform NAT for its private subnet. The following example commands are for the earlier example:

```
echo 1 > /proc/sys/net/ipv4/ip_forward
iptables -P FORWARD DROP
iptables -t nat -A POSTROUTING -o ppp0 -j MASQUERADE
iptables -A FORWARD -i eth0 -j ACCEPT
iptables -A FORWARD -m state --state ESTABLISHED,RELATED -j ACCEPT
```

This example applies to an internal Ethernet network on eth0 sharing a PPP Internet connection (ppp0). Change these to suit your network.

When using NAT, remember that it's essentially a hack. In a perfect world, we would all be using IPv6 (the next-generation Internet), and we could get permanent subnets from our ISPs without any pain. In the meantime, though, you have to deal with these NAT limitations:

- Internet hosts cannot connect to services inside the private network without special port forwarding help from the NAT router. Of course, the hosts in the private network may have network security vulnerabilities, so this limitation may be more of a blessing than a drawback.

- Because Internet hosts cannot connect to internal hosts, some services need even more complicated packet dissection to work.

- NAT works for TCP, UDP, and some ICMP, but not necessarily all transport layer protocols.

- NAT requires much more memory and computing power than normal IP routing, so the computer acting as the router cannot be completely underpowered. In addition, there is always some connection overhead and latency. However, modern computers are more than fast enough to handle this, and the overhead and latency don't really matter unless you're running a big operation.

## 5.15 Wireless Ethernet

The proliferation of notebook computers and other portable computing devices has given rise to wireless Ethernet (also irritatingly known as "Wi-Fi") that you do not need to physically plug into a switch or hub. There are two popular consumer versions of the standard: 802.11b (maximum speed 11 Mbps) and 802.11g (54 Mbps).

In principle, wireless Ethernet isn't much different than any other kind of Ethernet, except that it uses radio waves instead of copper wires or fiber. You can configure a wireless card's network interface with traditional tools, such as ifconfig and dhclient. And wireless Ethernet cards have MAC addresses just like their wired counterparts.

With a wireless network, you typically want to be able to send packets out to some wired network. To accomplish this, you can buy a wireless base station to bridge (or link) a wireless network to a wired network — it's almost like adding more ports to a hub or switch by plugging another hub or switch into one of the ports. A wireless base station contains both wired and wireless networking hardware; it physically plugs into the wired network and can also communicate wirelessly with wireless network devices. (You can make a regular computer do the work of a wireless base station, but it's hardly worth the trouble.)

Linux has an additional tool called iwconfig for setting up a few technical details of a wireless network. For example, if someone else has a wireless network next door, you need to differentiate yours from theirs with an Extended Service Set Identifier (ESSID) string identifier.

To enable iwconfig, your kernel needs the wireless LAN extensions that you'll find in the kernel configuration's networking support options (see Chapter 10). Running iwconfig with no options yields output like this:

```
lo        no wireless extensions.

eth0      no wireless extensions.

eth1      IEEE 802.11-DS  ESSID:"some net"  Nickname:"HERMES I"
          Mode:Managed  Frequency:2.437GHz  Access Point: 00:04:5A:CE:BF:17
          Bit Rate:11Mb/s   Tx-Power=15 dBm   Sensitivity:1/3
          RTS thr:off    Fragment thr:off
          Power Management:off
          Link Quality:44/92  Signal level:-49 dBm  Noise level:-93 dBm
          Rx invalid nwid:0  invalid crypt:0  invalid misc:7255
```

As you can see, wireless settings are attached to network interfaces. The most important settings are as follows:

**ESSID** A string identifier for the network. Your wireless access point should have this setting.

**Mode** A setting that defines the type of network and the network interface's role in the network. Most wireless networks are managed networks, meaning that there is at least one interface that serves as an access point and oversees the nodes on the network. Your interface can act as a client, the master access point, a secondary access point, or a repeater. However, there are also ad hoc networks that have no access points.

**Access point** The MAC address of your current wireless access point's wireless interface (if you're on a managed network).

**Encryption key** The wireless network card's current Wired Equivalent Privacy (WEP) key.

You can manually set these parameters just as you would with ifconfig:

```
iwconfig eth1 essid mynet mode managed
```

In the preceding example, iwconfig configures the eth1 interface with an ESSID of mynet and a network topology of managed. The important iwconfig parameters are listed in Table 5-5. See the iwconfig(8) manual page for a complete list of parameters.

**Table 5-5:** iwconfig Parameters

| Parameter | Value |
| --- | --- |
| essid | The ESSID string, or any. |
| ap | The MAC address of your access point, or any. |
| mode | Managed, Master, Repeater, Secondary, or Auto. |
| channel | A channel number (each channel has a predetermined frequency); run iwlist *interface* channel to get a list of available channels. |
| freq | A direct frequency specification (for example, 2.412G for 2.412 GHz). |
| key | Normally, the hexadecimal value of the WEP key, or off to disable WEP. |

For wireless plug-in PC cards, most distributions support the PC card utilities in /etc/pcmcia, where you will find a configuration file called wireless.opts. When you plug a wireless card into your machine, the PC card services daemon described in Section 11.6 runs /etc/pcmcia/wireless. wireless runs iwconfig based on the parameters in wireless.opts, which is a Bourne shell case statement, making decisions primarily based on your wireless card's MAC address. The wireless.opts configuration file has many sample entries that you should examine.

To create an entry in this file for a wireless card with MAC address 00:02:2D:B0:EE:E4, you could use the following:

```
*,*,*,00:02:2D:B0:EE:E4)
    INFO="My Home Network"
    ESSID="my network"
    MODE="Managed"
    RATE="auto"
    KEY="268B645297"
    ;;
```

You must place this entry in the *case* statement in `wireless.opts` before these lines:

```
# NOTE : Remove the following four lines to activate the samples below ...
# --------- START SECTION TO REMOVE -----------
*,*,*,*)
    ;;
# ---------- END SECTION TO REMOVE ------------
```

### 5.15.1 A Lecture on Wireless Security

Unfortunately, using radio waves as a medium is absurdly insecure. Anyone with any kind of wireless Ethernet device, even something as small as a Sharp Zaurus, can sidle up near your network and waltz all around your packets. Without any additional protective measures, anyone can get access to your network, snoop around your packets, or do something much worse. For example, if your wireless network is connected to the Internet, anyone can use your network for a wide variety of very illegal activities.

There are several ways to make it considerably tougher to access your wireless network, and you'd think that most people would use them. Shockingly, the overwhelming majority do not. It's easy to set up a completely insecure wireless network, whereas to make the network more secure you need to enter a whole bunch of numbers into any computer that wants to use it. Who wants to go through all of that trouble when the network works just fine out of the box? Not to mention that it's a continuous hassle, especially when one of your friends comes over with a notebook.

Everyone thinks, "Hey, all of this bad stuff can't happen to me." But it can and will if you choose not to have any security. Fortunately, even the weakest kind of wireless security, WEP, drives off virtually all would-be intruders. If nothing else, you should enable WEP on your access points and wireless network interfaces. Yes, this does mean typing in a bunch of numbers, but do you really want to risk being caught in the middle of a legal mess?

You should know that WEP is not terribly secure. Given five to ten million packets, someone snooping on your network can figure out your WEP key with a program such as AirSnort. Of course, sniffing five to ten million packets takes a while, but if this concerns you, change your keys every now and then (like, say, every three million packets).

In any case, *never* transmit any sensitive data across your network without serious encryption like SSL or SSH, even if you are using WEP. This is especially true if you do not control your network, and also holds for wired networks.

If you have a good reason to be paranoid about security, WEP isn't going to help you much. You should require IPSec or SSH port forwarding for all traffic on your wireless network. Many administrators use a virtual private network (VPN) to implement an IPSec-based system.

# NETWORK SERVICES

Chapter 5 explained all layers of Internet networks except the application layer. Network applications (clients and servers) interact with the operating system by using a transport layer protocol and interface, such as TCP. This chapter covers basic network servers, including the inetd superserver and SSH servers. In addition, you will see some tools that will help you debug the servers.

Unix network servers come in many forms. A server may listen to a port on its own, or it may use a superserver such as inetd. Servers have no common configuration database, and they vary widely in features. Most servers have a configuration file to control their behavior (though with no common format), and most use the operating system's syslog service for message logging.

If you understand the system of TCP and UDP ports described in Section 5.12, you won't run into much trouble with network servers. Let's start out by getting an idea of how network clients talk to network servers.

## 6.1 The Basics of Services

TCP services are among the easiest to understand because they are simple, uninterrupted data streams. For example, you can talk directly to a Web server on TCP port 80 to get an idea of how data comes across the connection. Run the following command to connect to a Web server:

```
telnet www.nytimes.com 80
```

You should get a response like this:

```
Trying some address...
Connected to www.nytimes.com.
Escape character is '^]'.
```

Now type this:

```
GET /
```

Press ENTER twice. The server should send a bunch of HTML text as a response, and then terminate the connection.

There are two important lessons here:

- The remote host has a Web server process *listening* on TCP port 80.
- telnet was the client that initiated the connection.

**NOTE**  telnet *is a program originally meant to enable logins to remote hosts. Although the non-Kerberos* telnet *remote login server is completely insecure (as you will learn later), the* telnet *client is useful for debugging remote services.* telnet *does not work with UDP or any other transport layer other than TCP. See Section 6.5.3 for information on* netcat, *a powerful general-purpose network client.*

## 6.2 Stand-Alone Servers

Stand-alone network servers are no different than any other server daemons on your system (such as cron), except that they listen on network ports. In fact, you already saw syslogd in Chapter 4, which accepts UDP packets on port 514 if it is started with the -r option.

Here are some other common network servers that you may find running on your system:

**httpd**   Web server

**lpd**   Print server (see Chapter 12)

**postfix, qmail, sendmail**   Mail servers

**sshd**   Secure shell daemon (see Section 6.4)

**nfsd, mountd**   Network filesystem daemons

**smbd, nmbd**   Windows file-sharing daemons (see Chapter 14)

**portmap**   Remote procedure call (RPC) portmap service daemon

## 6.3 The inetd Daemon

Implementing stand-alone servers for every single service is somewhat inefficient, because each server must know all about the network interface API, have its own port configuration system, and so on. In many respects, the API for talking to TCP is not much different than the standard I/O system. TCP servers read from network ports and return output back to those ports — this is similar to the behavior of cat with no arguments in Section 1.2 is similar.

The inetd daemon is a *superserver* that standardizes network port access and interfaces between regular programs and network ports. After you start inetd, it reads the inetd.conf file and then listens on the network ports defined in that file, attaching a newly started process to every new incoming connection.

Each line in inetd.conf looks something like this:

```
ident       stream   tcp   nowait   nobody   /usr/sbin/identd identd -i
```

There are seven fields here:

**Service name**   The service name from /etc/services (see Section 5.12).

**Socket type**   This is usually stream for TCP and dgram for UDP.

**Protocol**   The transport protocol, such as tcp or udp.

**Datagram server behavior**   For UDP, this is wait or nowait. Services using any other transport protocol should use nowait.

**User**   The username that should run the service. Add .*group* if you want to set a group.

**Executable**   The program that inetd should connect to the service.

**Arguments**   The arguments for the executable in the preceding field. The first argument should be the name of the program.

A # sign in inetd.conf denotes a comment. To deactivate an inetd service, place a # before its entry in /etc/inetd.conf and then run the following command to make inetd re-read its configuration file:

```
kill -HUP `cat /var/run/inetd.pid`
```

inetd has several built-in services that you might see at the beginning of your inetd.conf, including echo, chargen, discard, daytime, and time. You can use these for testing, but otherwise they aren't important.

### 6.3.1 TCP Wrapper: tcpd, /etc/hosts.allow, /etc/hosts.deny

Before lower-level firewalls took off in popularity, many administrators used the *TCP wrapper* library for host control over network services. In fact, even if you run an IP firewall, you should still use TCP wrappers on any service that does not have its own logging mechanism (and many inetd services do not have such capabilities).

The tcpd program is the TCP wrapper utility for linking inetd with a server. An administrator can modify the inetd.conf file to include tcpd, like this:

```
finger  stream  tcp      nowait  nobody  /usr/sbin/tcpd  /usr/sbin/in.fingerd
```

When someone makes a connection to the finger port, the following happens:

1. inetd runs tcpd as the name /usr/sbin/in.fingerd.
2. tcpd verifies the executable /usr/sbin/in.fingerd.
3. tcpd consults /etc/hosts.allow and /etc/hosts.deny to see if the remote machine has permission to connect.
4. tcpd logs its decision.
5. If tcpd decides that the remote host is okay, it runs /usr/sbin/in.fingerd. Otherwise, tcpd terminates, dropping the connection.

Here is an example hosts.deny file:

```
ALL: .badguys.example.com
in.fingerd: nofinger.example.com
portmap: ALL
```

You can interpret this as follows:

- No one in the subdomain .badguys.example.com may connect to any TCP wrapper–enabled program.
- The host nofinger.example.com may not run in.fingerd.
- No one may access portmap (see Section 6.6 for more information on this service).

The TCP wrapper library reads /etc/hosts.allow before /etc/hosts.deny. If a rule in /etc/hosts.allow matches an incoming connection, the TCP wrapper library allows the connection, ignoring /etc/hosts.deny. For example, the following line in /etc/hosts.allow enables portmap access to the subdomain goodguys.example.com:

```
portmap: .goodguys.example.com
```

**NOTE**    *Using domain names in a TCP wrapper configuration has the disadvantage that it uses DNS. Forcing DNS lookups can hinder performance. It's also not extremely secure; it's possible to affect DNS lookups.*

### 6.3.2 xinetd

Some Linux distributions come with an enhanced version of inetd named xinetd (http://www.xinetd.org/). You can read about the xinetd improvements at the Web site, but to summarize, xinetd offers built-in TCP wrapper support, better logging, and extended access control.

If you currently have inetd, should you run xinetd? If you need its features, sure. However, if you only have one local server (for example, FAM for the GNOME desktop), and you firewall the external traffic to this server anyway, there are probably better things you can do with your time. xinetd administrators should also keep careful track of security advisories, because this package has not seen as widespread use as the old inetd.

xinetd does not read inetd.conf, but if you understand the fields in inetd.conf, you won't have trouble using xinetd. If you want an alternative to /etc/xinetd.d, you can also use itox to convert your inetd.conf to a xinetd.conf file that xinetd can read.

To add a new service to xinetd, create a file in /etc/xinetd.d with the name of the service. For example, the /etc/xinetd.d/finger file might look like this:

```
service finger
{
    socket_type = stream
    protocol    = tcp
    wait        = no
    user        = nobody
    passenv     =
    server      = /usr/sbin/in.fingerd
    server_args =
}
```

To make xinetd recognize the changes, run kill -USR1 on the xinetd process ID.

## 6.4 Secure Shell (SSH)

The secure shell (SSH) is now the de facto standard for remote logins to other machines. It replaces old, insecure programs like telnet and rlogin. In addition to being a good example of a stand-alone server (for the purposes of this book, at least), SSH has these features:

- Encrypts your password and all other session data, protecting you from snoopers.

- Tunnels other network connections, including those from X Window System clients. *Tunneling* is the process of packaging and transporting a network connection using another network connection. The advantages of using SSH to tunnel X Window System connections are that SSH sets up the display environment for you and encrypts the X data inside the tunnel.

- Has clients for almost every operating system.
- Uses keys for host authentication.

OpenSSH (http://www.openssh.com/) is a popular free SSH implementation for Unix. The OpenSSH client is ssh and the server is sshd. OpenSSH uses public key cryptography for authentication and less complex ciphers for its session data. SSH does not come without its disadvantages; in particular, you need the remote host's public key, and you do not necessarily get it in a secure way (however, you can check it manually if you think you're being spoofed). If you would like to know how cryptography works, get your hands on *Applied Cryptography* [Schneier].

There are two main SSH protocol versions: 1 and 2. OpenSSH supports both, with version 2 being the default.

## 6.4.1 Installing OpenSSH

You can install a precompiled binary version of OpenSSH, such as an .rpm file in a Red Hat distribution, or you can get the "portable" source code from the OpenSSH Web site to install from source. If you install from source code, you need a version of the SSL (Secure Socket Layer) library, preferably OpenSSL.

In either case, you need to know your OpenSSH configuration directory — it's usually /etc or /usr/local/etc. If you install from source code, you can override the default configuration directory by using the --sysconfdir=*dir* parameter to configure (see Chapter 9 for more information on compiling software from source code).

## 6.4.2 The SSHD Server

To run sshd, you need a configuration file and host keys in the configuration directory. The configuration filename is sshd_config. It's easy to confuse this filename with the client's ssh_config setup file, so look out. You shouldn't need to change anything in sshd_config, but it never hurts to check.

The file consists of keyword-value pairs, as shown in this fragment:

```
Port 22
#Protocol 2,1
#ListenAddress 0.0.0.0
#ListenAddress ::
HostKey /usr/local/etc/ssh_host_key
HostKey /usr/local/etc/ssh_host_rsa_key
HostKey /usr/local/etc/ssh_host_dsa_key
```

Lines beginning with # are comments. Many comments in your sshd_config may indicate default values. The sshd_config(5) manual page contains descriptions of all possible values, but these are the most important:

**HostKey** *file*   Uses *file* as a host key (host keys are described shortly).

**SyslogFacility** *name*   Logs messages with syslog facility *name*.

**LogLevel** *level*   Logs messages with syslog level *level*.

**PermitRootLogin** *value*   Permits the superuser to log in with SSH if *value* is set to yes; set *value* to no if you do not want to allow this.

**X11Forwarding** *value*   Enables X Window System client tunneling if *value* is set to yes.

**XAuthLocation** *path*   Provides a path for xauth; X11 tunneling does not work without xauth. If xauth isn't in /usr/X11R6/bin, set *path* to the full path-name for xauth.

### Host Keys

OpenSSH has three different host key sets: one for protocol version 1, and two for protocol 2. Each set has a *public key* (with a .pub file extension) and a *private key* (with no extension). Do not let anyone see your private key, even on your own system. If someone gets your host's private key, SSH provides no protection against password snooping. SSH version 1 has RSA keys only, and SSH version 2 has RSA and DSA keys. RSA and DSA are public key cryptography algorithms. SSH version 2 provides both because there are always debates over which one is better.

The key filenames are as follows:

**Table 6-1:** OpenSSH Key Files

| | |
|---|---|
| ssh_host_rsa_key | Private RSA key (version 2) |
| ssh_host_rsa_key.pub | Public RSA key (version 2) |
| ssh_host_dsa_key | Private DSA key (version 2) |
| ssh_host_dsa_key.pub | Public DSA key (version 2) |
| ssh_host_key | Private RSA key (version 1) |
| ssh_host_key.pub | Public RSA key (version 1) |

Normally, you do not need to build the keys, because the OpenSSH installation program should do this for you. However, this isn't always a given, and you may need to know how to create keys if you plan to use programs like ssh-agent.

To create SSH protocol version 2 keys, use the ssh-keygen program that comes with OpenSSH:

```
ssh-keygen -t rsa -N '' -f ssh_host_rsa_key
ssh-keygen -t dsa -N '' -f ssh_host_dsa_key
```

For the version 1 keys, use this command:

```
ssh-keygen -t rsa1 -N '' -f ssh_host_key
```

The SSH server (and clients) also use another key file, ssh_known_hosts, which contains public keys from other hosts. If you intend to use host-based authentication, the server's ssh_known_hosts file must contain the host keys of all trusted clients.

### Starting the SSH Server

Running sshd as root starts the server. You may put this in an init.d script to start at boot time. There is also a way to start sshd from inetd, but this is usually not a good idea, because the server occasionally needs to generate key files, and this process can take a long time.

sshd writes its PID to /var/run/sshd.pid, so you can terminate the server at any time with this command:

```
kill `cat /var/run/sshd.pid`
```

## 6.4.3 The SSH Client

To log in to a remote host, run this command:

```
ssh remote_username@host
```

You may omit *remote_username@* if your local username is the same as on *host*. You can also run pipelines to and from an ssh command.

The SSH client configuration file is ssh_config, and it should be in the same place as your sshd_config file. As with the server configuration file, the client configuration file has key-value pairs, but you should not need to change anything in there.

The most frequent problem with using SSH clients occurs when an SSH version 1 public key in your local ssh_known_hosts or .ssh/known_hosts file does not match the key on the remote host. Bad keys cause errors or warnings like this:

```
@@@@@@@@@@@@@@@@@@@@@@@@@@@@@@@@@@@@@@@@@@@@@@@@@@@@@@@@@@@
@    WARNING: REMOTE HOST IDENTIFICATION HAS CHANGED!    @
@@@@@@@@@@@@@@@@@@@@@@@@@@@@@@@@@@@@@@@@@@@@@@@@@@@@@@@@@@@
IT IS POSSIBLE THAT SOMEONE IS DOING SOMETHING NASTY!
Someone could be eavesdropping on you right now (man-in-the-middle attack)!
It is also possible that the RSA host key has just been changed.
The fingerprint for the RSA key sent by the remote host is
38:c2:f6:0d:0d:49:d4:05:55:68:54:2a:2f:83:06:11.
Please contact your system administrator.
```

```
Add correct host key in /home/user/.ssh/known_hosts to get rid of this message.
Offending key in /home/user/.ssh/known_hosts:12
RSA host key for host has changed and you have requested
strict checking.
Host key verification failed.
```

This usually just means that the remote host's administrator changed the keys, but it never hurts to check with the administrator if you don't know. In any case, look at this line of the preceding message:

```
Offending key in /home/user/.ssh/known_hosts:12
```

This tells you exactly where the bad key is: line 12 of a user's known_hosts file. If you do not suspect foul play, just remove the offending line or replace it with the correct public key.

### SSH File Transfer Clients

OpenSSH comes with replacement programs for rcp and ftp called scp and sftp.

You can use scp to transfer files from a remote machine to your machine, the other way around, or from one host to another. It works much like the cp command. Here are some examples:

```
scp user@host:file .
scp file user@host:dir
scp user1@host1:file user2@host2:dir
```

sftp works much like the command-line ftp client, with get and put commands. The remote host must have a sftp-server program, but this shouldn't be a problem if the remote host also uses OpenSSH.

### SSH Clients for Non-Unix Platforms

There are SSH clients for all popular operating systems. The index at the OpenSSH Web page (http://www.openssh.com/) gives a full list, but you may wonder which one to choose for Windows or the Mac. PuTTY is a good Windows client that includes a secure file-copy program. MacSSH works well for Mac OS 9. Mac OS X is based on Unix and includes OpenSSH.

## 6.5 Diagnostic Tools

netstat is one of the most basic network service debugging tools, telling you what ports are open and whether any programs are listening on ports. For example, if you want to view all open TCP ports, run this command:

```
netstat -t
```

Table 6-2 lists the netstat options.

**Table 6-2:** netstat Options

| Option | Description |
|--------|-------------|
| -t | Prints TCP port information |
| -u | Prints UDP port information |
| -l | Prints listening ports |
| -a | Prints every active port |
| -n | Disables name lookups (useful if DNS isn't working) |

Being able to list open and listening ports is good, but our good old friend lsof can go one step further.

## 6.5.1 lsof

In Section 4.8.1 you saw how lsof can track open files, but lsof can also list the programs currently using or listening to ports. For a complete list, run this command:

```
lsof -i
```

The output should look something like this:

```
COMMAND  PID   USER    FD   TYPE DEVICE SIZE NODE NAME
portmap  520 daemon    3u   IPv4   150       UDP  *:sunrpc
portmap  520 daemon    4u   IPv4   151       TCP  *:sunrpc (LISTEN)
inetd    522   root    4u   IPv4   188       TCP  *:discard (LISTEN)
inetd    522   root    5u   IPv4   189       UDP  *:discard
inetd    522   root    6u   IPv4   190       TCP  *:daytime (LISTEN)
inetd    522   root    7u   IPv4   191       UDP  *:daytime
inetd    522   root    8u   IPv4   192       TCP  *:time (LISTEN)
inetd    522   root    9u   IPv4   193       UDP  *:time
inetd    522   root   11u   IPv4   195       TCP  *:auth (LISTEN)
sshd     853   root    3u   IPv4   696       TCP  *:ssh (LISTEN)
X        900   root    1u   IPv4   791       TCP  *:6000 (LISTEN)
```

If you're looking for one port in particular (that is, if you know that a process is using a particular port and you want to know what that process is), use this version of the command:

```
lsof -i :port
```

The full syntax is

```
lsof -i protocol@host:port
```

*protocol*, *@host*, and *:port* are all optional. Specifying any of these parameters filters the lsof output accordingly. As with most other network utilities, *host* and *port* can be either names or numbers.

You can disable host-name resolution with the -n option. Finally, lsof -P forces numeric port listings.

**NOTE**    *If you don't have* lsof *on your system, you can run* netstat -p *to get the processes associated with ports. This is a Linux-specific* netstat *feature, but* lsof *is still far more flexible.*

### 6.5.2 tcpdump

If you need to know what's happening on your network, tcpdump puts your network interface card into *promiscuous mode* and reports on every packet that crosses the wire.

tcpdump with no arguments produces output resembling the following sample, which includes an ARP request and Web connection:

```
tcpdump: listening on eth0
20:36:25.771304 arp who-has mikado.example.com tell duplex.example.com
20:36:25.774729 arp reply mikado.example.com is-at 0:2:2d:b:ee:4e
20:36:25.774796 duplex.example.com.48455 > mikado.example.com.www: S
3200063165:3200063165(0) win 5840 <mss 1460,sackOK,timestamp 38815804[|tcp]>
(DF)
20:36:25.779283 mikado.example.com.www > duplex.example.com.48455: S
3494716463:3494716463(0) ack 3200063166 win 5792 <mss 1460,sackOK,timestamp
4620[|tcp]> (DF)
20:36:25.779409 duplex.example.com.48455 > mikado.example.com.www: . ack 1 win
5840 <nop,nop,timestamp 38815805 4620> (DF)
20:36:25.779787 duplex.example.com.48455 > mikado.example.com.www: P
1:427(426) ack 1 win 5840 <nop,nop,timestamp 38815805 4620> (DF)
20:36:25.784012 mikado.example.com.www > duplex.example.com.48455: . ack 427
win 6432 <nop,nop,timestamp 4620 38815805> (DF)
20:36:25.845645 mikado.example.com.www > duplex.example.com.48455: P
1:773(772) ack 427 win 6432 <nop,nop,timestamp 4626 38815805> (DF)
20:36:25.845732 duplex.example.com.48455 > mikado.example.com.www: . ack 773
win 6948 <nop,nop,timestamp 38815812 4626> (DF)

9 packets received by filter
0 packets dropped by kernel
```

You can tell tcpdump to be more specific by adding some filtering arguments. You can filter based on source and destination hosts, networks, Ethernet addresses, protocols at many different layers in the network model, and much more. Among the many packet protocols that tcpdump recognizes are ARP, RARP, ICMP, TCP, UDP, IP, IPv6, AppleTalk, and IPX packets. For example, if you want tcpdump to output only TCP packets, run this command:

```
tcpdump tcp
```

If you want to see Web packets and UDP packets, use this command:

```
tcpdump udp or port 80
```

In the preceding examples, tcp, udp, and port 80 are called *primitives*. The most important primitives are in Table 6-3:

**Table 6-3:** tcpdump Primitives

| Primitive | Packet Specification |
| --- | --- |
| tcp | TCP packets |
| udp | UDP packets |
| port *port* | TCP and/or UDP packets to/from port *port* |
| host *host* | Packets to or from *host* |
| net *network* | Packets to or from *network* |

As you saw in the example, or is an operator. Other operators include and and !; you may use parentheses for grouping. If you're going to do any serious work with tcpdump, make sure that you read the manual page, especially the section that describes the primitives.

**NOTE** *Use good judgment when using* tcpdump. *The output shown earlier in this section includes only packet TCP (transport layer) and IP (Internet layer) header information, but you can also make* tcpdump *print the entire packet contents. Even though many network operators make it far too easy to look at their network packets, it doesn't mean that you should. Don't snoop around on networks other than the ones you own, unless you happen to be in the espionage business and understand the risks of having sensitive wiretapped data.*

If you find that you need to do a lot of packet sniffing, you should probably consider a GUI alternative to tcpdump named Ethereal.

### 6.5.3 Netcat

If you need more flexibility in connecting to a remote host than a command such as telnet *host port* allows, use netcat (or nc). Netcat can connect to remote TCP/UDP ports, specify a local port, listen on ports, scan ports, redirect standard I/O to and from network connections, and more.

To open a TCP connection to a port, run this command:

```
netcat host port
```

netcat does not terminate until the other side of the connection ends the connection. This can confuse you if you redirect standard input to netcat. You can end the connection at any time by pressing CONTROL-C.

To listen on a port, run this command:

```
netcat -1 -p port
```

**NOTE** *There are two versions of netcat. The somewhat quirky original has just one executable name,* nc, *with a final version number of around 1.10. However, there is a newer GNU version using the name* netcat, *though the current version numbers are lower than the original. The new version includes several improvements, not the least of which is a manual page.*

The netcat utility is very specific in its treatment of the network connection; in particular, it does not like to exit until the network connection has terminated. If this behavior doesn't suit your application (in particular, if you'd like the program and network connection to terminate based on the standard input stream), try the sock program instead.

## 6.6 Remote Procedure Call (RPC)

RPC stands for *remote procedure call.* The basic idea is that programs call functions on remote programs (identified by program numbers), and the remote programs return a result code or message.

RPC implementations use transport protocols such as TCP and UDP, and they require a special intermediary service to map program numbers to TCP and UDP ports. The server is called portmap, and it must be running on any machine that wants to use RPC services.

If you want to know what RPC services your computer has, run this command:

```
rpcinfo -p localhost
```

RPC is one of those protocols that just doesn't seem to want to die. The unpleasant Network File System (NFS) and Network Information Service (NIS) systems use RPC, but they are completely unnecessary on stand-alone machines. But whenever you think that you've eliminated all need for portmap, something else comes up, such as File Access Monitor (FAM) support in GNOME.

## 6.7 Network Security

Because Linux is a very popular Unix flavor on the PC platform, it attracts more unpleasant characters who try to break into computer systems. Section 5.13 talked about firewalls, but this isn't really the whole story on security.

Network security attracts extremists. Those who are interested in breaking into systems do so because they *really* like to, and those who come up with elaborate schemes to protect themselves do so because they *really* like to swat away people trying to break into their systems.

Most people would rather just not have to deal with it, but that attitude and a broadband connection will get your system compromised in no time. Fortunately, you don't need to know very much to keep your system safe. Here are a few basic rules of thumb:

**Run as few services as possible**  Intruders can't break into services that don't exist on your system. If you know what a service is, and you're not using it at the moment, don't turn it on just in case you might want it sometime.

**Block as much as possible with a firewall**  Unix systems have a number of internal services that you may not know about, such as TCP port 6000 for the X Window System server. No other system in the world needs to know about these services, and no other system in the world *should* know about them, either. Furthermore, it is very difficult to track and regulate the services on your system, because many different kinds of programs listen on ports. You can prevent intruders from discovering internal services with effective firewall rules. Refer to Section 5.13.1 for an example firewall.

**Keep on top of the services that you offer to the entire Internet**  If you run an SSH server or Postfix or other services, make sure that you have the ability to stay up to date with the software and get appropriate alerts. See Section 6.7.4 for some online resources.

**Don't give an account to anyone who doesn't need an account**  It's much easier to gain superuser access from a local account than it is to break in remotely. In fact, given the huge base of software (and the resulting bugs and design flaws) available on most systems, it's almost laughably easy to gain superuser access to a system after you get to a shell prompt. Don't assume that your friends know how to protect their passwords (or to choose good passwords in the first place).

**Avoid installing dubious binary packages**  They can contain Trojan horses.

That's the practical end of protecting yourself. You should know a few basics on why it is important to do so. There are three basic kinds of network attacks:

**Full compromise**  This means getting superuser access (full control) of a machine. An intruder can accomplish this by trying a service attack, such as a buffer overflow exploit, or by taking over a poorly protected user account, and then trying to exploit a poorly written setuid program.

**Denial-of-service (DoS) attacks**  These prevent a machine from carrying out its network services, or they force a computer to malfunction in some other way without any special access. These attacks are harder to prevent, but they are easier to respond to.

**Virus or worm**   Linux users are mostly immune to email worms and viruses, simply because their email clients aren't so stupid as to actually run programs that they get in message attachments, and Linux isn't as attractive a target as Windows. However, you can create a Linux virus; it's been done before, and as Linux gains popularity, it will happen with increasing frequency. Avoid binary software distributions, especially from places that you've never heard of. Some network services have been susceptible to worms before, and history is doomed to repeat itself.

### 6.7.1 Where Linux Distributions Stand

Not long ago, installing certain Linux distributions on easily accessible networks (such as university networks) practically ensured security compromises. These distributions activated every single service by default and had no default firewalling. It wasn't just Linux, either — Solaris was remarkably good at leaving the door open, not to mention the hundreds of Windows exploits, and so on.

Linux distributions are better now; they do not activate every possible service, and they tend to come with preconfigured firewalls. There is no doubt that the firewalls do most of the work. Programmers delight in adding new network services, especially for GUI applications and support, but security often takes a backseat. Better authentication (such as the Kerberos system) would help tremendously, but this happens to be one of the weakest and most disorganized areas of most applications.

A firewall isn't necessarily the ideal solution, but it does offer a uniform way to block *all* network traffic. The only thing that ever came close to this in the past was the TCP wrapper system, but that only worked for inetd servers and applications that specifically included wrapper support.

In a perfect world, programmers would write invulnerable code, but while you wait for a perfect world, you need to know what to look out for.

### 6.7.2 Typical Vulnerabilities

There are two important kinds of vulnerabilities that you need to worry about: direct attacks and clear-text password sniffing. Direct attacks just try to take over your machine without being terribly subtle. The most common type of direct attack is a buffer overflow exploit, where a careless programmer doesn't check the bounds of a buffer array. The attacker fabricates a stack frame inside a huge chunk of data, dumps it to the remote server, then hopes that the program overwrites its program data and eventually executes the new stack frame. It's a somewhat complicated attack, but easy to replicate.

On the other hand, clear-text passwords can allow intruders to log in to your machine. From there, they will inevitably try to gain superuser access locally (which is much easier than making a remote attack), try to use the machine as an intermediary for attacking other hosts, or both.

*If you have a service that you need to encrypt, but the service offers no native support, you can try Stunnel (http://www.stunnel.org/), an encryption wrapper package much like TCP wrappers. Like* tcpd, *Stunnel is especially good at wrapping* inetd *services.*

Some servers are chronic targets of attacks because of poor implementation and design. You should deactivate the following services if you ever come across them:

**sendmail**   I would usually not rail against a specific program, but Sendmail has an exceptionally long history of exploitation. There are two very good alternative mail servers, Postfix (http://www.postfix.org/) and qmail (http://www.qmail.org/).

**ftpd**   For whatever reason, all FTP servers seem plagued with vulnerabilities. In addition, most FTP servers use clear-text passwords. If you have to move files from one machine to another, consider an SSH-based solution or an rsync server.

**telnetd, rlogind, rexecd**   All of these pass remote session data (including passwords) in clear-text form. Avoid them unless you happen to have a Kerberos-enabled version.

**fingerd**   Intruders can get user lists and other information with the finger service.

### 6.7.3 Port Scanning

Listing your open ports and firewall configuration with netstat and iptables is a good start for staying on top of unwanted traffic, but you may want to go a step further with Nmap (Network Mapper), a program that scans all of the ports on a machine or network of machines, looking for potential vulnerabilities. Nmap gives you a view from the *outside* and eliminates guessing which ports are open. Most intruders use Nmap, and you can get it at http://www.insecure.org/.

**WARNING**   *If someone else controls the network that you want to Nmap (or run Nmap from), ask that person if it's all right that you do so. Network administrators watch for port scans and delight in stomping on any machine that runs a scan.*

Just run nmap *host* to run a generic scan on a host. Here's an example scan:

```
Starting nmap 3.30 ( http://www.insecure.org/nmap/ ) at 2003-08-04 16:25 PDT
Interesting ports on host (10.1.2.2):
(The 1636 ports scanned but not shown below are in state: closed)
Port     State     Service
9/tcp    open      discard
13/tcp   open      daytime
22/tcp   open      ssh
37/tcp   open      time
111/tcp  open      sunrpc
```

```
113/tcp     open        auth
6000/tcp    open        X11

Nmap run completed -- 1 IP address (1 host up) scanned in 0.594 seconds
```

The host in this example probably doesn't have any kind of firewall running, because it has quite a few open ports.

Nmap can do much more — have a look at its manual page and the considerable online resources.

### 6.7.4 Security Resources

Here are three good security sites:

**http://www.sans.org/**  Offers training, services, a free weekly newsletter of the top current vulnerabilities, sample security policies, and more.

**http://www.cert.org/**  A place to look for the most severe problems.

**http://www.insecure.org/**  This is the place to go for Nmap and pointers to all sorts of network exploit testing tools. It's much more open and specific about exploits than many other sites.

# INTRODUCTION TO SHELL SCRIPTS

If you can enter commands into the shell, you can write Bourne shell scripts. A script is a series of commands written in a file, and the shell reads the commands from the file just as it would if you typed them into a terminal.

As with any program on Unix systems, you need to set the executable bit for the script file, but you must also set the read bit. The easiest way to do this is as follows:

```
chmod +x script
```

This chmod command allows other users to read and execute *script*. If you don't want that, use the absolute mode 700 instead (and refer back to Section 1.17 for a refresher on permissions).

## 7.1 Shell Script Basics

All Bourne shell scripts should start with the following line, indicating that the /bin/sh program should execute the commands in the script file:

```
#!/bin/sh
```

Make sure that no whitespace appears at the beginning of the script file. You can list any commands that you want the shell to execute following the #!/bin/sh line. Here is a very simple example:

```
#!/bin/sh
#
# Print something, then run ls

echo About to run the ls command.
ls
```

A # character at the beginning of a line indicates that the line is a comment; that is, the shell ignores anything on a line after a #. Use comments to explain parts of your scripts that are not easy to understand.

After creating a script and setting its permissions, you can run the script by placing the script file in one of the directories in your command path and then running the script name on the command line. Alternatively, you can run *./script* if the script is located in your current working directory.

### 7.1.1 Limitations of Shell Scripts

The Bourne shell manipulates commands and files with relative ease. You already saw the way the shell can redirect output in Section 1.14; this is one of the important elements of shell script programming. However, shell scripts are not the be-all and end-all of Unix programming. If you're trying to pick apart strings or do arithmetic computations, or if you want functions or complex control structures, you're better off using a scripting language like Perl, Python, or awk, or perhaps even a compiled language like C.

Be aware of your shell script sizes. Bourne shell scripts aren't meant to be big (though you will undoubtedly encounter some monstrosities in your time).

## 7.2 Quoting

A *literal* is a string that you want the shell to leave alone and pass to the command line. To see where a literal is useful, consider how the shell normally expands * to all files and directories in the current directory, then passes all those items on to the current command line. If you just want a star (*) to be used by a command, as you would for grep and other programs that use regular expressions, you need special notation to pass a literal *.

The easiest way to make the shell leave a string alone is to enclose the entire string in single quotes. Here's an example with grep and *:

```
grep 'r.*t' /etc/passwd
```

*All* characters located between the two single quotes, including any spaces, make up a single literal. Therefore, the following command does *not* work, because it asks the grep command to search for the string r.*t /etc/passwd from the standard input (because there is only one parameter):

```
grep 'r.*t /etc/passwd'
```

Double quotes (") work just like single quotes, except that the shell expands any variables that appear within double quotes, whereas it does not expand variables located between single quotes. You can see the difference by running the following command and then replacing the double quotes with single quotes and running it again.

```
echo "There is no * in my path: $PATH"
```

One tricky part to using literals with the Bourne shell is passing a literal single quote to a command. One way to do this is to place a backslash before the single quote character:

```
echo I don\'t like contractions inside shell scripts.
```

The backslash and quote *must* appear outside any pair of single quotes. A string such as 'don\'t results in a syntax error. However, oddly, you can enclose the single quote inside double quotes, as the following example shows (the output is identical to that of the preceding command):

```
echo "I don't like contractions inside shell scripts."
```

## 7.3 Special Variables

Most shell scripts understand command-line parameters and interact with the commands that they run. To take your scripts from simple lists of commands to more flexible programs, you need to know how to use the special Bourne shell variables. Using special variables is not much different than using any other shell variable (see Section 1.8), but you cannot change the value of certain special variables.

After reading the next few sections, you will understand why shell scripts accumulate many special characters as they are written. If you're trying to understand a shell script and you come across a line that looks completely incomprehensible, pick it apart piece by piece.

### 7.3.1 $1, $2, ...

$1, $2, and all variables named as positive nonzero integers contain the values of the script parameters, or arguments.

Let's say the name of the following script is named pshow:

```
#!/bin/sh
echo First argument: $1
echo Third argument: $3
```

Running pshow one two three produces this output:

```
First argument: one
Third argument: three
```

The built-in shell command shift is used with argument variables. This command removes the first argument ($1) and advances the rest of the arguments forward — that is, $2 becomes $1, $3 becomes $2, and so on. Assume that the name of the following script is shiftex:

```
#!/bin/sh
echo Argument: $1
shift
echo Argument: $1
shift
echo Argument: $1
shift
```

Run shiftex one two three. This output appears:

```
Argument: one
Argument: two
Argument: three
```

## 7.3.2 $#

The $# variable holds the number of arguments passed to the script. This variable is especially important when running shift in a loop to pick through arguments; when $# is 0, no arguments remain, so $1 is empty. (See Section 7.6 for a description of loops.)

## 7.3.3 $@

The $@ variable represents all of the script's arguments, and it is very useful for passing all of a script's arguments to one of the commands inside the script. For example, you will learn in Section 12.6 that the arguments to Ghostscript (gs) are complicated. Suppose that you want a shortcut for rasterizing a PostScript file at 150 dpi, using the standard output stream, but also leaving the door open for passing other options to gs. You could write a script like the following that allows for additional command-line options:

```
#!/bin/sh
gs -q -dBATCH -dNOPAUSE -dSAFER -sOutputFile=- -sDEVICE=pnmraw $@
```

*If a line in your shell script gets too long for your text editor, you can split it up with a backslash (\). For example, you can alter the preceding script as follows:*

```
#!/bin/sh
gs -q -dBATCH -dNOPAUSE -dSAFER \
   -sOutputFile=- -sDEVICE=pnmraw $@
```

A double-quoted $@ ("$@") expands to the parameters separated by spaces.

### 7.3.4 $0

The $0 variable holds the name of the script, and it is useful for generating diagnostic messages. Let's say that your script needs to report an invalid argument that is stored in the $BADPARM variable. You can print the diagnostic message with the following line so that the script name appears in the error message:

```
echo $0: bad option $BADPARM
```

You should send diagnostic error messages to the standard error. Recall from Section 1.14.1 that 2>&1 redirects the standard error to the standard output. For writing to the standard error, you can reverse the process with 1>&2. To do this for the preceding example, use this:

```
echo $0: bad option $BADPARM 1>&2
```

### 7.3.5 $$

The $$ variable holds the process ID of the shell.

### 7.3.6 $?

The $? variable holds the exit code of the last command that the shell executed. Exit codes are critical to mastering shell scripts, and they're discussed next.

## 7.4 Exit Codes

When a Unix program finishes, it leaves an *exit code* for the parent process that started the program. The exit code is a number and is sometimes called an *error code*. When the exit code is zero (0), this means that the program ran without problems. However, if the program has an error, it usually exits with some number other than 0.

The exit code of the last command is held in the $? special variable, so you can check it out for yourself at your shell prompt:

```
$ ls / > /dev/null
$ echo $?
0
$ ls /asdfasdf > /dev/null
ls: /asdfasdf: No such file or directory
$ echo $?
1
```

You can see that the successful command returned 0 and the unsuccessful command returned 1.

If you intend to use the exit code of a command, you *must* use or store the code immediately after running the command. For example, if you run a third echo $? just after the preceding series of commands, the result would be 0 because the second of the two echo commands completed successfully.

When writing shell code that aborts a script abnormally, you should use something like exit 1 to pass an exit code of 1 back to whatever parent process ran the script. You don't necessarily have to use 1; for example, you may want to use different numbers for different conditions.

**NOTE** *A few programs like* diff *and* grep *use nonzero exit codes to indicate normal conditions. For example,* grep *returns 1 if it finds something matching its pattern in its input, and 0 if not. In this case, the nonzero exit code is not an error. These commands use other exit codes for errors:* grep *and* diff *use 2 for real problems. If you think a program is using a nonstandard exit code, read its manual page. The exit codes are usually explained in the DIAGNOSTICS section.*

## 7.5 Conditionals

The Bourne shell has special constructs for conditionals, such as if/then/else and case statements. Here is a simple script with an if conditional that checks to see if the script's first argument is hi:

```
#!/bin/sh
if [ $1 = hi ]; then
    echo 'The first argument was "hi"'
else
    echo -n 'The first argument was not "hi" -- '
    echo It was '"'"$1'"'
fi
```

The words if, then, else, and fi in the preceding script are shell keywords. Everything else is a command. This is an extremely important point, because one of the commands is [ $1 = "hi" ]. The [ character is an actual program on a Unix system; it is *not* special shell syntax. All Unix systems have a command called [ that performs tests for shell script conditionals. This program is also known as test — careful examination of [ and test should reveal that they share an inode, or one is a symbolic link to the other.

Now you can see why the exit codes in Section 7.4 are so important, because this is how the whole process works:

1. The shell runs the command after the if keyword and collects the exit code of that command.

2. If the exit code is 0, the shell executes whatever commands follow the then keyword, stopping when it reaches an else or fi keyword.

3. If the exit code is not 0 and there is an else clause, the shell runs the commands after the else keyword.

4. The conditional ends at fi.

**NOTE** *There is a slight problem with the conditional in the preceding example — a very common mistake. $1 could be empty, because the user might not enter a parameter. Without a parameter, the test reads [ = "hi" ], and the [ command aborts with an error. You can fix it by enclosing the parameter in quotes in one of the two following ways (both are common):*

```
if [ "$1" = hi ]; then
if [ x"$1" = x"hi" ]; then
```

It is worth repeating that the stuff following if is always a command. You need a semicolon (;) after the test command — if you skip the semicolon, the shell passes then as a parameter to the test command. (If you don't like the semicolon, you can put the then keyword on a separate line.)

Here is an example that uses grep instead of the [ command:

```
#!/bin/sh
if grep -q daemon /etc/passwd; then
    echo The daemon user is in the passwd file.
else
    echo There is a big problem. daemon is not in the passwd file.
fi
```

There is also an elif keyword that lets you string if conditionals together like this:

```
#!/bin/sh
if [ $1 = "hi" ]; then
    echo 'The first argument was "hi"'
elif [ $2 = "bye" ]; then
    echo 'The second argument was "bye"'
else
    echo -n 'The first argument was not "hi" and the second was not "bye"-- '
    echo They were '"'$1'"' and '"'$2'"'
fi
```

Don't get too carried away with `elif`, because the `case` construct that you will see in Section 7.5.3 is usually more appropriate.

### 7.5.1 && and || Logical Constructs

There are two quick one-line conditional constructs that you may see from time to time: `&&` ("and") and `||` ("or").

The `&&` construct works like this:

```
command1 && command2
```

Here, the shell runs *command1*, and if the exit code is 0, it also runs *command2*.

The `||` construct is similar; if the command before a `||` returns a nonzero exit code, the shell runs the second command.

`&&` and `||` often find their way into use in `if` tests. In both cases, the exit code of the last command run determines how the shell processes the conditional. In `&&`, if the first command fails, the shell uses its exit code for the `if` statement, but if the first command is successful, the shell uses the exit code of the second command for the conditional. For `||`, the shell uses the exit code of the first command if successful, or the exit code of the second if the first is unsuccessful.

Here is an example:

```
#!/bin/sh
if [ "$1" = hi ] || [ "$1" = bye ]; then
    echo 'The first argument was "'$1'"'
fi
```

If your conditionals include the test (`[`) command (as here), you can use `-a` and `-o` instead of `&&` and `||`, as described in the next section.

### 7.5.2 Testing Conditions

You have already seen how `[` works; the exit code is 0 if the test is true and nonzero when the test fails. You also know how to test string equality with `[ str1 = str2 ]`.

However, remember that shell scripts are well suited to operations on entire files. An important reason for this is that the most useful `[` tests involve file properties. For example, the following line checks whether *file* is a regular file (not a directory or special file):

```
[ -f file ]
```

In a script, you might see the `-f` test in a loop similar to this next one, which tests all of the items in the current working directory:

```
for filename in *; do
    if [ -f $filename ]; then
        ls -l $filename
        file $filename
    else
        echo $filename is not a regular file.
    fi
done
```

You can invert a test by placing the ! operator before the test. For example, [ ! -f *file* ] returns true if *file* is *not* a regular file. Furthermore, the -a and -o flags are the and and or operators (for example, [ -f *file1* -a *file2* ]).

There are dozens of test operations that fall into three general categories: file tests, string tests, and arithmetic tests. The info pages contain complete online documentation, but the test(1) manual page is also a fast reference. The following sections outline the main tests (some of the less common tests have been omitted).

### File Tests

Most file tests, like -f, are called *unary* operations because they require only one argument — the file to test.

Here are two important file tests:

-e   Returns true if a file exists

-s   Returns true if a file is not empty

Several operations inspect a file's type, meaning that they can determine whether something is a regular file, a directory, or some kind of special device. Those operations are listed in Table 7-1. There are also a number of unary operations that check a file's permissions, as listed in Table 7-2 on the next page (see Section 1.17 for an overview of permissions).

**Table 7-1:** File Type Operators

| Operator | Tests For |
|----------|-----------|
| -f | Regular file |
| -d | Directory |
| -h | Symbolic link |
| -b | Block device |
| -c | Character device |
| -p | Named pipe |
| -S | Socket |

**NOTE**   *Except for* -h, test *follows symbolic links. That is, if* link *is a symbolic link to a regular file,* [ -f link ] *returns an exit code of true (0).*

**Table 7-2:** File Permissions Operators

| Operator | Returns True if the File Is: |
|----------|------------------------------|
| -r | Readable |
| -w | Writable |
| -x | Executable |
| -u | Setuid |
| -g | Setgid |
| -k | "Sticky" |

Finally, there are three *binary* operators (tests that need two files as arguments) that are used in file tests, but they are not terribly common. Consider this command that includes -nt (newer than):

```
[ file1 -nt file2 ]
```

This exits true if *file1* has a newer modification date than *file2*. The -ot (older than) operator does the opposite. And if you need to detect identical hard links, -ef compares two files and returns true if they share inode numbers and devices.

### String Tests

You have already seen the binary string operator =, which returns true if its operands are equal. The != operator returns true if its operands are not equal.

There are two unary string operations:

- **-z**  Returns true if its argument is empty ([ -z "" ] returns 0)
- **-n**  Returns true if its argument is not empty ([ -n "" ] returns 1)

### Arithmetic Tests

It's important to recognize that = looks for *string* equality, not *numeric* equality. Therefore, [ 1 = 1 ] returns 0 (true), but [ 01 = 1 ] returns false. If you want to work with numbers, use -eq instead — [ 01 **-eq** 1 ] returns true. Table 7-3 provides the full list of numeric comparison operators.

**Table 7-3:** Arithmetic Comparison Operators

| Operator | Returns True When the First Argument Is . . . the Second |
|----------|-----------------------------------------------------------|
| -eq | Equal to |
| -ne | Not equal to |
| -lt | Less than |
| -gt | Greater than |
| -le | Less than or equal to |
| -ge | Greater than or equal to |

### 7.5.3 Matching Strings with case

The case keyword forms another conditional construct that is exceptionally useful for matching strings. case does not execute any test commands and therefore does not evaluate exit codes. Here is an example that should tell most of the story:

```
#!/bin/sh
case $1 in
    bye)
        echo Fine, bye.
        ;;
    hi|hello)
        echo Nice to see you.
        ;;
    what*)
        echo Whatever.
        ;;
    *)
        echo 'Huh?'
        ;;
esac
```

The shell executes this as follows:

1.  The script matches $1 against each case value demarcated with the ) character.
2.  If a case value matches $1, the shell executes the commands below the case until encountering ;;. The shell then skips to the esac keyword.
3.  The conditional ends with esac.

For each case value, you can match a single string (such as bye in the preceding example), multiple strings with | (hi|hello returns true if $1 equals hi or hello), or make use of the * or ? wildcards (what*). If you want to make a case that catches all possible values other than the case values specified, use a single *, as shown by the final case in the preceding example.

**NOTE**  *Each case must end with a double semicolon (;;). You risk a syntax error otherwise.*

## 7.6 Loops

There are two kinds of loops in the Bourne shell; for loops and while loops. The for loop is much more common; it is actually a "foreach" loop. Here's an example:

```
#!/bin/sh
for str in one two three four; do
    echo $str
done
```

Here, for, in, do, and done are all shell keywords. The shell executes the code as follows:

1. The shell sets the variable str to the first of the four space-delimited values following the in keyword (one).

2. The shell runs the echo command between the do and done.

3. The shell goes back to the for line, setting str to the next value (two), runs the commands between do and done, and repeats the process until it is through with the values following the in keyword.

Therefore, the output of this script looks like this:

```
one
two
three
four
```

The Bourne shell's while loop uses exit codes, like the if conditional. This example does ten iterations:

```
#!/bin/sh
FILE=/tmp/whiletest.$$;
echo firstline > $FILE

while tail -10 $FILE | grep -q firstline; do
    echo -n Number of lines in $FILE:' '
    wc -l $FILE | awk '{print $1}'
    echo newline >> $FILE
done

rm -f $FILE
```

Here, the exit code of grep -q firstline is the test. As soon as the exit code is nonzero (in this case, when the string firstline no longer appears in the last ten lines in $FILE), the loop exits. You can break out of a while loop with the break statement.

The Bourne shell also has an until loop that works just like while, except that it breaks the loop when it encounters a zero exit code rather than a nonzero exit code. This said, you shouldn't need to use the while and until loops often. The somewhat obscure example in this section is indicative of the nature of while loops; if you need to use while, you should probably be using a language like awk or Perl instead.

## 7.7 Command Substitution

The Bourne shell can redirect a command's standard output back to the shell's own command line. That is, you can use a command's output as an argument to another command, or you can store the command output in a shell variable. You do this by enclosing a command in backquotes (`).

Here's an example that stores a command inside a variable, FLAGS:

```
#!/bin/sh
FLAGS=`grep ^flags /proc/cpuinfo | sed 's/.*://' | head -1`
echo Your processor supports:
for f in $FLAGS; do
    case $f in
        fpu)    MSG="floating point unit"
                ;;
        3dnow)  MSG="3DNOW graphics extensions"
                ;;
        mtrr)   MSG="memory type range register"
                ;;
        *)      MSG="unknown"
                ;;
    esac
    echo $f: $MSG
done
```

The second line contains the command substitution, in bold type. This example is somewhat complicated, because it demonstrates that you can use both single quotes and pipelines inside the command substitution backquotes. The result of the grep command is sent to the sed command (more about sed later), which removes anything matching the expression .*:, and the result of sed is then passed to head.

It's too easy to go overboard with command substitution. For example, don't use `ls` in a script, because using the shell to expand * is faster. Also, if you want to invoke a command on several filenames that you get as a result of a find command, you may want to consider using a pipeline to xargs rather than command substitution (see Section 7.10.4).

## 7.8 Temporary File Management

Sometimes it is necessary to create a temporary file to collect output for use by a later command. When making such a file, you must make sure that the filename is unique enough that no other programs will accidentally write to the temporary file.

You should know how to use the mktemp command to create temporary filenames. Here is a script that shows you what device interrupts have occurred in the last two seconds:

```
#!/bin/sh
TMPFILE1=`mktemp /tmp/im1.XXXXXX`
TMPFILE2=`mktemp /tmp/im2.XXXXXX`

cat /proc/interrupts > $TMPFILE1
sleep 2
cat /proc/interrupts > $TMPFILE2
diff $TMPFILE1 $TMPFILE2
rm -f $TMPFILE1 $TMPFILE2
```

The argument to mktemp is a template. mktemp converts the XXXXXX to a unique set of characters and creates an empty file with that name (without the XXXXXX, the command fails). Notice that this script uses variable names to store the filenames, so that you only have to change one line if you want to change a filename.

**NOTE** *Not all Unix flavors come with* mktemp. *If you're having portability problems, you might want use the* $$ *special variable to construct a temporary filename based on the process ID.*

Another problem is that scripts that employ temporary files are vulnerable to signals that abort the script and leave temporary files behind. In the preceding example, pressing CONTROL-C before the second cat command leaves a temporary file in /tmp. You want to avoid this if possible. Use the trap command to create a signal handler to catch the signal that CONTROL-C generates. The handler removes the temporary files:

```
#!/bin/sh
TMPFILE1=`mktemp /tmp/im1.XXXXXX`
TMPFILE2=`mktemp /tmp/im2.XXXXXX`
trap "rm -f $TMPFILE1 $TMPFILE2; exit 1" INT
  ...
```

Notice that you must use exit in the handler to explicitly end script execution. Otherwise, the shell continues running as usual after running the signal handler.

## 7.9 Here Documents

Sometimes you want to print a large section of text or feed a lot of text to another command. Rather than using several echo commands, you can employ the shell's *here document* feature.

The following is a script that shows how here documents work:

```
#!/bin/sh
DATE=`date`
cat <<EOF
Date: $DATE

The output above is from Unix date command.
It's not a very interesting command.
EOF
```

The items in bold control the here document. `<<EOF` tells the shell to redirect all lines that follow to the standard input of the command that precedes `<<EOF`, which in this case is `cat`. The redirection stops as soon as the `EOF` marker occurs on a line by itself. The marker that you use doesn't have to be `EOF` — use any string that you like, but remember that you must use the same marker at the beginning and end of the here document, and that convention dictates that the marker be in all uppercase letters.

Notice also that there is a shell variable in the here document. The shell expands shell variables inside here documents. This is especially useful when you're printing out some kind of report and have many variables to put into a larger form.

## 7.10 Important Shell Script Utilities

There are several programs that are particularly useful in shell scripts. Some utilities (such as `basename`) are really only practical when used in conjunction with other programs, and therefore usually don't find a place outside of shell scripts, but others, such as `awk`, can be quite useful on the command line too.

### 7.10.1 basename

If you need to strip the extension off of a filename or get rid of the directories in a full pathname, use the `basename` command.

Try these examples on the command line to get a feel for how the command works:

```
basename example.html .html
basename /usr/local/bin/example
```

In both cases, `basename` returns `example`. The first command strips the `.html` suffix from `example.html`, and the second removes the directories from the full pathname.

Here is an example of how you can use `basename` in a script to convert GIF image files to the PNG format:

```
#!/bin/sh
for file in *.gif; do
    # exit if there are no files
```

```
      if [ ! -f $file ]; then
          exit
      fi
      b=`basename $file .gif`
      echo Converting $b.gif to $b.png...
      giftopnm $b.gif | pnmtopng > $b.png
done
```

### 7.10.2 awk

You may have seen the awk command already. This is not a simple single-purpose command — it's a powerful programming language. Perhaps unfortunately, awk is now something of a lost art due to larger languages such as Perl.

However, entire books do exist on the subject of awk, including *The AWK Programming Language* [Aho 1988]. This said, you will see many, many people use awk to pick a single field out of an input stream like this:

```
ls -l | awk '{print $5}'
```

This command prints the fifth field of the ls output (the file size); the result is a list of file sizes.

### 7.10.3 sed

sed stands for stream editor, and it is an automatic text editor that takes an input stream (a file or the standard input), alters it according to some expression, and prints the results to standard output. In many respects, sed is somewhat similar to ed, the original Unix text editor. It has dozens of operations, matching tools, and addressing capabilities. Like awk, there are books about sed, including one that covers both utilities, *sed & awk* [Dougherty].

Although sed is a big program, and an in-depth analysis is beyond the scope of this book, it's easy to see how it works. In general, sed takes an address and an operation as one argument. The address is a set of lines, and the command determines what to do with the lines.

For example, the following command reads /etc/passwd, deletes lines three through six and sends the result to the standard output:

```
sed 3,6d /etc/passwd
```

In this example, 3,6 is the address (a range of lines), and d is the operation (delete). If you omit the address, sed operates on all lines in its input stream. The two most common sed operations are probably s (search and replace) and d.

Let's go through a few more sed examples. In all of the examples, single quotes are necessary to prevent the shell from expanding special characters like * and $.

The following command replaces the regular expression *exp* with *text* (see Section 1.5.1 for basic information on regular expressions):

```
sed 's/exp/text/'
```

The preceding command replaces only one instance of the expression *exp* per line. To replace all instances of *exp*, use the g modifier at the end of the operation:

```
sed 's/exp/text/g'
```

You can also use a regular expression as the address. The following command deletes any line that matches the regular expression *exp*:

```
sed '/exp/d'
```

## 7.10.4 xargs

If you ever have to run one command on a huge number of files, the command or shell sometimes responds that it can't fit all of the arguments in its buffer. Use xargs to get around this problem. xargs runs a command on each filename in its standard input stream.

Many people use xargs in conjunction with the find command. Here is an example that can help you verify that every file in the current directory tree that ends with .gif is actually in the GIF format:

```
find . -name '*.gif' -print | xargs file
```

In the preceding example, xargs runs the file command. However, this invocation can cause errors or leave your system open to security problems, because filenames can include spaces and newlines. If you're writing a script or need extra security, use the following form instead, which changes the find output separator and the xargs argument delimiter from a newline to a NULL character:

```
find . -name '*.gif' -print0 | xargs -0 file
```

Keep in mind that if you have a large list of files, xargs starts a *lot* of processes. Don't expect great performance.

**NOTE** *You may need to add two hyphens (--) to the end of your* xargs *command if there is a possibility that any of the target files start with -. The -- is a way to tell a program that any arguments that follow the -- are filenames, not options. However, keep in mind that not all programs support --.*

### 7.10.5 expr

If you need arithmetic operations in your shell scripts, the expr command can help you (and even do some string operations). The command expr 1 + 2 prints 3; run expr --help for a full list of operations.

expr is a clumsy, slow way of doing math. If you find yourself using expr frequently, it probably means that you should be using a language like Perl, Python, or awk instead of a shell script.

### 7.10.6 exec

The exec command is a built-in shell feature that replaces the current shell process with the program you name after exec. This is a feature for saving system resources, but remember that there's no return; once you run exec in a shell script, the script and shell running the script are gone, replaced by the new command.

You can test it in a shell window. Try running exec cat. After you press CONTROL-D or CONTROL-C to terminate the cat program, your window disappears because its child process no longer exists.

## 7.11 Subshells

Sometimes you need to alter the environment in a shell slightly, but don't want a permanent change. You can change and restore a part of the environment (such as the path or working directory) using shell variables, but that is a clumsy way to go about things. The easy way around these kinds of problems is to use a *subshell*, an entirely new shell process that you can create just for the purpose of running a command or two. The new shell has a copy of the original shell's environment, and when the new shell exits, any changes you made to its shell environment disappear, leaving the initial shell to run as normal.

To use a subshell, put the commands to be executed by the subshell in parentheses. For example, the following line executes the command uglyprogram in uglydir, leaving the original shell intact:

```
(cd uglydir; uglyprogram)
```

Here's another example, showing how to add a component to the path that might cause problems as a permanent change:

```
(PATH=/usr/confusing:$PATH; uglyprogram)
```

Pipes and background processes work with subshells too. The following example uses tar to make an archive of the entire directory tree within *orig* and then unpacks the archive into the new directory *target*, effectively duplicating the files and folders in *orig*:

```
tar cf - orig | (cd target; tar xvf -)
```

**WARNING**   *Double-check this sort of command before you run it, because you want to make sure that the* target *directory exists and is completely separate from the* orig *directory.*

## 7.12 Including Other Files in Scripts

If you need to include another file in your shell script, use the . operator. For example, this runs the commands in the file config.sh:

```
. config.sh
```

This "include" file syntax does not start a subshell, and it can be useful for a group of scripts that need to use a single configuration file.

## 7.13 Reading User Input

The read command reads a line of text from the standard input and stores the text in a variable. For example, the following command stores the input in $*var*:

```
read var
```

This is a built-in shell command. It's useful to a certain extent, and when used in conjunction with other shell features not mentioned in this book, you can do some more interesting things, but at a certain point you have to ask yourself when enough is enough.

## 7.14 Too Much?

The shell is so feature-rich that it's difficult to condense its important elements into a single chapter. If you're interested in what else the shell can do, you might want to look at some of the books on shell programming, such as *Unix Shell Programming* [Kochan], or the shell script discussion in *The UNIX Programming Environment* [Kernighan].

Above all, remember what shell scripts do best — manipulate files and commands. If you find yourself writing something that looks convoluted, especially if it involves string or arithmetic operations, then you should probably look to a scripting language like Perl, Python, or awk.

# DEVELOPMENT TOOLS

Unix is very popular with programmers not just due to the overwhelming array of tools and environments available, but also because the system is exceptionally well documented and transparent. On a Unix machine, you don't have to be a programmer to take advantage of development tools, and when working with the system, you *must* know something about programming tools because they play a larger role in Unix systems management than in other operating systems. At the very least, you should be able to identify development utilities and have some idea of how to run them.

This chapter packs a lot of information into a small space, but you do not need to master everything here. Furthermore, you can easily leave the material and come back later.

## 8.1 The C Compiler

Knowing how to run the C compiler can give you a great deal of insight into the origin of the programs that you see on your Linux system. The source code for nearly all Linux utilities, and for many applications on Linux systems, is written in the C programming language. C is a compiled language, and C programs follow the traditional development process: you write programs, you compile them, and they run. After you write a C program, you must *compile* the source code that you wrote into a *binary* low-level form that the computer understands.

The C compiler on most Unix systems is named cc (on Linux, this is usually a link to gcc), and C source code files end with .c. Take a look at the single, self-contained C source code file called hello.c that you can find in *The C Programming Language* [Kernighan and Ritchie]:

```
#include <stdio.h>

main() {
    printf("Hello, World.\n");
}
```

To compile this source code, run this command:

```
cc hello.c
```

The result is an executable named a.out, which you can run like any other executable on the system. However, you should probably give the executable another name (such as hello). To do this, use the compiler's -o option:

```
cc -o hello hello.c
```

For small programs, there isn't much more to compiling than that. You may need to add an extra include directory or library (see Sections 8.1.2 and 8.1.3), but let's look at slightly larger programs before getting into those topics.

### 8.1.1 Multiple Source Files

Most C programs are too large to reasonably fit inside one single source code file. Mammoth files become too disorganized for the programmer, and compilers sometimes even have trouble parsing large files. Therefore, developers group components of the source code together, giving each piece its own file.

To compile the .c files, use the compiler's -c option on each file. Let's say that you have two files, main.c and aux.c. The following two commands would do most of the work of building the program:

```
cc -c main.c
cc -c aux.c
```

The preceding two compiler commands compile the two source files into two object files (`main.o` and `aux.o`). An *object file* is a nearly complete binary that a processor can almost understand, except that there are still a few loose ends. First, the operating system does not know how to run an object file by itself, and second, you may need to combine several object files to make a complete program.

To build a fully functioning executable from one or more object files, you must run the *linker* — the `ld` command in Unix. Programmers rarely use `ld` on the command line, because the C compiler knows how to run the linker program properly. To create an executable called `myprog` from the two object files above, run this command to links them:

```
cc -o myprog main.o aux.o
```

Although you can compile multiple source files by hand, as the preceding example shows, it can be hard to keep track of them all during the compiling process when the number of source files multiplies. The `make` system described in Section 8.1.5 is the Unix standard for managing compiles. This system is especially important in managing the files described in the next two sections.

## 8.1.2 Header (Include) Files and Directories

C *header files* are additional source code files that usually contain type and library function declarations. For example, `stdio.h` is a header file (see the simple program in Section 8.1).

Unfortunately, a great number of compiler problems crop up with header files. Most glitches occur when the compiler can't find header files and libraries. There are even some cases where a programmer forgets to include a required header file, so some of the source code may not compile.

Tracking down the correct include files isn't always easy. Sometimes there are several include files with the same names in different directories, and it's not clear which is the correct one. When the compiler can't find an include file, the error message looks like this:

```
badinclude.c:1: notfound.h: No such file or directory
```

This message reports that the compiler cannot not find the `notfound.h` header file that the `badinclude.c` file references. This specific error is a direct result of this directive on line 1 of `badinclude.c`:

```
#include <notfound.h>
```

The default include directory in Unix is /usr/include; the compiler always looks there unless you explicitly tell it not to (for example, with gcc -nostdinc). However, you can make the compiler look in other include directories (most paths that contain header files have include somewhere in the name).

For example, let's say that you find notfound.h in /usr/junk/include. You can make the compiler see this directory with the -I option:

```
cc -c -I/usr/junk/include badinclude.c
```

Now the compiler should no longer stumble on the line of code in bad-include.c that references the header file.

You should also be careful of includes that use double quotes (" ") instead of angle brackets (< >), like this:

```
#include "myheader.h"
```

Double quotes mean that the header file is not in a system include directory, but that the compiler should otherwise search its include path. It often means that the include file is supposed to be in the same directory as the source file. If you encounter a problem with double quotes, you're probably trying to compile incomplete source code.

### What Is the C Preprocessor (cpp)?

The *C preprocessor* is a program that the compiler runs on your source code before parsing the actual program. The preprocessor rewrites source code into a form that the compiler understands; it's a tool for making source code easier to read (and for providing shortcuts).

Preprocessor commands in the source code are called *directives*, and they start with the # character. There are three basic types of directives:

**Include files**   An #include directive instructs the preprocessor to include an entire file. Note that the compiler's -I flag is actually an option that causes the preprocessor to search a specified directory for include files, as you saw in the previous section.

**Macro definitions**   A line such as #define BLAH something tells the preprocessor to substitute something for all occurrences of BLAH in the source code. Convention dictates that macros appear in all uppercase, but it should come as no shock that programmers sometimes use macros whose names look like functions and variables. (Every now and then, this causes a world of headaches. Many programmers make a sport out of abusing the preprocessor.)

Note that instead of defining macros within your source code, you can also define macros by passing parameters to the compiler: -DBLAH=something works like the directive above.

**Conditionals** You can mark out certain pieces of code with #ifdef, #if, and #endif. The #ifdef MACRO directive checks to see if the preprocessor macro MACRO is defined, and #if *condition* tests to see if *condition* is non-zero. For both directives, if the condition following the "if statement" is false, the preprocessor does not pass any of the program text between the #if and the next #endif to the compiler. If you plan to look at any C code, you'd better get used to this.

An example of a conditional directive follows. When the preprocessor sees the following code, it checks to see if the macro DEBUG is defined, and if so, passes the line containing fprintf() on to the compiler. Otherwise, the preprocessor skips this line and continues to process the file after the #endif:

```
#ifdef DEBUG
  fprintf(stderr, "This is a debugging message.\n");
#endif
```

**NOTE** *The C preprocessor doesn't know anything about C syntax, variables, functions, and other elements. It understands only its own macros and directives.*

On Unix, the C preprocessor's name is cpp, but you can also run it with gcc -E. However, you will rarely need to run the preprocessor by itself.

### 8.1.3 Linking with Libraries

The C compiler does not know enough about your system to create a useful program all by itself. Modern systems require *libraries* to build complete programs. A C library is a collection of common precompiled functions that you can build into your program. For example, many executables use the math library because it provides trigonometric functions and the like.

Libraries come into play primarily at link time, when the linker program creates an executable from object files. For example, if you have a program that uses the math library, but you forget to tell the compiler to link against that library, you'll see errors like this:

```
badmath.o(.text+0x28): undefined reference to `sin'
badmath.o(.text+0x36): undefined reference to `pow'
```

The most important parts of these error messages are in bold. When the linker program examined the badmath.o object file, it could not find the math functions that appear in bold, and as a consequence, it could not create the executable. In this particular case, you might suspect that you forgot the math library because the missing functions refer to mathematical operations (sine and exponentiation).

**NOTE** *Undefined references do not always mean that you're missing a library. One of the program's object files could be missing in the link command. It's usually easy to differentiate between library functions and functions in your object files, though.*

To fix this problem, you must first find the math library and then use the compiler's -l option to link against the library. As with include files, libraries are scattered throughout the system (/usr/lib is the system default location), though most libraries reside in a subdirectory named lib. For the preceding example, the math library file is libm.a (in /usr/lib), so the library name is m. Putting it all together, you would link the program like this:

```
cc -o badmath badmath.o -lm
```

You must tell the linker about nonstandard library locations; the parameter for this is -L. Let's say that the badmath program requires libcrud.a in /usr/junk/lib. To compile and create the executable, use a command like this:

```
cc -o badmath badmath.o -lm -L/usr/junk/lib -lcrud
```

**NOTE**    *If you want to search a library for a particular function, use the* nm *command. Be prepared for a lot of output. For example, try this:* nm /usr/lib/libm.a

### 8.1.4 Shared Libraries

A library file ending with .a (such as libm.a) is a *static library*. Sadly, the story on libraries doesn't end here.

When you link a program against a static library, the linker copies machine code from the library file into your executable. Therefore, the final executable does not need the original library file to run.

However, the ever-expanding size of libraries has made static libraries wasteful in terms of disk space and memory. *Shared libraries* counter this problem. When you run a program linked against a shared library, the system loads the library's code into the process memory space only when necessary. Furthermore, many processes can share the same shared library code in memory.

Shared libraries have their own costs: difficult management and a somewhat complicated linking procedure. However, you can bring shared libraries under control if you know four things:

- How to list the shared libraries that an executable needs
- How an executable looks for shared libraries
- How to link a program against a shared library
- What the common shared library pitfalls are

The following sections tell you how to use and maintain your system's shared libraries. If you're interested in how shared libraries work, or if you want to know about linkers in general, you can look at *Linkers and Loaders* [Levine], or at "The Inside Story on Shared Libraries and Dynamic Loading," [Beazley/Ward/Cooke]. The ld.so(8) manual page is also worth a read.

## Listing Shared Library Dependencies

Shared library files usually reside in the same places as static libraries. The two standard library directories on a Linux system are /lib and /usr/lib. The /lib directory should not contain static libraries.

A shared library has a suffix that contains .so, as in libc-2.3.2.so and libc.so.6. To see what shared libraries a program uses, run ldd *prog*, where *prog* is the executable name. Here is the output of ldd /bin/bash:

```
libreadline.so.2 => /lib/libreadline.so.2 (0x40019000)
libncurses.so.3.4 => /lib/libncurses.so.3.4 (0x40045000)
libdl.so.2 => /lib/libdl.so.2 (0x4008a000)
libc.so.6 => /lib/libc.so.6 (0x4008d000)
/lib/ld-linux.so.2 => /lib/ld-linux.so.2 (0x40000000)
```

Executables alone do not know the locations of their shared libraries; they know only the names of the libraries, and perhaps a little hint. A small program named ld.so (the *runtime dynamic linker/loader*) finds and loads shared libraries for a program at runtime. The preceding ldd output shows the library names on the left — that's what the executable knows. The right side shows where ld.so finds the library.

## How ld.so Finds Shared Libraries

The first place that the dynamic linker *should* normally look for shared libraries is an executable's preconfigured *runtime library search path* (if one exists). You will see how to create this path shortly.

Next, the dynamic linker looks in a system cache, /etc/ld.so.cache, to see if the library is in a standard location. This is a fast cache of the names of library files found in directories listed in the cache configuration file /etc/ld.so.conf. Each line in this file is a directory that you want to include in the cache. The list of directories is usually short, containing something like this:

```
/usr/X11R6/lib
/usr/lib/libc5-compat
```

The standard library directories /lib and /usr/lib are implicit — you don't need to include them in /etc/ld.so.conf.

If you alter ld.so.conf or make a change to one of the shared library directories, you must rebuild the /etc/ld.so.cache file by hand with the following command:

```
ldconfig -v
```

The -v option provides detailed information on libraries that ldconfig adds to the cache and any changes that it detects.

There is one more place that ld.so looks for shared libraries: the environment variable LD_LIBRARY_PATH. Before discussing this variable, let's look at the runtime library search path.

## Linking Programs Against Shared Libraries

Don't get into the habit of adding stuff to /etc/ld.so.conf. You should know what shared libraries are in the system cache, and if you put every bizarre little shared library directory into the cache, you risk conflicts and an extremely disorganized system. When you compile software that needs an obscure library path, give your executable a built-in runtime library search path.

Let's say that you have a shared library named libweird.so.1 in /opt/bizarresoft/lib that you need to link myprog against. Link the program as follows:

```
cc -o myprog myprog.o -Wl,-rpath=/opt/obscure/lib -L/opt/obscure/lib -lweird
```

The -Wl,-rpath option tells the linker to include a following directory into the executable's runtime library search path. However, even if you use -Wl,-rpath, you still need the -L flag.

## Problems with Shared Libraries

Shared libraries provide remarkable flexibility, not to mention some really incredible hacks, but it's also possible to abuse them to the point where your system is an utter and complete mess. Three particularly bad things can happen:

- Missing libraries
- Terrible performance
- Mismatched libraries

The number one cause of all shared library problems is an environment variable named LD_LIBRARY_PATH. Setting this variable to a colon-delimited set of directory names makes ld.so search the given directories *before* anything else when looking for a shared library. This is a cheap way to make programs work when you move a library around, if you don't have the program's source code, or if you're just too lazy to recompile the executables. Unfortunately, you get what you pay for.

*Never* set LD_LIBRARY_PATH in shell startup files or when compiling software. When the dynamic runtime linker encounters this variable, it must often search through the entire contents of each specified directory more times than you would care to know. This causes a big performance hit, but more importantly, you can get conflicts and mismatched libraries because the runtime linker looks in these directories for *every* program.

If you *must* use LD_LIBRARY_PATH to run some crummy program for which you don't have the source (or an application that you'd rather not compile, like Mozilla or some other beast), use a wrapper script. Let's say that your executable is /opt/crummy/bin/crummy.bin and it needs some shared libraries in /opt/crummy/lib. Write a wrapper script called crummy that looks like this:

```
#!/bin/sh
LD_LIBRARY_PATH=/opt/crummy/lib
export LD_LIBRARY_PATH
exec /opt/crummy/bin/crummy.bin $@
```

Avoiding `LD_LIBRARY_PATH` prevents most shared library problems. But one other significant problem that occasionally comes up with developers is that a library's application programming interface (API) may change slightly from one minor version to another, breaking installed software. The best solutions here are preventive: either use a system like Encap (see Section 9.4) to install shared libraries with `-Wl,-rpath` to create a runtime link path, or simply use the static versions of obscure libraries.

### 8.1.5 Make

A program with more than one source code file or requiring strange compiler options is too cumbersome to compile by hand. This problem has been around for years, and the traditional Unix compile management utility that eases these pains is called make. You need to know a little about make if you're running a Unix system, because system utilities sometimes rely on make to operate. However, this chapter is only the tip of the iceberg. The classic guide for compiled languages and make is *The UNIX Programming Environment* [Kernighan and Pike].

make is a big system, and there are entire books on the subject (such as *Managing Projects with make* [Oram]), but it's not very difficult to get an idea of how it works. When you see a file named Makefile or makefile, you know that you're dealing with make. (Try running make to see if you can build anything.)

The basic idea behind make is the *target*, a goal that you want to achieve. A target can be a file (a .o file, an executable, and so on) or a label. In addition, some targets depend on other targets — for instance, you need a complete set of .o files before you can link your executable. The targets on which another target depends are called *dependencies*.

To build a target, make follows a *rule*, such as a rule for how to go from a .c source file to a .o object file. make already knows several rules, but you can customize these existing rules and create your own.

The following is a very simple Makefile that builds a program called myprog from aux.c and main.c:

```
OBJS=aux.o main.o
# object files

all: myprog

myprog: $(OBJS)
        $(CC) -o myprog $(OBJS)
```

The first line of the Makefile is just a macro definition; it sets the OBJS variable to two object filenames. This will be important later. For now, take note of how you define the macro and also how you reference it later ($(OBJS)).

The # in the next line denotes a comment.

The next item in the Makefile contains its first target, all. The first target is always the default, the target that make wants to build when you run make by itself on the command line.

The rule for building a target comes after the colon. For all, this Makefile says that you need to satisfy something called myprog. This is the first dependency in the file; all depends on myprog. Note that myprog can be an actual file or the target of another rule. In this case, it is both (it is the rule for all and the target of OBJS).

To build myprog, this Makefile uses the macro $(OBJS) in the dependencies. The macro expands to aux.o and main.o, so myprog depends on these two files (they must be actual files, because there aren't any targets with those names anywhere in the Makefile).

This Makefile assumes that you have two C source files named aux.c and main.c in the same directory. Running make on the Makefile yields the following output, showing the commands that make is running:

```
cc    -c -o aux.o aux.c
cc    -c -o main.o main.c
cc -o myprog aux.o main.o
```

So how does make know how to go from aux.c to aux.o? After all, aux.c is not in the Makefile. The answer is that make follows its built-in rules. It knows to look for a .c file when you want a .o file, and furthermore, it knows how to run cc -c on that .c file to get to its goal of creating a .o file.

The final step of getting to myprog is a little tricky, but the idea is clear enough. Once you have the two object files in $(OBJS), you can run the C compiler according to the following line (where $(CC) expands to the compiler name):

```
        $(CC) -o myprog $(OBJS)
```

Pay special attention to the whitespace before $(CC). This is a tab. You must put a tab before any real command, and it must be on a line by its own. Watch out for this:

```
Makefile:7: *** missing separator.  Stop.
```

An error like this means that the Makefile is broken. The tab is the separator, and if there is no separator or there's some other interference, you will see this error.

### Staying Up to Date

One last make fundamental is that targets should be up to date with their dependencies. If you type make twice in a row for the preceding example, the first command builds myprog, but the second command yields this output:

```
make: Nothing to be done for `all'.
```

For this second time through, make looked at its rules and noticed that myprog already exists. To be more specific, make did not build myprog again because none of the dependencies had changed since the last time it built myprog. You can experiment with this as follows:

1. Run touch aux.c.
2. Run make again. This time, make figures out that aux.c is newer than the aux.o already in the directory, so it must compile aux.o again.
3. myprog depends on aux.o, and now aux.o is newer than the preexisting myprog, so make must create myprog again.

This type of chain reaction is very typical.

### Command-Line Options

You can get a great deal of mileage from make if you know how its command-line options work.

The most common make option is specifying a single target on the command line. For the preceding Makefile, you can run make aux.o if you want only the aux.o file.

You can also define a macro on the command line. Let's say that you want to use a different compiler called my_bad_cc. Try this:

```
make CC=my_bad_cc
```

Here, make uses your definition of CC instead of its default compiler, cc. Command-line macros come in handy when you're testing out preprocessor definitions and libraries, especially with the CFLAGS and LDFLAGS macros explained later.

You don't even need a Makefile to run make. If built-in make rules match a target, you can just ask make to try to create the target. For example, if you have the source to a very simple program called blah.c, try make blah. The make run tries the following command:

```
cc   blah.o   -o blah
```

This use of make works only for the most elementary C programs; if your program needs a library or special include directory, you're probably better off writing a Makefile.

Running make without a Makefile is actually most useful when you aren't dealing with a C program, but with something like Fortran, lex, or yacc. It can be a real pain to figure out how the compiler or utility works, so why not let make try to figure it out for you? Even if make fails to create the target, it will probably still give you a pretty good hint as to how you might use the tool.

Two more make options stand out from the rest:

**-n**  Prints the commands necessary for a build, but prevents make from actually running any commands

**-f** *file*  Tells make to read from *file* instead of Makefile or makefile

### Standard Macros and Variables

make has many special macros and variables. It's difficult to tell the difference between a macro and a variable, so this book uses the term *macro* to mean something that usually doesn't change after make starts building targets.

As you saw earlier, you can set macros at the start of your Makefile. The following list includes the most common macros:

**CFLAGS**  C compiler options. When creating object code from a .c file, make passes this as an argument to the compiler.

**LDFLAGS**  Like CFLAGS, but for the linker when creating an executable from object code.

**LDLIBS**  If you use LDFLAGS but do not want to combine the library name options with the search path, put the library name options in this file.

**CC**  The C compiler. The default is cc.

**CPPFLAGS**  C *preprocessor* options. When make runs the C preprocessor in some way, it passes this macro's expansion on as an argument.

**CXXFLAGS**  GNU make uses this for C++ compiler flags. Like C++ source code extensions (and nearly everything else associated with C++), this isn't standard and probably won't work with other make variants unless you define your own rule.

A make *variable* changes as you build targets. Because you don't ever set variables by hand, the following list includes the $.

**$@**  When inside a rule, this expands to the current target.

**$***  Expands to the *basename* of the current target. For example, if you're building blah.o, this expands to blah.

The most comprehensive list of the make variables on Linux is the make info page.

**NOTE**  *Keep in mind that GNU make has many extensions, built-in rules, and features that other variants do not have. This is fine as long as you're running Linux, but if you step off onto a Sun or BSD machine and expect the same stuff to work, you might be in for a surprise.*

### Conventional Targets

Most Makefiles contain several standard targets that perform auxiliary tasks related to compiles.

- The clean target is ubiquitous; a make clean usually instructs make to remove all of the object files and executables so that you can make a fresh start or pack up the software. Here is an example rule for the myprog Makefile:

```
clean:
        rm -f $(OBJS) myprog
```

- A Makefile created with the GNU autoconf system always has a distclean target to remove everything that wasn't part of the original distribution, including the Makefile. You will see more of this in Section 9.2.3. On very rare occasions, you may find that a developer opts not to remove the executable with this target, preferring something like realclean instead.

- install copies files and compiled programs to what the Makefile thinks is the proper place on the system. This can be dangerous, so you should always run a make -n install first to see what will happen without actually running any commands.

- Some developers provide test or check targets to make sure that everything works after you perform a build.

- depend creates dependencies by calling the compiler with a special option (-M) to examine the source code. This is an unusual-looking target because it often changes the Makefile itself. This is no longer common practice, but if you come across some instructions telling you to use this rule, make sure that you do it.

- all is often the first target in the Makefile; you will often see references to this target instead of an actual executable.

### Organizing a Makefile

Even though there are many different Makefile styles, there are still some general rules of thumb to which most programmers adhere.

In the first part of the Makefile (inside the macro definitions), you should see libraries and includes grouped according to package:

```
X_INCLUDES=-I/usr/X11R6/include
X_LIB=-L/usr/X11R6/lib -lX11 -Xt

PNG_INCLUDES=-I/usr/local/include
PNG_LIB=-L/usr/local/lib -lpng
```

Each type of compiler and linker flag often gets a macro like the following:

```
CFLAGS=$(CFLAGS) $(X_INCLUDES) $(PNG_INCLUDES)
LDFLAGS=$(LDFLAGS) $(X_LIB) $(PNG_LIB)
```

Object files are usually grouped according to executables. Let's say that you have a package that creates executables called boring and trite. Each has its own .c source file and requires the code in util.c. You might see something like this:

```
UTIL_OBJS=util.o

BORING_OBJS=$(UTIL_OBJS) boring.o
TRITE_OBJS=$(UTIL_OBJS) trite.o

PROGS=boring trite
```

The rest of the Makefile might look like this:

```
all: $(PROGS)

boring: $(BORING_OBJS)
        $(CC) -o $@ $(BORING_OBJS) $(LDFLAGS)

trite: $(TRITE_OBJS)
        $(CC) -o $@ $(TRITE_OBJS) $(LDFLAGS)
```

You could combine the two executable targets into one rule, but this is usually not good practice because you would not easily be able to move a rule to another Makefile, delete an executable, or group executables differently. Furthermore, the dependencies would be incorrect — if you had just one rule for boring and trite, trite would depend on boring.c, and boring would depend on trite.c, and make would always try to rebuild both programs whenever you changed one of the two source files.

**NOTE**    *If you need to define a special rule for an object file, put the rule for the object file just above the rule that builds the executable. If several executables use the same object file, put the object rule above all of the executable rules.*

## 8.2 Debuggers

The standard debugger on Linux systems is gdb, with DDD as a graphical user frontend. To enable full debugging in your programs, you must run the compiler with the -g option to write a symbol table and other debugging information into the executable. To start gdb on an executable named *program*, run this command:

```
gdb program
```

You should get a (gdb) prompt. To run *program* with the command-line arguments *options*, type this at the (gdb) prompt:

```
run options
```

If the program works, it should start, run, and exit as normal. However, if there's a problem, gdb stops, prints a stack trace and the failed source code, and throws you back to the (gdb) prompt. Because the source code fragment often gives you a hint about the problem, you often want to print the value of a particular variable that the trouble may be related to (print also works for arrays and C structures):

```
print variable
```

If you want to make gdb stop the program at any point in the original source code, use the breakpoint feature. In the following command, *file* is a source code file, and *line_num* is the line number in that file where gdb should stop:

```
break file:line_num
```

To tell gdb to continue executing the program, use this command:

```
continue
```

To clear a breakpoint, type this:

```
clear file:line_num
```

This section provides only the briefest introduction to the debugger. gdb comes with a very extensive manual that you can read online, print, or buy as *Debugging with GDB* [Stallman/Pesch/Shebs].

**NOTE** *If you're interested in rooting out memory problems and running profiling test, try Valgrind (http://valgrind.kde.org/).*

## 8.3 Lex and Yacc

You may encounter lex and yacc when compiling programs that read configuration files or commands.

- Lex is a *tokenizer* that transforms text into numbered tags with labels. The Linux version of lex is named flex. You may need a -ll or -lfl linker flag in conjunction with lex.
- Yacc is a *parser* that attempts to read tokens according to a *grammar*. The GNU parser is bison; to get yacc compatibility, run bison -y. You may need the -ly linker flag.

## 8.4 Scripting Languages

A long time ago, the average Unix systems manager didn't have to worry much about scripting languages other than the Bourne shell and awk. Shell scripts (discussed in Chapter 7) continue to be an important part of Unix, but as stated earlier, awk has faded somewhat from the scripting arena. However, many powerful successors have arrived, and many systems programs have actually switched from C to scripting languages (such as the sensible version of the whois program). Let's look at some scripting basics.

The very first thing that you need to know about any scripting language is that the first line of a script looks similar to a Bourne shell script. For example, a Perl script starts out like this:

```
#!/usr/bin/perl
```

In Unix, *any* executable text file that starts with #! is a script. The pathname following this prefix is the scripting language interpreter executable. When Unix tries to run an executable file that starts with #!, it runs the program following the #!, and then sends the script file to the new program's standard input. Therefore, even this is a script:

```
#!/bin/tail +2
This program prints this line...
and this line, too.
```

The first line of a shell script often contains one of the most common basic script problems — an invalid path to the scripting language interpreter. Let's say that you named the previous script myscript. Now, what if tail were actually in /usr/bin on your system (not /bin)? When you tried to run myscript, you would get this error:

```
myscript: No such file or directory
```

Most Unix error messages aren't confusing, misleading, or otherwise incomplete, but this one certainly qualifies on all three counts. First of all, myscript *does* exist — you can see it right in front of your eyes with ls. Is there a problem with your filesystem? No. The system *really* meant to say that it couldn't find /bin/tail, but it just had a small communication breakdown.

The worst case occurs when a script is in some system binary directory. You can locate the script with a utility like which or find, and you *think* that the program is in your path, yet you get that error message. The only real clue you have is the error message: "No such file or directory." If the script were actually missing from your path, the error message would be "command not found."

Another script "gotcha" is that you shouldn't expect any more than one argument in the script's first line to work. That is, the +2 in the preceding example may work, but if you add another argument, the system might decide to treat the +2 *and* the new argument as one big argument, spaces and all. This can vary from system to system; don't test your patience on something as insignificant as this.

### 8.4.1 Perl

The most important third-party Unix scripting language today is Perl — Larry Wall's Practical Extraction and Report Language. This tool has been called the "Swiss Army Chainsaw" of programming tools, and it is capable of an incredible variety of tasks, from networking to database access. It excels at text processing, conversion, and file manipulation.

It's hard to describe what Perl code looks like; it's kind of like an imperative-style mix of C, Bourne shell, sed, awk, LISP, and others. It can be a little hairy (using every single special character on your keyboard), but it is as fast and powerful as it is ugly. If you want to be on top of your Unix system, you need to know a little bit of this language. Have a look at *Learning Perl* [Schwartz] for a tutorial-style introduction; the larger reference is *Programming Perl* [Wall]. Getting a grasp of Perl is well worth it, not just because you will be able to do remarkable things with text files, but also because many of the concepts (such as associative arrays) carry over to other scripting languages.

Nearly all Unix and Linux systems in the world have Perl installed somewhere. Most administrators maintain it as /usr/bin/perl, even if they insist on keeping all other third-party software away from /usr. There is extensive online documentation in the manual pages; the perl(1) page has an index of the other pages.

If you're having trouble with a Perl script, here are some suggestions:

- Look at it to see if you can tell when the script was written. It might require a newer version of Perl than you have.

- If it's an old script, you may have to put backslashes in front of the @ characters in strings and comments.

- It might require a module that you do not have (in particular, a database module).

When all else fails, run perl -w *script* to turn on warning mode.

### 8.4.2 Python

Python is a newer scripting language with a fairly strong following, enough to make it the implementation language for packages such as GNU Mailman. It offers many of the same system features as Perl, but it has a powerful interactive mode and a somewhat more organized object model.

Python's executable is python, but there's no telling where it is on your system. Therefore, when you get a Python program, you may have to modify the first line in the script to match your Python installation.

Although it was written for slightly older versions, *Python Essential Reference* [Beazley] is a good reference with a small tutorial at the beginning to get you started.

### 8.4.3 Other Scripting Languages

There are some other scripting languages that you might encounter:

**PHP** This is a powerful hypertext processing language often found in dynamic Web scripts. Some people use PHP for stand-alone scripts. The PHP Web site is at http://www.php.net/.

**Tcl** Tcl (tool command language) is a simple scripting language usually associated with the Tk graphical user interface toolkit and Expect, an automation utility. Although Tcl does not enjoy the widespread use that it once did, you should not discount its power. Many veteran developers prefer Tcl, especially for its embedded capabilities. Refer to http://www.tcl.tk/ for more information on Tcl.

**m4** This is a macro processing language.

**Ruby** Object-oriented fanatics enjoy programming in this language (http://www.ruby-lang.org/).

**Matlab** This is a commercial matrix and mathematical programming language and library. There is a very similar open source project called octave.

**Mathematica, Maple** These are more commercial mathematical programming languages with libraries.

## 8.5 Java

Although some application programmers love Java, Unix systems programmers avoid it, and you may not even need it on your system. However, you should still have an idea of how it works on a typical Linux system.

There are two kinds of Java compilers: native compilers for producing machine code for your system (like a C compiler), and bytecode compilers for use by a bytecode interpreter (usually called a *virtual machine*, even though it's more of an *abstract machine*). You will invariably encounter bytecode on Linux.

Bytecode files end in .class. The Java runtime environment (JRE) contains all of the programs you need to run Java bytecode. To run a bytecode file, use this command:

```
java file.class
```

You may also encounter bytecode files that end in .jar, which are collections of archived .class files. To run a .jar file, use this syntax instead:

```
java -jar file.jar
```

Sometimes you need to set the JAVA_HOME environment variable to your Java installation prefix. If you're really unlucky, you may need to use CLASSPATH to include any directories containing classes that your program expects. This is a colon-delimited set of directories like the regular PATH variable for executables.

If you need to compile a .java file into bytecode, you need the Java Development Kit (JDK). You can run the javac compiler from JDK to create some .class files:

```
javac file.java
```

JDK also comes with jar, a program that can create and pick apart .jar files. It works like tar.

# 8.6 Assembly Code and How a Compiler Works

If you want to use a compiler's advanced features, you should have an idea of how the compiler operates. Here is a brief summary:

1.  The compiler reads a source code file and builds an internal representation of the code inside the file. If there's a problem with the source code, the compiler states the error and exits.

2.  The compiler analyzes the internal representation and generates assembly code for the target processor.

3.  An *assembler* converts the assembly code into an object file.

4.  The linker gathers object files and libraries into an executable.

You may be specifically interested in steps 2 and 3 of this process. Assembly code is one step away from the raw binary machine code that the processor runs; it is a textual representation of the processor instructions. Here is an excerpt of a program in x86 assembly code:

```
.L5:
        movl  -8(%ebp),%eax
        imull -16(%ebp),%eax
        movl  -4(%ebp),%edx
        addl  %eax,%edx
        movl  %edx,-12(%ebp)
        incl  -16(%ebp)
        jmp   .L3
        .p2align 4,,7
```

Each line of assembly code usually represents a single instruction. To manually generate assembly code from a C source file, use the compiler's -S option:

```
cc -S -o prog.S prog.c
```

Here, *prog*.c is the C source file and *prog*.S is the assembly code output. You can turn an assembly code file into an object file with the assembler, as:

```
as -o prog.o prog.S
```

For more information about x86 assembly code, see *The Art of Assembly Language* [Hyde]. RISC assembly code is a little more comprehensible; see *MIPS RISC Architecture* [Kane]. If you are interested in how to design and implement a compiler, two good books are *Compilers: Principles, Techniques, and Tools* [Aho 1986] and *Modern Compiler Implementation in ML* [Appel].

# COMPILING SOFTWARE
# FROM SOURCE CODE

Most nonproprietary third-party Unix software packages come as source code that the administrator can compile and install. One reason for this tradition is that Unix has so many different flavors and architectures that it would be difficult to distribute binaries for all possible platform combinations. Widespread source code distribution throughout the Unix community encouraged users to contribute bug fixes and new features to the software, and eventually this gave rise to the term "open source."

You can get everything you see on a Linux system comes as source code — this means everything from the kernel and C library to the Web browsers. This means it is possible to update and augment your entire system by (re-)installing parts of your system from the source code. However, you probably *shouldn't* update your machine by installing *everything* from source code unless you really enjoy the process. Linux distributions provide easier means to update core parts of the system (such as the programs in /bin).

Don't expect your distribution to provide everything for you. When you install binary packages from a distribution, you have no control over configuration options, including where the software goes. Some packages are not available as binaries, and furthermore, binary packages will not necessarily match the shared libraries on your system (see Section 8.1.4).

You should understand everything in Chapter 8 before proceeding with this chapter. Installing a package from source code usually involves the following steps:

1. Unpacking the source code archive.

2. Configuring the package.

3. Running make to build the programs.

4. Running make install to install the package.

## 9.1 Unpacking Source Packages

A package's source code distribution usually comes as a .tar.gz or .tar.bz2 file, and you should unpack the file as described in Section 1.18.

Before you unpack, though, verify the contents of the archive with tar tvf, because some packages don't create their own subdirectories in the directory where you extract the archive. Output like the following means that the package is probably okay to unpack:

```
package-1.23/Makefile.in
package-1.23/README
package-1.23/main.c
package-1.23/bar.c
...
```

However, you might see that not all of the files are in a common directory (like package-1.23 in the preceding example):

```
Makefile
README
main.c
...
```

Extracting an archive like this one can leave a big mess in your current directory. To avoid this, create a new directory and cd there before extracting the contents of the archive.

Watch out for a test listing with absolute pathnames like this:

```
/etc/passwd
/etc/inetd.conf
```

You likely won't come across anything like this, but if you do, remove the archive from your system, because it probably contains a Trojan horse or some other malicious code.

### 9.1.1 Where to Start

After you extract the contents of a source archive and have a bunch of files in front of you, try to get a feel for the package. In particular, look for these files: README and INSTALL.

Always look at any README files first. They often contain a description of the package, a small manual, installation hints, and other useful information. Many packages also come with INSTALL files that contain instructions on how to compile and install the package. Check for special compiler options and definitions.

Apart from the README and INSTALL files, you will find other package files that fall into roughly three categories:

- Files relating to the make system, such as Makefile, Makefile.in, and configure. Some packages come with a Makefile that you may need to modify. However, most modern packages use GNU autoconf and come with a configure script to generate a Makefile from Makefile.in based on your system settings and configuration options.

- Source code files ending in .c, .h, or .cc. C source code files may appear just about anywhere in a package directory. C++ source code files usually have .cc, .C, or .cxx suffixes.

- Object files ending in .o or binaries. Normally there aren't any object files in source code distributions. However, you may find object files in rare cases when the package maintainer is not allowed to release certain source code, and you may need to do something special to use the object files. In most cases, object (or binary executable) files in a source distribution mean that the package wasn't put together too well, and you should run make clean to make sure that you get a fresh compile.

## 9.2 GNU Autoconf

Even though C source code is usually fairly portable, there are still differences on each platform that make it impossible to compile most packages with a single Makefile. An early solution to this problem was to provide individual Makefiles for every operating system, or to provide a Makefile that was easy to modify. This approach somehow evolved into scripts that generate Makefiles based on an analysis of the system used to build the package.

GNU autoconf is now the most popular system for automatic file generation. Packages using this system come with files named configure, Makefile.in, and config.h.in. To generate a Makefile, run configure to check your system for prerequisites:

```
./configure
```

You should get a lot of diagnostic output like this:

```
checking build system type... i586-pc-linux-gnu
checking host system type... i586-pc-linux-gnu
checking for a BSD-compatible install... /bin/install -c
checking whether build environment is sane... yes
...
...
```

**NOTE**   *configure creates a cache file (*config.cache*) so that it does not need to run certain tests more than once. In addition,* configure *consults* config.cache *on subsequent runs (this may come up if your system requires special options).*

If all goes well, configure creates one or more Makefiles and config.h:

```
configure: creating ./config.status
config.status: creating Makefile
...
...
config.status: creating config.h
```

**NOTE**   *If you're looking for a package to test, get the coreutils package from the GNU FTP site (ftp://ftp.gnu.org/pub/gnu/coreutils/). Coreutils includes common system programs like* ls *and* cat.

Now you can type make to compile the package. A successful configure step doesn't necessarily mean that the make step will work, but the chances are pretty good (see Section 9.6 for troubleshooting failed configures and compiles).

After the build completes, you might want to try running a program from the package, just to see if it works. To install the program, run this command:

```
make install
```

### 9.2.1 configure Script Options

The configure script that comes with autoconf-enabled packages has several useful options. The most important of these is the installation directory. By default, the install target uses a *prefix* of /usr/local — that is, binary programs go in /usr/local/bin, libraries go in /usr/local/lib, and so on.

If you want to use a prefix other than /usr/local, run configure with this option:

```
./configure --prefix=new_prefix
```

For example, if you specify --prefix=/tmp/test, a make install puts binaries in /tmp/test/bin, libraries in /tmp/test/lib, and so on.

Most versions of configure have a --help option that lists other configuration options. Unfortunately, the list is usually so long that it's sometimes hard to figure out what might be important. Here are some other options:

**--bindir=*directory***   Installs executables in *directory*.

**--sbindir=*directory***   Installs system executables in *directory*.

**--libdir=*directory***   Installs libraries in *directory*.

**--disable-shared**   Prevents the package from building shared libraries. Depending on the library, this can save hassles later on (see Section 9.4.1).

**--with-*package*=*directory***   Tells configure that *package* is in *directory*. This is handy when a necessary library is in a nonstandard location. Unfortunately not all configure scripts recognize this type of option, and furthermore, it can be difficult to determine the exact syntax.

You can create separate build directories if you want to experiment with some of these options. To do this, create a new directory anywhere on the system, and from that directory, run the configure script in the original package source code directory. You will find that configure then makes a symbolic link farm in your new build directory, where all of the links point back to the source tree in the original package directory. Some developers actually prefer that you build packages this way.

## 9.2.2 Environment Variables

You can influence configure with environment variables that the configure script puts into make variables. The most important variables are CPPFLAGS, CFLAGS, and LDFLAGS. Be aware that configure can be very picky about environment variables. For example, you should always use CPPFLAGS instead of CFLAGS for header file directories, because configure often runs the preprocessor independently of the compiler.

In bash, the easiest way to send an environment variable to configure is by placing the variable assignment in front of ./configure on the command line. For example, to define a DEBUG macro for the preprocessor, use this command:

```
CPPFLAGS=-DDEBUG ./configure
```

Environment variables are especially handy when configure doesn't know where to look for third-party include files and libraries. For example, to make the preprocessor search in *include_dir*, run this command:

```
CPPFLAGS=-Iinclude_dir ./configure
```

As shown in Section 8.1.5, to make the linker look in *lib_dir*, use this command:

```
LDFLAGS=-Llib_dir ./configure
```

If *lib_dir* has shared libraries (see Section 8.1.4), the previous command probably won't set the runtime dynamic linker path. In that case, use the -rpath linker option in addition to -L:

```
LDFLAGS="-Llib_dir -Wl,-rpath=lib_dir" ./configure
```

Be careful when setting variables. A small slip can trip up the compiler and cause *configure* to fail. Let's say that you forget the - in -I, as in this example:

```
CPPFLAGS=Iinclude_dir ./configure
```

This yields an error like this:

```
checking for C compiler default output... configure: error: C compiler
cannot create executables
See `config.log' for more details.
```

Digging through config.log yields this:

```
configure:2161: checking for C compiler default output
configure:2164: gcc Iinclude_dir  conftest.c  >&5
gcc: Iinclude_dir: No such file or directory
```

### 9.2.3 Autoconf Targets

In addition to the standard all and install, an autoconf-generated Makefile has these targets:

**make clean**   As described in Section 8.1.5, make clean removes all object files, executables, and libraries.

**make distclean**   This is similar to make clean, but it removes all automatically generated files, including Makefiles, config.h, config.log, and so on. The idea is that the source tree should look like a newly unpacked distribution after running make distclean.

**make check**   Some packages come with a battery of tests to verify that the compiled programs work properly; the command make check runs the tests.

**make install-strip**   This is like make install, but it strips the symbol table and other debugging information from executables and libraries when installing. Stripped binaries require much less space.

### 9.2.4 Autoconf Log Files

If something goes wrong during the `configure` process and the cause isn't obvious, you can examine `config.log` to find the problem. Unfortunately, `config.log` is often a gigantic file, making it difficult to locate the exact source of the problem.

The best approach is to go to the very end of `config.log` (for example, by pressing G in `less`), and then page back up until you see the problem. However, there is still a lot of stuff at the end, because `configure` dumps its entire environment there, including output variables, cache variables, and other definitions.

You can also try running a search for the error message, starting from the end of the file. For example, let's say that `configure` fails, terminating with this message:

```
See `config.log' for more details.
```

Search backward for the string "for more details" (or "config.log," or anything that looks reasonably unique); it's a pretty good bet that the error is nearby.

## 9.3 Other Systems

If a package does not use GNU autoconf for platform-specific configuration, you should expect that the package uses one of these three systems:

- A customizable Makefile and/or `config.h`. At one time, administrators had to configure nearly all third-party Unix software by editing Makefiles. GNU autoconf has made this practice nearly extinct, but you still may come across custom configuration in older packages or very Linux-specific packages.
- Imakefiles. Many X Window System applications use `imake` to create Makefiles from Imakefiles.
- "Anybody's guess." Some developers just have to be different.

In addition, many packages, including those using the three types listed above, now rely on the `pkg-config` program for compiler and linker options. You will see how these work in Section 9.3.3.

### 9.3.1 Custom Makefiles

When you need to customize a Makefile, make a copy of the original Makefile (to `Makefile.dist`, for example) before changing anything. This ensures that you can always refer to a pristine original when you delete or alter a line that you shouldn't have touched.

A typical custom Makefile might look like this:

```
# CC=gcc
CFLAGS=-g
# use -O to enable optimizer
# CFLAGS=-O

DESTDIR=/usr/local
BINDIR=$(DESTDIR)/bin
MANDIR=$(DESTDIR)/man/man1

# To enable X11 support, use -DHAS_X11
# X11FLAGS=-DHAS_X11
# XINC=-I/usr/X11R6/include
# XLIB=-L/usr/X11R6/lib -lX11 -lXt
#
# Don't edit below this line
```

As you learned in Chapter 8, # is a comment in a Makefile. Custom Makefiles often include macros that are commented out; and uncommenting those macros allows you to override defaults and add extra features.

The XINC and XLIB macros in the preceding example illustrate use of a third-party library. Macros like DESTDIR are analogous to the --prefix parameter in the GNU autoconf system. Don't expect all Makefiles to have such a mechanism, though.

Finally, some particularly old configuration files ask you to specify whether your system is a BSD-like or SVR4 (System V Release 4) system. At one time, most Unix flavors were derived from one or the other. Linux leans more toward SVR4, but depending on the nature of the package, there are many BSD-isms on Linux that you might need to take into account.

### 9.3.2 Imake

Many X Window System applications use imake to create Makefiles from Imakefiles. The Imake system attempts to produce valid Makefiles from Imakefile template files with the help of predefined default values for the C compiler, options, and so on. The imake program uses the C preprocessor for its dirty work.

Imake is standard on any platform that has an X Window System installation (usually located in /usr/X11R6). Imake's ubiquity is its only advantage. The system's disadvantages are that it's not very flexible (it usually requires installing packages with a /usr/X11R6 prefix) and it's not very smart (it doesn't dig around in your system and verify that things actually work as advertised).

To build and install a package that comes with an Imakefile, do the following:

1. Run xmkmf or xmkmf -a (use -a if there are subdirectories) to create the valid Makefile.

2. Run make to compile the package.

3. Run `make install` to install the executables and libraries.

4. Run `make install.man` to install the manual pages.

### X Resource Files

Many packages that have Imakefiles also use application default ("app-defaults") files to store default configuration data. A program window missing an app-defaults file may look "plain" or extremely bad.

App-defaults files are usually in `/usr/X11R6/lib/X11/app-defaults`. Some packages give you an option for installing their app-defaults file in a place other than the default. Unfortunately, most do not, and you might have to resort to this ugly trick in order to install the package in a nonstandard location:

1. Identify the programs to be installed with `make -n install`.

2. Identify the app-defaults file (it usually ends with `.ad`). Your `make -n install` from the previous step should tell you the name of the installed file, though in the `make -n install` output the app-defaults filename normally does not have the `.ad` extension.

3. Install the program by hand.

4. Install the app-defaults file without a `.ad` extension.

5. Rename the program with a `.bin` extension.

6. Write a wrapper script like the following and name it *program* without the `.bin` extension (*app_defaults_path* is where you installed the app-defaults file, and *prog_path/program*`.bin` is the binary program):

```
#!/bin/sh
XUSERFILESEARCHPATH=app_defaults_path/%N%S:$XUSERFILESEARCHPATH
export XUSERFILESEARCHPATH
exec prog_path/program.bin
```

## 9.3.3 pkg-config

The number of third-party libraries has risen dramatically in recent years. Because keeping all add-on libraries in a common location can be messy, you may wish to install each with a separate prefix. However, doing so can lead to problems when building packages that require these third-party libraries. For example, if you want to compile OpenSSH, you need the OpenSSL library. How do you tell the OpenSSH configuration process the nonstandard location of the OpenSSL header files and libraries?

Many libraries now use the `pkg-config` program not only to advertise the locations of their include files and libraries, but also to specify the exact flags that you need to compile and link a program. The syntax is as follows:

```
pkg-config options package1 package2 ...
```

For example, to find the include files for OpenSSL, you can run this command:

```
pkg-config --cflags openssl
```

The output should be something like this:

```
-I/opt/openssl/include
```

If you want the linker flags, use --ldflags instead. This should yield a library location and the names of the individual libraries, as in this example for OpenSSL:

```
-L/opt/openssl/lib -lssl -lcrypto -ldl
```

To see all libraries that pkg-config knows about, run this command:

```
pkg-config --list-all
```

If you look behind the scenes, you will find that pkg-config finds package information by reading configuration files that end with .pc. For example, here is openssl.pc, from the OpenSSL socket library:

```
prefix=/opt/openssl
exec_prefix=${prefix}
libdir=${exec_prefix}/lib
includedir=${prefix}/include

Name: OpenSSL
Description: Secure Sockets Layer and cryptography libraries and tools
Version: 0.9.7b
Requires:
Libs: -L${libdir} -lssl -lcrypto  -ldl
Cflags: -I${includedir}
```

You can change this file if you like — for example, you may wish to add -Wl,-rpath=${libdir} to the library flags to set a runtime dynamic linker path. However, the bigger question is how pkg-config finds the .pc files in the first place. What happens is that pkg-config looks in the lib/pkgconfig directory of its installation prefix. A pkg-config installed with a /usr/local prefix looks in /usr/local/lib/pkgconfig.

Unfortunately, pkg-config does not read any .pc files outside of its installation prefix by default. The previous OpenSSL example .pc file would reside at /opt/openssl/lib/pkgconfig/openssl.pc, almost certainly out of the reach of any stock pkg-config installation.

There are two basic ways to show pkg-config the .pc files that are located outside of the pkg-config installation prefix:

- Make symbolic links (or copies) from the actual `.pc` files to the central `pkgconfig` directory.

- Set your `PKG_CONFIG_PATH` environment variable to include any extra `pkgconfig` directories. This strategy does not work well on a system-wide basis.

## 9.4 Installation Practice

Knowing *how* to build and install software is good, but knowing *when* and *where* to install your own packages is what proves to be useful. Linux distributions try to cram in as much software as possible on installation. You should always ask yourself if you should install a package by yourself instead.

Here are the advantages of doing it yourself:

- You can customize package defaults.
- Custom software usually survives operating system upgrades.
- When installing a package, you often get a much clearer picture of how to use the package.
- You always get the latest releases.
- It's easier to back up a custom package.
- It's easier to distribute self-installed packages across a network.

These are the disadvantages:

- It takes time.
- If you don't actually use the package, you're wasting your time.
- There is a potential for misconfiguring packages.

Consider the C library and the coreutils package (`ls`, `cat`, and so on) — there really is no point in building these by yourself unless you have some real obsession with the build process. On the other hand, if you have a vital interest in network servers such as Apache, the best way to get complete control is to install the servers yourself.

### 9.4.1 Where to Install

The default prefix in GNU autoconf and many other packages is `/usr/local`, the traditional directory for locally installed software. Operating system upgrades ignore `/usr/local`, so you won't lose anything installed there during an operating system upgrade.

For small local software installations, `/usr/local` is fine. However, if you have a lot of custom software installed, this can turn into a terrible mess. Thousands of odd little files can make their way into the `/usr/local` hierarchy, and you may have no idea where the files came from.

There are several schemes that help manage software packages. I like the Encap system (http://www.encap.org/) because it requires no extra software.

### Encap

Encap abuses symbolic links, but that's a small price to pay for the features you get:

- You can identify everything in /usr/local by package name.
- You can keep old versions of a software package intact, so you can always downgrade, run the old version, and or use the old version as a model.
- It is easy to remove old versions and entire packages.
- You can easily transport packages to another partition or another machine.
- Encap requires very little extra configuration.

The main idea behind Encap is that you *encapsulate* a package installation before making it available in /usr/local. To start, you must have a common installation root (most administrators use /usr/local/encap or /opt; this book uses /opt because it's shorter).

Let's say that you are installing bogon-3.2.3. Here's what you would do with Encap:

1. Configure, build, and install the package with an installation prefix that reflects the package and version. For example, the package uses GNU autoconf, so run this command:

   ```
   ./configure --prefix=/opt/bogon/bogon-3.2.3
   ```

2. Go to /opt/bogon and make a symbolic link to the install you just made from default:

   ```
   cd /opt/bogon
   ln -s /opt/bogon/bogon-3.2.3 default
   ```

3. If there are binary programs in /opt/bogon/default/bin, run this command:

   ```
   ln -s /opt/bogon/default/bin/* /usr/local/bin
   ```

4. If there are binary programs in /opt/bogon/default/sbin, run this command:

   ```
   ln -s /opt/bogon/default/sbin/* /usr/local/sbin
   ```

5. Run the appropriate variant of the following command for each section in which there are manual pages (the example works for man section 1):

   ```
   ln -s /opt/bogon/default/man/man1/* /usr/local/man/man1
   ```

Now the bogon package binaries and manual pages are available in /usr/local via symbolic links. Furthermore, you can now do the following:

- If you ever need to know the originating package of an item in /usr/local/bin, you need only run ls -l on the link to see where it points.

- To remove a package, you can remove the symbolic links and its directory in /opt. For example, to remove the bogon symbolic links in /usr/local/bin, run this:

```
cd /opt/bogon/default/bin
for file in *; do
  rm -f /usr/local/bin/$file
done
```

### Should You Compile Shared Libraries?

Shared libraries (see Section 8.1.4) cause trouble with custom installations, primarily because a shared library upgrade can break a large number of programs at once. For this reason, you should *never* make links to shared libraries in /usr/local/lib when using Encap. Leave shared libraries in their installed location.

Even with this precaution, you still have these problems:

- It's hard to tell if you can actually delete an old shared library, because some program may depend on the library.

- It's difficult to link programs against the shared library. You must use the -Wl,-rpath=*path* linker option.

- When linking against a shared library, you should specify a path that includes a version number. For example, use /opt/bogon/bogon-3.2.3/lib instead of /opt/bogon/default. You risk library version mismatches otherwise.

In fact, shared libraries can cause so many problems that you should always think twice before installing them. If the library is fairly small (such as libpng and libtiff), there's no problem in opting for static libraries over shared libraries. Use this configure option to disable shared libraries for packages that use GNU autoconf:

```
./configure --disable-shared
```

### Encap, pkg-config, and Shared Libraries

You can't get away with static libraries for everything. Enormous libraries such as GNOME components demand shared libraries. In the worst cases, you need to slug it out with LDFLAGS Makefile and environment variables. Happily, many larger libraries also use pkg-config, described in Section 9.3.3.

You can make Encap work with `pkg-config` if you put in a little extra effort. To set it up, you need to know which `lib/pkgconfig` directory `pkg-config` searches for `.pc` files. Let's say that you're trying to install the shared libraries from `bogon-3.2.3` with Encap:

1. Configure, compile, and install the package as usual.
2. Carry out the Encap steps discussed earlier. In particular, you need the default symbolic link to point to `bogon-3.2.3`.
3. Go to `/opt/bogon/default/lib/pkgconfig`. You should see a file named `bogon.pc`.
4. Edit `bogon.pc`. Look for this line:

```
Libs: -L${libdir} -lbogon
```

Change that line to reflect a runtime link path:

```
Libs: -Wl,-rpath=${libdir} -L${libdir} -lbogon
```

5. Now tell `pkg-config` about the package. If *pcpath* is where `pkg-config` keeps its `.pc` files (for example, *pcpath* could be `/usr/local/lib/pkgconfig`), create a symbolic link:

```
ln -s /opt/bogon/default/lib/pkgconfig pcpath
```

6. Test `pkg-config` on `bogon`:

```
pkg-config --libs bogon
```

The output should include `-Wl,-rpath`.

## 9.5 Applying a Patch

Every now and then, you might get a *patch* that you need to apply against source code to fix bugs or add features. You may also see the term *diff* used as a synonym for patch, because the `diff` program produces the patch.

The beginning of a patch looks something like this:

```
--- src/file.c.orig    2003-07-17 14:29:12.000000000 +0100
+++ src/file.c    2003-09-18 10:22:17.000000000 +0100
@@ -2,16 +2,12 @@
```

Patches usually contain alterations to more than one file. Search the patch for three dashes in a row (`---`) if you want to see the files that have alterations.

You should always look at the beginning of a patch to determine the required working directory. Notice that the preceding example refers to src/file.c. Therefore, you should change to the directory that *contains* src before applying the patch, *not* to the src directory itself.

To apply the patch, run the patch command:

```
patch -p0 < patch_file
```

If everything goes well, patch exits without a fuss, leaving you with an updated set of files. However, watch out if patch asks you this question:

```
File to patch:
```

This usually means that you are not in the correct directory. However, it could also indicate that your source code does not match the source code in the patch. In this case, you're probably out of luck — even if you could identify some of the files to patch, others would not be properly updated, leaving you with source code that you cannot compile.

In rare cases, you might come across a patch that refers to a package version like this:

```
--- package-3.42/src/file.c.orig    2003-07-17 14:29:12.000000000 +0100
+++ package-3.42/src/file.c   2003-09-18 10:22:17.000000000 +0100
```

If you have a slightly different version number (or you just renamed the directory), you can tell patch to strip leading path components. Let's say that you were in the directory that contains src (as before). To make patch ignore the package-3.42/ part of the path (that is, to strip one leading path component), use -p1:

```
patch -p1 < patch_file
```

## 9.6 Troubleshooting Compiles and Installations

If you understand the difference between compiler errors, compiler warnings, linker errors, and shared library problems as described in Chapter 8, then you should not have too much trouble fixing many of the glitches that arise when building software. This section covers some other common problems.

Before getting into specifics, you should learn to read make output. You first need to know the difference between an error and an ignored error. The following is a real error that you need to investigate:

```
make: *** [target] Error 1
```

However, some Makefiles suspect that an error condition may occur but know that these errors are harmless. You can usually disregard any messages like this:

```
make: *** [target] Error 1 (ignored)
```

Furthermore, GNU make often calls itself many times in large packages, with each instance of make in the error message marked with [N], where N is a number. You can often find the error quickly by looking at the make error that comes *directly* after the compiler error message. Here is an example:

```
[compiler error message involving file.c]
make[3]: *** [file.o] Error 1
make[3]: Leaving directory `/home/src/package-5.0/src'
make[2]: *** [all] Error 2
make[2]: Leaving directory `/home/src/package-5.0/src'
make[1]: *** [all-recursive] Error 1
make[1]: Leaving directory `/home/src/package-5.0/'
make: *** [all] Error 2
```

The first three lines practically give it away — the trouble centers around file.c located in /home/src/package-5.0/src. Unfortunately, there is so much extra output that it can be difficult to spot the important details. Learning how to filter out the subsequent make errors goes a long way toward digging out the real cause.

### 9.6.1 Specific Errors

*Problem:* Compiler error message:

```
src.c:22: conflicting types for `item'
/usr/include/file.h:47: previous declaration of `item'
```

*Explanation and Fix:* The programmer made an erroneous redeclaration of *item* on line 22 of src.c. You can usually fix this by removing the offending line (with a comment, an #ifdef, or whatever works).

*Problem:* Compiler error message:

```
src.c:37: `time_t' undeclared (first use this function)
...
src.c:37: parse error before `...'
```

*Explanation and Fix:* The programmer forgot a critical header file. The manual pages are the best way to find the missing header file. First, look at the offending line (in this case, it's line 37 in src.c). It's probably a variable declaration like the following:

```
time_t v1;
```

Search forward for v1 in the program for its use around a function call. For example:

```
v1 = time(NULL);
```

Now run man 2 time or man 3 time to look for system and library calls named time(). In this case, the section 2 manual page has what you need:

```
SYNOPSIS
     #include <time.h>

     time_t time(time_t *t);
```

This means that time() requires time.h. Place #include <time.h> at the beginning of src.c and try again.

*Problem:* Compiler (preprocessor) error message:

```
src.c:4: pkg.h: No such file or directory
(long list of errors follows)
```

*Explanation and Fix:* The compiler ran the C preprocessor on src.c, but could not find the *pkg*.h include file. The source code likely depends on a library that you need to install, or you may just need to provide the compiler with the nonstandard include path (see Section 9.2.2 if the package uses GNU autoconf). In most cases, you just need to add a -I include path option to the C preprocessor flags (CPPFLAGS). Keep in mind that you may also need a -L linker flag to go along with the include files.

If you are using a graphics application and see Xm and Mrm in the error message, you are missing the Motif library. LessTif is a free replacement for Motif; if it is not on your system, you can get it at http://www.lesstif.org/.

If it doesn't look as though you're missing a library, there's also an outside chance that you are attempting a compile for an operating system that this source code does not support. Check the Makefile and README files for details about platforms.

*Problem:* make error message:

```
make: prog: Command not found
```

*Explanation and Fix:* To build the package, you need *prog* on your system. If *prog* is something like cc, gcc, or ld, you don't have the development utilities installed on your system. On the other hand, if you think *prog* is already installed on your system, try altering the Makefile to specify the full pathname of *prog*.

In rare cases, make builds *prog* and then uses *prog* immediately, assuming that the current directory (`.`) is in your command path. If your `$PATH` does not include the current directory, you can edit the Makefile and change *prog* to *./prog*. Alternatively, you could append `.` to your path temporarily.

*Problem:* Undefined symbols that start with `SM_` and `ICE_`.

*Explanation and Fix:* Some packages that link against X Window System libraries also need the `-lSM` and `-lICE` linker flags.

# 10

# MAINTAINING THE KERNEL

As mentioned in Section 2.2, the kernel is the core of the operating system. In some respects, the Linux kernel is no different than any other software package. You can configure, build, and install the kernel because it comes as source code. However, the procedure for doing so is substantially different than for any other software package because the kernel *runs* like no other package.

There are four basic topics pertaining to kernel management:

**Configuring and compiling a new kernel**   Your end goal here is to build an image file, ready for the boot loader.

**Manipulating loadable kernel modules**   You don't have to build the kernel as one massive chunk of code. Kernel modules let you load drivers and kernel services as you need them.

**Configuring a boot loader such as GRUB or LILO** Your kernel is useless if you can't load it into memory.

**Learning miscellaneous utilities and procedures** There are many facilities that tweak runtime kernel parameters and extend kernel features. You have already seen some examples of these in previous chapters, including the /proc filesystem and the iptables command.

## 10.1 Do You Need to Build Your Own Kernel?

Before running head-first into a kernel build, you need to ask yourself if it is worth it. Administrators who compile their own kernels have the following goals in mind:

- Installing the latest drivers
- Using the latest kernel features (especially with respect to networking and filesystems)
- Having fun

However, if you need a driver or feature, and your distribution offers a straightforward upgrade, you might opt for that instead, for several reasons:

- You can make mistakes in configuring your own kernel, and your distribution probably offers a well-rounded kernel.
- Compiling a new kernel takes a long time.
- It's far too easy to mess up the boot loader, making your system unable to boot.

Even if you choose not to build your own kernel, though, you should still learn how boot loaders and modules work.

## 10.2 What You Need to Build a Kernel

As with any package, the kernel source includes documentation explaining what you need to compile a functional kernel. These three aspects of your system are particularly important for building a kernel:

- A C compiler (gcc). Most distributions put the C compiler in a development tools package. Make sure that your C compiler agrees with the recommendations in the kernel source code, specifically the README file. Kernel developers have not been eager to adopt the latest versions of gcc. Some distributions have a separate compiler named kgcc for compiling the kernel.
- Disk space. A new kernel source tree can easily unpack to more than 100MB even before building any object files.
- A relatively fast computer with plenty of memory. Otherwise, the compile will take some time.

Your first step is to get the source code.

# 10.3 Getting the Source Code

Linux kernel versions have three components. Suppose you have kernel release 2.6.3. Here's what the numbers mean:

- 2 is the *major* release number.
- 6 is the *minor* release number.
- 3 is the *patchlevel.* Kernels with the same major and minor numbers but with different patchlevels belong to a *release series.*

There are two different kinds of kernel releases:

- *Production releases* have minor version numbers that are even (for example, 1.**2**.*x*, 2.**0**.*x*, 2.**2**.*x*, 2.**4**.*x*, 2.**6**.*x*, and so on). These versions are meant to be as stable as possible. Within a single production release series, there are no radical feature or interface changes.
- *Development releases* have minor version numbers that are odd (such as 2.**5**.). Don't use a developer release if you aren't willing to take risks. Kernel developers intentionally break code, introduce new features, and may inadvertently make the kernel unstable in a development series. Stay away from development releases unless you know exactly what you're doing.

You can get the latest Linux kernel source code at http://www.kernel.org/. The releases have names like linux-*version*.tar.bz2 for bzip2 compression or linux-*version*.tar.gz for GNU Zip compression. Bzip2 archives are smaller.

In addition to the full releases available in the kernel archives, you will also find patches containing just the changes between two consecutive kernel patchlevel releases. Unless you are obsessed with upgrading your kernel with every single release, you probably won't be able to do much with a patch.

## 10.3.1 Unpacking the Source Archive

You can unpack kernels with zcat/bzip2 and tar. To get started, go to /usr/src and make your permissions less restrictive if necessary:

```
cd /usr/src
umask 022
```

Then run one of these commands to extract the source files, depending on whether you are using bzip2 or GNU Zip:

```
bzip2 -dc linux-version.tar.bz2 | tar xvf -
zcat linux-version.tar.gz | tar xvf -
```

**WARNING**    *If your kernel release is 2.4.18 or lower, the kernel unpacks into a directory named* linux *rather than* linux-version. *Rename any existing* linux *directory before unpacking one of these kernels (the new name does not matter, as long as it is different than the old one).*

### 10.3.2 A Look Around the Kernel Source

If you've never seen the Linux kernel source code before, it helps to take a look around first. The top-level directory includes several subdirectories and files, including these:

**README**   This file is a general introduction to the Linux kernel source and what you need to get started. This document explains the version of the C compiler that you need to compile the kernel.

**Documentation**   This directory contains a wealth of documents. Most of the documents here are in plain-text format, and they may describe anything from user-level programs to low-level programming interfaces. One of the most important files in this directory is Changes, which describes recent changes to the kernel and identifies utility programs you may need to upgrade to get full functionality.

**include**   You'll find the kernel header files in this directory. If you feel comfortable with your kernel, you can use the header files in include/linux as your system /usr/include/linux header file set.

**arch**   This directory contains architecture-specific kernel build files and targets. After a kernel build on a PC system, the final kernel image is in arch/i386/boot/bzImage.

### 10.3.3 Distribution Kernels

Linux distributions come with generic kernels intended to run on almost any processor type. These kernels tend to be a little larger than custom kernels, and they rely heavily on loadable modules.

However, many of the Linux kernels that come with the various Linux distributions omit complete source code in their default installations, and furthermore, distribution kernels often differ from the official standard kernels at kernel.org. For example, Red Hat adds another component to the patchlevel to distinguish their kernels (for example, 2.4.20-**20**). If you wish to install a distribution kernel from source code, you need to use the distribution's kernel source package. In Red Hat Linux, the package name is kernel-source-*version*.rpm.

If your distribution has a /usr/src/linux directory, this does *not* mean that you have the entire kernel source. It is possible that you only have the header files. The kernel source takes up dozens of megabytes; run du -s /usr/src/linux for a quick check on what you have.

## 10.4 Configuring and Compiling the Kernel

You need to configure the options that you want to have in your kernel before you build it. Your goal is to have an appropriate .config file in your kernel source distribution. Here's an excerpt of a typical .config file:

```
# CONFIG_HIGHMEM64G is not set
# CONFIG_MATH_EMULATION is not set
CONFIG_MTRR=y
CONFIG_HAVE_DEC_LOCK=y
```

This file isn't easy to write with a text editor, so there are several configuration utilities that generate the file for you. An easy, standard way to set up a kernel is to run this command:

```
make menuconfig
```

After some initial setup, `make menuconfig` runs a text-based menu interface that is shown in Figure 10-1. The box in the center of the screen contains the options at the current configuration level. You can navigate the menu with the up- and down-arrow keys. An arrow next to an item (--->) indicates a submenu.

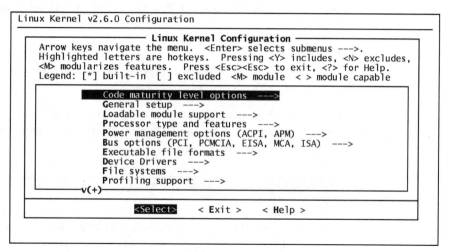

Figure 10-1: The make menuconfig kernel configuration menu.

The bottom of the menu contains three actions that you can navigate to with the left- and right-arrow keys. Pressing ENTER while one of the menu items is highlighted performs whichever of the three following actions is also highlighted:

**Select**  If the current menu item leads to a submenu, the configuration system activates the submenu.

**Exit**  Exits the current submenu. If you are at the top-level menu, the configuration system asks whether you would like to save the current configuration. You can activate the **Exit** option by pressing ESC.

**Help**  Shows any online help for the current item. You can also get at the help by pressing the ? key.

To get a general feel for how configuration options work, go into the **Processor type and features** submenu. You will see options such as these:

```
[ ] Math emulation
[*] MTRR (Memory Type Range Register) support
< > /dev/cpu/microcode - Intel IA32 CPU microcode support
```

You can alter an item's configuration value by moving to the item and pressing the SPACEBAR. The square brackets ([ ]) provide a simple on/off toggle:

[*] indicates that the feature is on.

[ ] indicates that the feature is off.

You may not configure on/off features as kernel modules. Active features go directly into the main kernel image.

By contrast, an item with angle brackets (< >) denotes a feature that you may compile as a module. You can use the SPACEBAR to toggle between these values:

<*> indicates that the feature is on.

<M> indicates that the feature is configured as a module.

< > indicates that the feature is off.

An item that includes regular parentheses like these, ( ), is a multiple-choice option or a number that you can customize. Press ENTER to see the option list, or enter a number.

### When Should You Compile a Driver as a Module?

There aren't many absolute rules for deciding which features to compile as modules and which features to compile as part of the main kernel image, but here are a few guidelines and rules that can help you:

- Always compile your root filesystem type directly into the kernel, not as a module. Your system won't boot otherwise.

- Most administrators prefer to compile crucial disk support (such as SCSI host adapter drivers) directly into the kernel. There is a way to get around this with an initial RAM disk, but that is more an ugly hack than anything else.

- Most administrators also compile network interface card drivers directly into the kernel. This isn't as crucial as disk support, though.

- Compile obscure filesystems as modules. You may need them at some point, but there is no point in wasting memory in the meantime.

When you are through with configuration and decide to exit, the menu system will ask if you would like to save the current configuration. If you choose **Yes**, the system backs up your previous .config file as .config.old and writes a new .config file.

## 10.4.1 Configuration Options

Most of the configuration options are fairly self-explanatory. For example, in the menu shown in Figure 10-1 on page 205, the items under **Device Drivers > SCSI device support > SCSI low-level drivers** correspond to device drivers for SCSI host controllers.

Some configuration options depend on other options, and until you activate the dependency options you cannot reach configuration options that have dependencies. For example, to reach the **SCSI low-level drivers** submenu, you must first activate **SCSI device support** in the previous menu. These dependencies are not always obvious; you may need to do a little bit of experimentation to find what you're looking for. If you're really stumped on a dependency, go to the source. Look at arch/i386/Kconfig, the master file for all options and online help for the kernel configuration.

The following sections outline the most significant kernel options that reside within the important top-level menus. Keep in mind that these options change with time; you may see items not listed here, or the items may be in a different place in the kernel that you decide to build.

### Code Maturity Level Options

Inside this menu item you will find an option named **Prompt for development and/or incomplete code/drivers**. To see the newest (but perhaps unstable) drivers and features when perusing the rest of the kernel configuration menus, select this option.

### General Setup

This section has three settings that you should turn on:

> **Support for paging of anonymous memory**   Enables swap disk and file support
>
> **System V IPC**   Enables interprocess communication
>
> **Sysctl support**   Enables kernel parameter changes through /proc

If you do not build your kernel with the support listed here, many major packages and utilities will not work, including the X Window System.

In addition to these options, the **General Setup** menu in kernel 2.6.0 and newer versions have an option named **Kernel .config support** to make the build process save the current .config file in the kernel image. If you enable this option, you will also have the opportunity to enable a second option that allows you to turn on access to the embedded .config file via

`/proc/config.gz`. These options increase your kernel size slightly, but they can come in extremely handy later on when you need to upgrade your kernel but can't remember what configuration options you selected.

### Loadable Module Support

You have some control over the kernel's module loader. In general, you should always activate the kernel module system with the **Enable loadable module support** option, as well as activating the kernel module loader option, **Automatic kernel module loading**, sometimes called the autoloader.

The only item in the kernel module support menu that you should be wary of is versioning support (at the moment, this is experimental). Kernels compiled with this option enabled may try to load modules built for a different kernel version, and this can cause trouble if you don't know exactly what you're doing.

### Processor Type and Features

The Linux kernel includes a number of optimizations and other enhancements that are specific to certain processors. You can choose your processor with the **Processor family** option. Be careful — a kernel built for a "primitive" CPU supports advanced processors, but a kernel tailored to an advanced CPU will likely not work on an older (or different brand of) CPU.

Other significant options in the processor category include:

**High memory support**   This is for machines with more than 2GB of physical memory.

**Symmetric multi-processing support**   This is for machines with more than one processor.

**MTRR support**   This permits optimizations that may improve certain kinds of graphics performance.

### Power Management Options

There are two types of power management in PC hardware: the older APM (Advanced Power Management) and the newer ACPI (Advanced Configuration and Power Interface). You can configure a kernel with both varieties. Appropriate power management support is essential on notebooks to preserve battery life, and it is a good idea for desktops so that your machine doesn't generate too much heat and use too much electricity.

Power management features enable interesting tricks with fans, processor speeds, and more. There's a lot to explore, but you may need additional software such as `apmd` or `acpid` to take advantage of the kernel features.

## Bus Options

You shouldn't need to change the bus options for most systems. Unless you have an extremely old or odd system, include PCI support (and if you'd like to list and diagnose devices on the PCI bus, install lspci, which is a part of the pci-utils package).

You should enable the **Support for hot-pluggable devices** option so that your system can take appropriate action when you attach and detach removable devices.

Newer kernels include base PCMCIA (PC Card/CardBus) drivers as configuration options in this menu — in previous systems, PCMCIA support was completely separate from the main kernel distribution. You still need the PCMCIA utilities if you intend to use PC cards, and at the moment, you can still leave out PCMCIA kernel support here and get it from these utilities, but this may change in the future.

## Executable File Formats

To start a process from an executable file on the disk, the kernel needs to know how to load the executable file, how to initialize the process in memory, and where to start running the process. An executable's file format determines these characteristics. Most binaries on a modern Linux system are ELF (Executable and Linkable Format) files. You probably do not need to support the ancient "a.out" executable format (you may not even have the shared libraries to support these binaries), but it does not take too much memory to include support, and you can build it as a module.

## Device Drivers

Configuring device drivers is a long process due to the wide variety of devices that Linux supports. Unfortunately, it's during this stage that you can get bogged down with all of the options and end up building a kernel that is far too large because you included drivers for devices that you will never have. If you're in doubt about whether you are going to use any particular driver (other than a disk driver), build it as a module so that it does not unnecessarily take up kernel memory.

The following sections describe the driver configuration options inside the **Device drivers** menu.

### Plug and Play Support

You must enable **Plug and Play support** if you want any reasonably modern built-in hardware in your computer to work. You may also need plug-and-play support in order to use network cards, internal modems, and sound cards.

### Block Devices

The **Block devices** section of the kernel configuration contains miscell-aneous random-access storage devices, such as floppy disks and RAM disks. These devices normally hold filesystems that you directly attach to your current system with the mount command. The interesting drivers here include the following:

**Normal floppy disk support**   A driver for the PC floppy disk drive.

**Loopback device support**   A simple driver that maps a file into a block device. This driver is very useful because it allows you to mount a filesystem on a disk image.

**Network block device support**   A driver that allows you to use a network server as a block device.

**RAM disk support**   A driver that designates a chunk of physical memory as disk space.

**Initial RAM disk (initrd) support**   A driver that provides a special kind of RAM disk that a boot loader gives to the kernel as the initial / parti-tion during the very first stages of init. Many distributions use an initial RAM disk for SCSI drivers and other modules that may not be in their stock kernels.

**Parallel port IDE device support**   A driver for certain older portable disk devices.

### ATA (IDE) Support

You should always compile ATA (IDE) support directly into your kernel unless you know exactly what you're doing. There are several kinds of IDE drivers that you can enable here:

**Disk support**   A driver required if you want hard drives to work. Need-less to say, you should compile this driver directly into the kernel.

**CD-ROM support**   A driver for ATAPI CD-ROM and DVD-ROM drives.

**Floppy support**   A driver for various removable-media drives with an ATAPI interface.

**SCSI emulation**   A driver for ATAPI CD-R and CD-RW drives. Older Linux CD-burning software worked exclusively with SCSI drivers; if your CD-burning software is up to date, you do not need this driver.

**Various chipsets**   Drivers for various specific chipsets. If your mother-board's IDE chipset is listed, you might be able to squeak out a little more performance with one of these drivers.

### SCSI Support

Even if you have no SCSI devices, you may still need SCSI support because many Linux device drivers work through emulated SCSI devices. For example, if you want to use USB mass storage, you need SCSI disk support.

These are the media drivers:

**SCSI disk support**    Covers all fixed and removable-media disk-like storage devices, except CD-ROM drives.

**SCSI tape support**

**SCSI CD-ROM support**

**SCSI generic support**    Allows applications talk to a SCSI device at a low level. You need SCSI generic support for a wide range of devices, including CD burners, changer devices on tape drives, SCSI scanners, and more.

A look inside the **SCSI low-level drivers** submenu reveals drivers for many kinds of SCSI host controllers. Some of the drivers are named after the SCSI chipset on the host controller, so you may have to look carefully at your hardware to find a match. The low-level driver list also includes support for some parallel port devices, such as Zip drives.

**NOTE**    *If your kernel and root partition are on a SCSI disk, compile SCSI support (including the disk and host controller drivers) directly into the kernel rather than as modules. This makes booting much easier, because you do not need to worry about loading SCSI modules from a disk that the kernel does not yet know how to access.*

### Networking Support

You need networking support for almost any system, even if you do not have an external network connection. Many applications use local network interface features.

Your first order of business is to pick the networking devices that you need. For most Ethernet devices, look under **Ethernet (10 or 100Mbit)**. There are many devices to choose from. If you're not too sure what you need, don't be afraid to configure several drivers as modules. In addition, if you plan to dial up to the Internet or use certain DSL connections, you need **PPP support**, along with asynchronous (serial port) or PPP over Ethernet (PPPoE) support. If you're not sure about PPP options, configure them as modules.

The configuration options inside the **Networking options** submenu represent the trickiest part of the kernel network configuration. You need to select all of the options and protocols that you intend to use. The essential options for many packages include the following:

**TCP/IP networking**

**Unix domain sockets**

**Packet socket** (for features such as promiscuous mode)

Not so obvious is **Network packet filtering**, which is required for any kind of firewall or NAT (Network Address Translation, or "IP masquerading") support. Just selecting this option is not enough because, in general, your kernel needs all of the connection tracking, NAT, and masquerade options if you want to use NAT. Therefore, you must enter the **Netfilter Configuration** submenu and choose more options there, such as these:

**Connection tracking** for NAT (be sure to include any protocols you need to track).

**IP tables support** for firewalling and NAT. Once you enable IP tables, you get several more options, including various **match** options for filtering. You don't have to worry about most of these, except for **Connection state** and **Connection tracking**, both of which you need for NAT. That's not the end of the things you need for NAT — look out for and enable **Full NAT** and **MASQUERADE target support**.

**Packet filtering** and **REJECT target support** for firewalls.

### Input Device Support

You need several configuration options to support your keyboard and mouse. There are two levels of support. The basic drivers support the PS/2 keyboard. Also, look for **PS/2 Mouse**.

### Character Devices and Parallel Port Support

Among the most important character devices are **Virtual terminals** (/dev/tty0, /dev/tty1, and so on). Unless you have a special type of server, you also need to put the console on the virtual terminal.

Here are some other things to check up on:

**Serial drivers**   Standard PC serial ports use or emulate 8250/16550 UART chips. You almost certainly need this support if you plan to use a modem.

**Unix98 PTY support**   Some programs now expect to see the dynamic Unix98 /dev/pts/* pseudo-terminal devices rather than old static names like /dev/ttyp*.

**Enhanced real time clock support**   This makes /dev/rtc available to programs like hwclock. You should enable this option for any modern machine.

**/dev/agpart**   This is for direct-rendered graphics (GLX and DRI) on AGP graphics cards.

**Parallel printer support**   This gives you /dev/lp* devices. To get this option, you must go back to the main kernel menu and enable **Parallel port support**. You also need **PC-style hardware** for any standard PC.

**NOTE**   *There is a section for **Mice** in the character device configuration, but you can probably safely ignore it, because the drivers there are for very old bus mice.*

### Sound

There are two parts to sound configuration: API support and drivers. The current sound system is called Advanced Linux Sound Architecture (ALSA), but you should also include the emulation support for the old OSS (Open Sound System), because many programs still use the OSS interface.

The driver configuration for sound devices is very similar to that for network devices — many of the sound drivers carry the names of the sound chipset.

### USB Support

When configuring USB, choose an interface driver first:

**UHCI** and **OHCI** are USB 1.1 interfaces. Even if you have a USB 2.0 motherboard, you need one of these. If you don't know which one your motherboard supports, pick both (modules are okay); the kernel will sort it out.

**EHCI** is a USB 2.0 interface.

You also want to enable the **USB device filesystem** option that can maintain USB device information in /proc/bus/usb.

Configuring the kernel to support USB devices is fairly straightforward, but there are two gotchas:

- The **Mass storage support** option requires that you also enable SCSI and SCSI disk support.
- The **Interface device support (HID)** option requires that you enable the input drivers described earlier. To get USB mouse and keyboard support, you need to enable **HID input layer support** in the USB support menu. Don't use the boot protocol drivers unless you know exactly what you're doing.

### Filesystems

You can add support for many different filesystems to your Linux kernel configuration. However, *make sure* that you compile your primary filesystem directly into the kernel. For example, if your root partition uses ext2, don't modularize ext2 support. Otherwise, your system will not be able to mount the root filesystem and therefore will not boot.

These are the most important filesystems:

**Second extended (ext2)**   The Linux standard for many years.

**Third extended (ext3)**   A journaled version of ext2; now the standard for many distributions.

**Reiserfs**   A high-performance journaled filesystem.

**DOS/FAT/NT** MS-DOS- and Windows-compatible filesystems. To get MS-DOS filesystem support, you need to enable FAT. VFAT is the extended filesystem introduced with Windows 95. You need VFAT if you plan to read images from the flash memory cards in digital cameras and similar devices.

**ISO9660** A standard CD-ROM filesystem. The Linux driver includes the Rock Ridge extensions. You can also add the Microsoft Joliet extensions.

**UDF** A newer CD-ROM and DVD filesystem.

**Minix** A filesystem that was the Linux standard a long time ago (it even predates Linux). It never hurts to include Minix filesystem support as a module.

**Pseudo filesystems** These are system interfaces, not storage mechanisms. The /proc filesystem is one of the best-known pseudo-filesystems, and one that you should *always* configure. You should also include the /dev/pts filesystem and the virtual memory filesystem.

**Network filesystems** These are used for sharing files with machines over the network.

There are also a couple important filesystem-related options:

**Kernel automounter support** Enables automatic filesystem mounting and unmounting. This is a popular solution for managing network filesystem access.

**Partition types** Allows Linux to read partitioning schemes other than the regular PC partition tables, including BSD disklabels and Solaris x86 partitions.

This wraps up the important kernel configuration options. You shouldn't really have to worry about the other options (such as the Profiling support used for kernel development); let's turn our focus to compiling the kernel.

## 10.4.2 Compiling the Kernel and Modules

After you save your kernel configuration, you're ready to build the kernel. To get a list of make targets, you can run this command:

```
make help
```

Your main goals are to compile the bzImage compressed kernel image and the kernel modules. Because these two are the default targets, you only need to run the following to build everything:

```
make
```

The compile takes some time. As it runs along, you see messages like this:

```
CC      init/version.o
```

If you see a message containing [M], it means that make is compiling a module:

```
CC [M]  net/sctp/protocol.o
```

The following output appears when make builds bzImage:

```
Kernel: arch/i386/boot/bzImage is ready
```

As the preceding message indicates, the build process creates your kernel image as arch/i386/boot/bzImage. The process also creates a file named System.map that contains kernel symbols and locations. You may have to wait a little while after the "Kernel ready" message appears, because make may still need to compile some kernel modules. Don't interrupt the build; make sure that you wait until you get your prompt back before installing the kernel.

**NOTE** *In kernel versions prior to 2.6, you had to run the following commands for a complete kernel build:*

```
make dep
make bzImage
```

### Failed Compiles

Recent kernels are very self-contained; there are only two primary things that can go wrong during the build process:

- If you get a parse error or some other sort of coherent compiler error, the compiler on your machine probably doesn't match the recommended compiler in the README file. Kernel code is very particular about the compiler, especially due to all of the assembly code involved.
- If the compiler dies unexpectedly midway through the build process, your hardware may be at fault. Compiling a kernel stresses a machine much more than almost any other task. Bad memory and overclocked or overheated processors are the main culprits.

If you need to see each command in the build process to track down a problem, use this command:

```
make V=1
```

### 10.4.3 Installing Modules

Before you install and boot from your new kernel, you should put the new kernel modules in /lib/modules with this command:

```
make modules_install
```

Your new modules should appear in /lib/modules/*version*, where *version* is your kernel version. If you fail to install the modules before booting your kernel, the kernel module utilities will not automatically recognize the new modules, and you may end up missing a few drivers.

The module installation builds a module dependency list in /lib/modules/version/modules.dep. If this stage fails, it's likely that your module utilities are out of date. As of this writing, the module utilities are in a package named module-init-tools.

### 10.4.4 Kernel Parameters

Sometimes you need to send extra parameters to the kernel at boot time in order to get devices or services working. For example, one of the most elementary kernel parameters is root=*partition*, which sets the initial root partition to *partition*.

You can enter a kernel parameter after the kernel image name. For example, at a LILO prompt where your kernel label is Linux, you can type this:

```
Linux root=/dev/hda3
```

Documentation/kernel-parameters.txt contains a list of all kernel parameters. Most of them are for hardware. In addition to root=*partition*, here are the most important parameters:

> **init=*path***  This starts *path* as the first process on the system in place of /sbin/init. For example, you can use init=/bin/sh to get out of a tight spot if your init does not work properly.

> **mem=*size***  This specifies that the machine has *size* memory; the kernel should not autodetect the memory size. For example, to specify 512MB of memory, you would use mem=512M.

> **rootfstype=*type***  This specifies that the root filesystem's type is *type*.

A number as a boot parameter indicates the init runlevel. You can use -s or S for single-user mode.

## 10.5 Installing Your Kernel with a Boot Loader

Boot loaders load kernel images into memory and hand control of the CPU over to the newly loaded kernel. To make your new kernel work, you must tell the boot loader about the kernel.

If you have never worked with a boot loader before, you need to know how a PC boots from the hard disk. On a normal Microsoft-based system, the boot process works like this:

1. After performing the power-on self test (POST), the BIOS loads sector 1 of the hard disk into memory and runs whatever landed in that memory. On most Windows-based systems, this sector is called the Master Boot Record (MBR).

2. The MBR extracts the partition table from the disk and identifies the "active" partition.

3. The MBR loads and runs yet another boot sector from the active partition, setting the operating system in motion.

On a Linux system, you can install the kernel boot loader on the active partition *or* you can replace the MBR with the boot loader. If you decide to replace the MBR with a boot loader such as GRUB or LILO, it is important to remember that the active partition has little meaning — these boot loaders address partitions based on their own configuration systems.

From a practical point of view, your decision to overwrite the MBR (and thus circumvent the active partition) makes little difference. If your machine runs Linux, you probably want GRUB or LILO as your default boot loader. Even if you have a dual-boot machine, you still want to use GRUB or LILO, because both boot loaders are capable of loading boot sectors from other operating systems.

The important point is that you know exactly where your boot loader resides. Let's say that your disk is /dev/hda and you have a Linux root partition at /dev/hda3. If you replace the MBR by writing GRUB to /dev/hda, you need to remember that the active partition is now irrelevant; GRUB uses its own configuration system to access partitions. However, if you decide to write the boot loader to /dev/hda3 instead, keeping the old MBR, your system will get to that boot loader only if /dev/hda3 is the active partition.

**NOTE** *If you need to replace the MBR on a hard disk, run the DOS command* FDISK /MBR.

When configuring a boot loader, be sure that you know the location of the root partition and any kernel parameters.

### 10.5.1 Which Boot Loader?

Because there are two popular Linux boot loaders, you may wonder which one you should choose:

**LILO**   Linux Loader. This was one of the very first Linux boot loaders. Its disadvantages are that it is not terribly flexible and that you must run lilo to install a new boot block every time you install a new kernel. However, LILO is fairly self-contained.

**GRUB**   Grand Unified Boot Loader. This is a newer boot system gaining in popularity, and it does not need a reconfiguration for every new kernel because it can read many kinds of filesystems. This feature is especially handy for situations where you might need to boot from an old kernel. Initially, GRUB is slightly trickier to configure than LILO, but it is much easier to deal with once installed, because you do not need to replace the boot sector for every new kernel. I recommend GRUB.

### 10.5.2 GRUB

With GRUB, you need only install the boot loader code on your machine once; after that, you can modify a GRUB menu file for any new kernel that you want to boot on a permanent basis.

The GRUB boot files are in /boot/grub. GRUB loads the various stage files into memory during the boot process. If you already have GRUB on your machine, you just need to modify the /boot/grub/menu.1st file when you add a new kernel image under a new name. (If you install a new kernel image with the same name as the old kernel, you do not need to modify the menu file.)

Some distributions preinstall GRUB but have a different name for menu.1st. You may need to dig around in /boot to find the correct filename. In any case, the menu file looks like this:

```
default 0
timeout 10

title Linux
  kernel (hd0,0)/boot/vmlinuz root=/dev/hda1

title backup
  kernel (hd0,0)/boot/vmlinuz.0 root=/dev/hda1
```

The parameters in the menu file are as follows:

**default**   The title entry that GRUB should boot by default. 0 is the first entry, 1 is the second, and so on.

**timeout**   How long GRUB should wait before loading the default image.

**title**   A label for a kernel.

**kernel**   The kernel image and parameters, possibly including the root device.

In GRUB, (hd0) is the first hard disk on your system, usually /dev/hda. GRUB assigns disk mappings in the order that they appear on your system, so if you have /dev/hda and /dev/hdc devices but no /dev/hdb, GRUB would assign (hd0) to /dev/hda and (hd1) to /dev/hdc. The first number in the GRUB name is for the disk, and the second is for the partition (if there is a partition). Check the /boot/grub/device.map file for your system's hard drive mapping.

The kernel images in the preceding example are on the root partition of the primary master ATA hard disk. There are two kernel images: a regular kernel at /boot/vmlinuz and a backup at /boot/vmlinuz.0.

### Root Device Confusion

You may find it odd that the root partition is actually specified twice in the kernel line in the preceding example (you can see (hd0,0) and /dev/hda1). This is easy to explain: the (hd0,0) is where GRUB expects to find the kernel image, and root=/dev/hda1 is a Linux kernel parameter that tells the kernel what it should mount as the root partition. These two locations are usually, but not always, the same. However, the GRUB and Linux device names are completely different, and so you need them in two places in the configuration file.

Unfortunately, you may see this alternate syntax in menu.lst:

```
root (hd0,0)
kernel /boot/vmlinuz.0 root=/dev/hda1
```

This is confusing, because GRUB does not pass its root parameter (hd0,0) to the Linux kernel. Omitting the GRUB root parameter can prevent some head scratching.

### Booting Other Operating Systems

There are all sorts of other things you can do with GRUB, like load splash screens and change the title (use info grub to see all of the options). However, the only other essential thing you should know is how to make a dual-boot system.

Here is a definition for a DOS or Windows system on /dev/hda3:

```
title dos
  rootnoverify (hd0,2)
  makeactive
  chainloader +1
```

Remember how the PC boot loaders usually work, by first loading whatever is on the first sector of the disk, then loading the first sector of the active partition.

### Installing GRUB

To put GRUB on your system for the first time, you must make sure that you have a menu.lst file. The GRUB installation process does not create menu.lst; you must come up with this file on your own. If you don't, you can still boot your system, but you must type a series of commands resembling entries in menu.lst to do so, as follows:

```
kernel (hd0,0)/boot/vmlinuz root=/dev/hda1
boot
```

To install the GRUB software, run this command to put the boot sector on your disk:

```
grub-install device
```

Here, *device* is your boot device, such as /dev/hda. However, if you have a special /boot partition, you need to do something like this:

```
grub-install --root-directory=/boot device
```

After running grub-install, review your /boot/grub/device.map file to make sure that the devices relevant to booting the kernel are in the map file and agree with your menu.1st file.

### 10.5.3 LILO

To load your kernel with LILO, you must settle on a permanent location for your kernel image and install a new boot block for every change you make to the kernel configuration.

Let's say that you want to boot /vmlinuz as your kernel with a root partition of /dev/hda1. Furthermore, you want to install the boot loader on /dev/hda (replacing the MBR). Do the following:

1.  Move the new image into place at /boot/vmlinuz.
2.  Create the LILO configuration file, /etc/lilo.conf. An elementary configuration might look like this:

```
boot=/dev/hda
root=/dev/hda1
install=/boot/boot.b
map=/boot/map
vga=normal
delay=20

image=/boot/vmlinuz
    label=Linux
    read-only
```

3.  Run lilo -t -v to test the configuration without changing the system.
4.  Run lilo to install the boot loader code at /dev/hda.

You can add more images and boot sectors to the LILO configuration. For example, if you saved your previous kernel as /boot/vmlinuz.0, you could add this to your lilo.conf to make the old image available as backup at the LILO prompt:

```
image=/boot/vmlinuz.0
    label=backup
    read-only
```

You can use the other keyword for foreign operating systems. The following addition to lilo.conf offers a Windows partition on /dev/hda3 as dos at the LILO prompt:

```
other=/dev/hda3
    label=dos
```

### LILO Parameters

Some of the most important lilo.conf parameters are listed here:

**boot=*bootdev*** Writes the new boot sector to the *bootdev* device.

**root=*rootdev*** Uses *rootdev* as the kernel's default root partition.

**read-only** Mounts the root partition initially as read-only. You should include this for normal boot situations (init remounts the root partition in read-write mode later).

**append="*options*"** Includes *options* as kernel boot parameters.

**delay=*num*** Displays the LILO prompt for *num* tenths of a second at boot time before booting the default kernel image.

**map=*map_file*** Stores the kernel's location in *map_file*. Don't delete this file.

**install=*file*** Specifies that *file* is the actual boot loader code that lilo writes to the boot sector.

**image=*file*** Defines a bootable kernel image with *file*. You should always use the label parameter directly following this definition to name the image.

**label=*name*** Uses *name* to label the current boot entry.

**other=*partition*** Defines another partition that contains a boot sector; analogous to image for other operating systems. Use label to define a label for the boot sector.

**linear** Remaps the boot sector load references when the BIOS disk geometry is different than the geometry that the Linux kernel sees. This is usually not necessary, because most modern BIOS code can recognize very large disks.

## 10.5.4 Initial RAM Disks

An *initial RAM disk* is a temporary root partition that the kernel should mount before doing anything else. Red Hat Linux uses initial RAM disks to support SCSI host controller drivers and other drivers that are compiled as modules.

**NOTE** *You do not need an initial RAM disk if you compile all the drivers necessary to mount your root filesystem directly into your kernel. The overwhelming majority of systems do not need an initial RAM disk.*

To install an initial RAM disk on a Red Hat Linux system, follow these steps:

1. Build your kernel and install the modules. Do not run any boot loader configuration or reboot just yet.

2. Run this command to create a RAM disk image (where *version* is your kernel version):

```
mkinitrd /boot/initrd-version    version
```

3. If your boot loader is LILO, add this line to your new kernel's section in lilo.conf and run lilo:

```
initrd=/boot/initrd-version
```

4. For GRUB, add the following to the appropriate kernel section:

```
initrd /boot/initrd-version
```

## 10.6 Testing the Kernel

When you boot your new kernel for the first time, you should take a careful look at the kernel diagnostic messages to make sure that all of your hardware shows up and that the drivers are doing what they are supposed to do. Unfortunately, kernel messages tend to fly by so quickly that you can't see them. You can run dmesg to see the most recent messages, but to see everything, you need to look at your log files.

Most /etc/syslog.conf files send kernel messages to a file such as /var/log/kernel.log. If you don't see it anywhere, add a line like this to your /etc/syslog.conf:

```
kern.*                          /var/log/kernel.log
```

Then run this command:

```
kill -HUP `/var/run/syslogd.pid`
```

You may wish to make a checklist for your new kernel to make sure that your system still operates as it should. Here's an example:

- Do the network interface and network firewalls work?
- Are all of your disk partitions still visible?
- Does the kernel see your serial, parallel, and USB ports?
- Does all of your external hardware work?
- Does the X Window System work?

## 10.7 Boot Floppies

You can also boot the kernel from a floppy disk. Creating a boot floppy can be useful when recovering a Linux system that has no active kernel.

To create a boot floppy, put a freshly formatted floppy disk in the drive, go to the kernel source directory, and run this command:

```
make bzdisk
```

Of course, this only works if the size of your bzImage is smaller than the floppy disk capacity.

You may also need to run rdev to set the floppy's default root device. For example, if your root partition is /dev/hda1, use this command:

```
rdev /dev/fd0 /dev/hda1
```

Again, boot floppies are primarily useful during a system recovery when there is no active kernel. For testing new kernels, it's far better just to use an advanced boot loader such as GRUB.

## 10.8 Working with Loadable Kernel Modules

Loadable modules are little pieces of kernel code that you can load and unload into the kernel memory space while the kernel is running.

The make modules_install command (discussed in the "Installing Modules" section) installs the kernel module object files in /lib/modules/*version*, where *version* is your kernel version number. Module object filenames end with .ko in kernel versions 2.6.0 and later, and .o in older releases.

All distributions use modules in some capacity. If you would like to see the modules currently loaded on your system, run this command:

```
lsmod
```

The output should look something like this:

```
Module            Size   Used by
es1370           24768   0 (autoclean)
appletalk        19696   13 (autoclean)
```

This output includes es1370 (a sound card driver) and appletalk (a network protocol driver). autoclean means that the kernel may try to automatically unload the module if it is not used for some time.

To load a module, use the modprobe command:

```
modprobe module
```

To remove a single module, use the -r option:

```
modprobe -r module
```

As mentioned earlier, you can find module dependencies in /lib/modules/*version*/modules.dep. Dependencies don't arrive on your system by magic; you must build an explicit list (the kernel module install process usually does this for you). You may need to create module dependencies by hand for all installed kernel versions after installing a module that doesn't come with the kernel. You can do this by running this command:

```
depmod -a
```

However, this doesn't always work, because depmod may try to read the symbol function memory address locations in the currently running kernel. This won't work if you're trying to build dependencies for kernels other than the one you're running. To zero in on a particular kernel version, find a System.map file that corresponds to that kernel, and then run this command:

```
depmod -a -F System.map version
```

As mentioned earlier, though, you do not need to run depmod under normal circumstances, because make modules_install runs it for you.

**HINT** *If you can't find the module that corresponds to a particular feature, go to the feature in the kernel configuration menu and press ? to get the help screen. This usually displays the module name.*

## 10.8.1 Kernel Module Loader

It's inconvenient to manually load a module every time you need to use a particular feature or driver. For example, if you compiled a certain filesystem as a module, it would be too much work to run a modprobe before a mount command that referenced the filesystem.

The Linux kernel provides an automatic module loader that can load most modules without additional modprobe or insmod commands. To use the loader, enable the **Kernel module loader** option in the kernel configuration. A kernel with the module loader runs modprobe to load modules that it wants.

There are limits to what the module loader can do without additional configuration. In general, it can load most modules that do not involve specific devices. For example, the module loader can load IP tables modules, and it can load filesystem modules as long as you specify the filesystem type with a mount command.

The module loader cannot guess your hardware. For instance, the module loader will not try to figure out what kind of Ethernet card is in your system. Therefore, you need to provide extra hints with the modprobe.conf file.

## 10.8.2 modprobe Configuration

The `modprobe` program reads `/etc/modprobe.conf` for important device information. Most entries are aliases such as this:

```
alias eth0 tulip
```

Here, the kernel loads the `tulip` module if you configure the `eth0` network interface. In other cases, you may need to specify drivers by their major device numbers, such as this entry for an Adaptec host controller:

```
alias block-major-8 aic7xxx
```

Wildcards are also possible in `modprobe.conf` aliases. For example, if all of your Ethernet interface cards use the `tulip` driver, you can use this line to catch all interfaces:

```
alias eth* tulip
```

**NOTE** *The module utilities discussed here are the ones that go with kernel version 2.6.0. These programs are part of the* `module-init-utils` *package. Earlier kernel versions used the* `modutils` *package. The most significant difference between the two sets of utilities is that the new package reads* `modprobe.conf` *instead of* `modules.conf`*. The syntax in both files is very similar.*

### Chaining Modules and the install Keyword

You can chain modules together with the `install` keyword. For example, if SCSI disk support isn't compiled directly into the kernel, you can force it, as in this example for `/dev/sda` on the Adaptec host controller from the preceding section:

```
alias block-major-8 my_scsi_modules
install my_scsi_modules /sbin/modprobe sd_mod; /sbin/modprobe aic7xxx
```

This works as follows:

1.  A process (or the kernel) tries to access `/dev/sda`. Assume that this device is not yet mapped to an actual device.

2.  The kernel sees that `/dev/sda` isn't mapped to its device, which has a block major number of 8. Therefore, the kernel runs this command:

    ```
    modprobe block-major-8
    ```

3.  `modprobe` searches though `/etc/modprobe.conf` for `block-major-8` and finds the alias line.

4.  The alias line says to look for my_scsi_modules, so modprobe runs itself, this time as follows:

```
modprobe my_scsi_modules
```

5.  The new modprobe sees install my_scsi_modules in modprobe.conf, and then runs the command(s) that follow in the file. In this case, these commands are two additional modprobe commands.

You can include any command that you like in an install line. If you need to debug something or just want to experiment, try adding an echo command.

**NOTE**    *There is a* remove *keyword that works like* install *but runs its command when you remove a module.*

### Module Options

Kernel modules can take various parameters with the options keyword, as shown in this example for a SoundBlaster 16:

```
alias snd-card-0 snd-sb16
options snd-sb16 port=0x220 irq=5 dma8=1 dma16=5 mpu_port=0x330
```

# CONFIGURING AND MANIPULATING PERIPHERAL DEVICES

This chapter covers various peripheral devices that may be attached to your computer. Although compiling and installing the low-level drivers for your kernel are the first steps in getting any device including peripherals working, you may also need additional utilities or servers to do anything useful with the device.

A great deal of the work involved when configuring peripherals is digging through kernel log messages to see exactly how the kernel assigns a device and whether the kernel recognizes the device correctly in the first place. Therefore, this chapter contains a great number of example kernel messages that you can use as a guide for your own installation.

# 11.1 Floppy Drives

When working with a PC floppy drive, you must remember that it is one of the most unreliable pieces of hardware that you can find on a PC. You can mount the first floppy drive using the device /dev/fd0, but this can be dangerous, because the kernel will not like any hardware errors. Using the mtools programs is a good alternative to mounting the filesystem directly.

The mtools programs look like their MS-DOS counterpart commands with an m at the beginning. For example, you can use mdir for a directory listing.

To copy a file from a floppy disk to the current directory, run this command:

```
mcopy a:file .
```

Copying files from the local system to the disk is similar:

```
mcopy file a:
```

You can also format a floppy with an MS-DOS filesystem using the mformat command:

```
mformat a:
```

For more options and commands, refer to the mtools(3) manual page.

## 11.1.1 Floppy Images

Sometimes it's more convenient to copy the entire image of a floppy disk to a file on your hard disk than it is to deal with individual floppy disk operations. You can perform the extraction with dd:

```
dd if=/dev/fd0 of=image_file bs=512
```

You might be able to make the extraction go a little faster by changing the bs parameter to 32k. After you have the image file, it's convenient to mount the image file on your system with a loopback block device. This example mounts an image of an MS-DOS filesystem:

```
mount -t vfat -oloop=/dev/loop0 image_file mount_point
```

**WARNING**   *Remember to unmount the image file after you finish, especially if you plan to alter the filesystem in the image.*

### 11.1.2 Low-Level Formatting a Floppy Disk

If you absolutely need to write to a floppy disk, but you keep getting I/O errors, you can try to format a disk with the `superformat` program (which is part of the fdutils package) or with `fdformat`.

## 11.2 CD Writers

Linux CD burning programs work with ATAPI devices and generic SCSI devices, such as `/dev/hdc` and `/dev/sg0`. The most popular command-line CD recording utility for Linux is named `cdrecord`.

Most CD burners on the market are ATAPI devices. At one time, Linux supported these devices with an IDE-to-SCSI emulation driver called ide-scsi. However, with Linux kernel version 2.6, this is no longer necessary, and the ide-scsi driver may not work well in newer kernel releases.

### 11.2.1 Verifying the Hardware

Before trying to write a CD, you should verify that the CD recorder drive exists and determine its device name and specification. For IDE devices, locating the device is easy; just use the standard device name for the entire disk (for example, `/dev/hdc`; see Section 2.3.4 for more information).

You can verify the existence and identity of a device with the `-inq` option to `cdrecord`. For example:

```
cdrecord -inq dev=device
```

If there is an ATAPI device at *device*, the output of the `cdrecord -inq` command looks like this:

```
Device type    : Removable CD-ROM
Version        : 0
Response Format: 1
Vendor_info    : 'PLEXTOR '
Identifikation : 'CD-R   PX-W4012A'
Revision       : '1.01'
Device seems to be: Generic mmc CD-RW.
```

You can search for a SCSI CD recorder device with this command:

```
cdrecord -scanbus
```

The output should look something like the following:

```
scsibus0:
    0,0,0    0) *
    0,1,0    1) *
    0,2,0    2) *
    0,3,0    3) *
    0,4,0    4) 'HP      ' 'C1533A              ' '9503' Removable Tape
    0,5,0    5) 'PLEXTOR ' 'CD-R    PX-R412C ' '1.04' Removable CD-ROM
    0,6,0    6) *
    0,7,0    7) *
```

A Linux SCSI device has a bus (for the host controller), a target, and a LUN (Logical Unit Number). Take a close look at the bold terms in the preceding output; these are the bus, target, and LUN numbers. You can see that the SCSI bus is 0, the target of the burner (a Plextor drive) is 5, and the LUN is 0. Therefore, the device you need to know is 0,5,0. Most burner devices do not have multiple units, so you can abbreviate the device to 0,5.

If you know the generic SCSI /dev/sg* device name of your CD-ROM, you can use that in place of the three-part numeric identifier. Look for messages like the following in your kernel logs to identify the generic device name. In this example, the device is /dev/sg1:

```
Vendor: PLEXTOR   Model: CD-R   PX-R412C   Rev: 1.04
  Type:   CD-ROM                           ANSI SCSI revision: 02
sr0: scsi3-mmc drive: 12x/12x writer cd/rw xa/form2 cdda caddy
Attached scsi CD-ROM sr0 at scsi0, channel 0, id 5, lun 0
Attached scsi generic sg1 at scsi0, channel 0, id 5, lun 0,  type 5
```

## 11.2.2 Creating a Filesystem Image and Writing a CD

To burn a CD, you need to create a new image of the filesystem to burn, then write that image to the CD writer. You can do this either with a temporary disk image file or in a pipeline.

### Using a Temporary Disk Image

ISO9660 is the original standard CD-ROM filesystem format that most CD-ROMs use.

To create an ISO9660 filesystem image from a directory on a Linux system, use mkisofs, like this:

```
mkisofs -r -o image.iso directory
```

The -r option enables the Rock Ridge extensions that transform the stark ISO9660 filesystem into one that looks more like a Unix filesystem. You should use this for any CD-ROM that you intend for use on Unix systems. (For Microsoft systems, you may want to consider using -J for the Joliet extensions.)

You can write an image to the burner with `cdrecord`:

```
cdrecord -v dev=device speed=speed image.iso
```

You can test a `cdrecord` command with the `-dummy` argument; this performs a recording run with the burning laser off.

Before writing an image to a CD, you may also wish to test it with the loopback device (just remember to unmount it when finished!):

```
mount -r -t iso9660 -oloop=/dev/loop0 image.iso /mnt
```

### Using a Pipeline

If you don't want to create a temporary image file, you can attempt to create the filesystem and write to the CD device in one pipeline:

```
mkisofs -r directory | cdrecord -v dev=device speed=speed -
```

The only problem you may encounter with this is a buffer underrun, where `mkisofs` can't produce data quickly enough for `cdrecord` to consume. If you run into a problem like this, one possible remedy is to lower *speed*, or you can see if there are any other processes on your system that are hogging the CPU.

## 11.3 Introduction to USB

Linux supports a wide variety of USB (universal serial bus) devices. A USB system on a PC consists of a host controller inside your computer, hubs that act as splitters to give you more ports, and the actual USB devices. The Linux kernel supports USB devices through three types of drivers:

- Host interface drivers
- USB device drivers
- Other drivers not necessarily related to USB, but required by a USB device driver (for example, the USB mass storage driver requires the SCSI disk support driver)

When the host interface driver recognizes a controller, the kernel logs messages such as these:

```
ohci_hcd: 2003 Oct 13 USB 1.1 'Open' Host Controller (OHCI) Driver (PCI)
ohci_hcd 0000:00:02.0: irq 9, pci mem d4806000
ohci_hcd 0000:00:02.0: new USB bus registered, assigned bus number 1
hub 1-0:1.0: USB hub found
hub 1-0:1.0: 2 ports detected
```

Notice that the controller has an integrated hub with two ports. Plugging in external hubs yields kernel messages like the following:

```
hub 1-0:1.0: new USB device on port 2, assigned address 3
hub 1-2:1.0: USB hub found
hub 1-2:1.0: 4 ports detected
```

**NOTE**    *Don't be surprised if you see hub-related log messages when plugging in a USB device, even if the device is not a hub. Some of these devices contain hubs.*

When you plug in a USB device, the kernel asks the various device drivers if they know how to talk to the device. If a driver recognizes the device, it can *claim* the device and take over its management.

### 11.3.1 USB Device Filesystem and Utilities

With the usbdevfs filesystem mounted at /proc/bus/usb on your system, you can take a look around this directory to see the details of the devices that are connected to your system. However, you can also get a short summary with the lsusb command from the usbutils package:

```
Bus 001 Device 005: ID 054c:002d Sony Corp. MSAC-US1 MemoryStick Reader
Bus 001 Device 003: ID 0451:2046 Texas Instruments TUSB2046 Hub
Bus 001 Device 002: ID 046d:c00c Logitech Inc. Optical Wheel Mouse
Bus 001 Device 001: ID 0000:0000 Virtual Hub
```

If you want to see the gory details of all of your devices, run lsusb -v. Be warned, though, that this prints an extremely verbose listing.

### 11.3.2 USB Input Devices

Basic USB keyboard and mouse support is not complicated. To use these devices on your system, you need the USB human input device (HID) driver in your kernel. The relevant kernel log message looks like this:

```
drivers/usb/input/hid-core.c: v2.0:USB HID core driver
```

With this in place, any USB keyboard that you plug into your computer should work with no further configuration. Here is the message that the kernel logs when you plug in an old Apple keyboard:

```
input: USB HID v1.00 Keyboard [Alps Electric Apple USB Keyboard] on
usb-0000:00:02.0-2.1
```

USB mice aren't much more difficult to configure; the only thing you need to do is to tell the X server or gpm where to find a USB mouse (look at your /etc/X11/XF86Config file and grep for gpm in your init.d directory). The kernel maps all mice to /dev/input/mice, using the PS/2 mouse driver. The kernel message that results from the hookup of a new mouse looks like this:

```
input: USB HID v1.10 Mouse [Logitech USB Optical Mouse] on usb-0000:00:02.0-1
```

### 11.3.3 USB Digital Cameras, External Flash Media, and External Disks

Linux accesses external USB storage devices, including flash memory, in blocks, presenting the storage as a SCSI disk. Therefore, you need the following drivers in your kernel if you would like to use such a device:

- SCSI disk support, compiled directly into your kernel or as the sd_mod kernel module

- A USB interface driver (see Section 11.3)

- USB mass storage support, compiled directly into your kernel or as the usb-storage module

Assuming that you have all of the drivers in place, you should see a kernel log message proclaiming that there is a new SCSI bus when you plug in a flash media card device or other external mass storage device:

```
scsi1 : SCSI emulation for USB Mass Storage devices
  Vendor: Sony      Model: MSAC-US1        Rev: 1.00
  Type:   Direct-Access                    ANSI SCSI revision: 02
  SCSI device sda: 15840 512-byte hdwr sectors (8 MB)
sda: Write Protect is off
sda: Mode Sense: 00 06 00 00
sda: assuming drive cache: write through
 sda: sda1
Attached scsi removable disk sda at scsi1, channel 0, id 0, lun 0
Attached scsi generic sg2 at scsi1, channel 0, id 0, lun 0,  type 0
```

Upon disconnecting the device, you will see a message like this:

```
usb 1-2.1: USB disconnect, address 4
```

Seeing the new SCSI bus in the kernel log does not necessarily mean that you have access to the attached USB device. If your system does not have hotplug support, you may need to run a script called rescan-scsi-bus.sh to get the kernel to recognize the new device. You can verify the geometry, partitions, and filesystems on the storage device with an fdisk command such as this:

```
fdisk -l /dev/sda
```

#### Flash Memory Filesystem Issues

The flash memory in most digital cameras contains an MS-DOS filesystem that you can easily mount when you see the device in the kernel logs.

**WARNING**    *You may wish to mount the filesystem in read-only mode, because it is too easy to remove flash media cards and devices before unmounting the filesystem. If you alter the filesystem, then remove the card before flushing the changes to the physical media with an unmount operation, you risk data corruption.*

## 11.4 IEEE 1394/FireWire Disks

IEEE 1394 (also known as FireWire) drivers are relatively new to Linux. The Linux IEEE 1394 driver system is similar to that of the USB system, and the Linux kernel support for IEEE 1394 includes the base module (ieee1394) and host interface drivers. One common interface is OHCI-1394 (which has a module name of ohci1394), and the TI PCILynx interface also has a driver (pcilynx).

Kernel messages like the following indicate that the host interface driver detected the hardware:

```
ohci1394_0: OHCI-1394 1.1 (PCI): IRQ=[26] MMIO=[9006000-90067ff] Max Packet=[2048]
ieee1394: Host added: ID:BUS[0-00:1023]  GUID[0001080020005cb4]
```

IEEE 1394 hard disks use SBP-2 (Serial Bus Protocol). As in the USB mass storage code, the Linux sbp2 driver masquerades as a SCSI host controller. When you plug in a drive, look for these kernel messages:

```
scsi0 : SCSI emulation for IEEE-1394 SBP-2 Devices
ieee1394: sbp2: Logged into SBP-2 device
ieee1394: sbp2: Node 0-02:1023: Max speed [S400] - Max payload [2048]
ieee1394: Node added: ID:BUS[0-02:1023]  GUID[0090a95000001796]
```

If your system does not have hotplug support (see Section 11.5), you may need to probe the SCSI bus with the rescan-scsi-bus.sh script described earlier in order to get the kernel to recognize the IEEE 1394 drive. Upon recognizing the drive, the kernel emits the usual SCSI drive messages:

```
Vendor: WDC       Model: FireWire/USB2.0 Rev: 4.17
 Type:   Direct-Access ANSI SCSI revision: 06
blk: queue fffffc001954b928, no I/O memory limit
Attached scsi disk sda at scsi0, channel 0, id 0, lun 0
SCSI device sda: 234441648 512-byte hdwr sectors (120034 MB)
 sda: sda1 sda2
```

**NOTE** *The Apple iPod is an SBP-2 device. To access the disk and its filesystem, you need appropriate filesystem support and possibly also the appropriate partition table support in your kernel. The PC version of the iPod uses the FAT32 filesystem, so you can use the vfat filesystem. The Macintosh version uses a completely different filesystem type, so you need the Macintosh partition map support in your kernel, as well as Macintosh filesystem (HFS) support as a module or compiled directly into the kernel.*

# 11.5 Hotplug Support

Now that we've covered Linux USB and IEEE 1394 support, you should learn a little about Linux *hotplug* support, a system that can handle the automatic configuration and cleanup of devices when you plug them into the system.

The idea is simple; the kernel runs /sbin/hotplug when you plug in a device. Here's the procedure:

1. You plug in a device. The kernel notices.
2. The kernel runs /sbin/hotplug *type*, where *type* is the device type (usb, ieee1394, scsi, and so on). The kernel sets a number of device-related environment variables in the new hotplug process.
3. The /etc/hotplug script runs /etc/hotplug/*type*.agent.
4. The /etc/hotplug/*type*.agent script tries to configure the device.

There really isn't much more to it than this. Each device type's .agent file has its own method of configuring devices. For example, usb.agent goes through these steps:

1. usb.agent looks in /etc/hotplug/usb.distmap and /etc/hotplug/usb.usermap to locate a kernel module for the devices.
2. Having identified a module, usb.agent attempts to load the module.
3. If /etc/hotplug/usb/*type* exists, usb.agent runs that program.

Linux hotplug is almost entirely script-driven, which means that the details are even more subject to change than the rest of Linux. However, keep in mind that if you ever have problems or questions you can always read the hotplug scripts to determine what they are trying to do, even if the documentation is inadequate or out of date.

# 11.6 PC Cards (PCMCIA)

Linux PCMCIA support is highly dependent on kernel versions. If you upgrade your kernel, you almost certainly need to upgrade your PCMCIA drivers and tools.

Although some of the core PCMCIA drivers are in the main Linux kernel distribution, you still need the pcmcia-cs package for additional drivers and system utilities. The components of the PCMCIA system include the following:

- Kernel modules for PC Card interface controllers and individual PC Cards. These modules go in /lib/modules/*version*/pcmcia.
- The /sbin/cardmgr daemon for managing configuration when you insert or remove a card.
- Various support utilities and services, located in /etc/pcmcia and /sbin.

There are too many pieces of the system to set up and configure by hand, so the pcmcia-cs package provides several scripts to get you on your way. The most important of these is an init.d script called pcmcia, where, depending on your distribution, you may need to modify a few lines to specify which PCMCIA interface controller chipset you have. Look at this section:

```
# Source PCMCIA configuration, if available
if [ -f /etc/pcmcia.conf ] ; then
    # Debian startup option file
    . /etc/pcmcia.conf
elif [ -f /etc/sysconfig/pcmcia ] ; then
    # Red Hat startup option file
    . /etc/sysconfig/pcmcia
else
    # Slackware startup options go right here:
    # Should be either i82365 or tcic
    PCIC=i82365
    # Put socket driver timing parameters here
    PCIC_OPTS=
    # Put pcmcia_core options here
    CORE_OPTS=
    # Put cardmgr options here
    CARDMGR_OPTS=
    # To set the PCMCIA scheme at startup...
    SCHEME=
fi
```

The mention of specific Linux distributions may seem confusing, so step back and recall your shell script essentials from Chapter 7. The script does the following checks and actions:

1.  If /etc/pcmcia.conf exists, the script reads configuration details from there and skips past the fi. This is probably the case if you're running Debian GNU/Linux.

2.  If step 1 fails, the script looks for /etc/sysconfig/pcmcia, which is the location of the pcmcia file in Red Hat Linux.

3.  If steps 1 and 2 both fail, the script directly sets PCIC, PCIC_OPTS, and so on. Note that this may apply to distributions other than Slackware Linux.

To get cardmgr talking to your PCMCIA interface controller, you should only need to set the PCIC variable. Check through your init.d and /etc files to find the file in which you need to set this variable (every distribution is different, so using grep PCIC may come in handy). If you don't know what sort of hardware you have, there is a pcic_probe program that comes with the pcmcia-cs source code that can help you. The value of PCIC should match one of the module filenames in /lib/modules/*version*/pcmcia; it's typically something like i82365 or tcic.

With the correct PCIC setting in place, you can manually load the interface controller driver and start cardmgr with this command:

```
pcmcia start
```

However, because pcmcia is an init.d script, you should create rc.d links to start and stop the PCMCIA services at boot and shutdown time (refer back to Section 3.1 if you're a little hazy on this process).

## 11.6.1 When You Insert a Card

The cardmgr program reads configuration data and activates scripts in /etc/pcmcia in response to cards being inserted and removed. The central card configuration database is /etc/pcmcia/config.

When you insert a PC Card, cardmgr does the following:

1. It reads the device identifier information from the PC Card.
2. It looks up the identifier in /etc/pcmcia/config, retrieving the kernel module name that contains the device driver.
3. It matches the kernel module name with a class name in /etc/pcmcia/config.
4. It loads the kernel module(s) and configures the PC Card with respect to the local options in /etc/pcmcia/config.opts.
5. It runs a class script located in the /etc/pcmcia directory, corresponding to the class name it found in /etc/pcmcia/config.

### /etc/pcmcia

Let's look at the /etc/pcmcia directory in more detail. Each kernel module has one or more matching PC Card definitions in the /etc/pcmcia/config file. For example, here is an entry that matches the 3c589_cs module against its vendor and version identifier strings:

```
card "Lucent Technologies WaveLAN Adapter"
  version "Lucent Technologies", "WaveLAN/PCMCIA"
  bind "wavelan_cs"
```

The bind in the last line means to bind the card definition to one or more kernel modules. However, the card definition does not always specify that version of the hardware. cardmgr can also identify the appropriate kernel module by using other hardware criteria, including the function parameter, as in this example:

```
card "ATA/IDE Fixed Disk"
  function fixed_disk
  bind "ide_cs"
```

Well-defined device interfaces such as disks, serial ports (modems), and flash memory usually have a function parameter, but don't expect this from all devices. In particular, Ethernet cards usually don't have a function parameter. You may also see manual device-identifier matches that use the manfid keyword.

Having identified the necessary kernel module(s), `cardmgr` then looks for the device driver module class, which are found in the first part of /etc/pcmcia/config. Here is a sample definition that maps `wavelan_cs` to the network driver class:

```
device "wavelan_cs"
  class "network" module "wavelan_cs"
```

Each driver class has a script in /etc/pcmcia that `cardmgr` runs after loading and configuring a card's module (you'll see more about class scripts shortly).

### Configuration Options

You should not modify /etc/pcmcia/config; instead, enter your local configuration data in /etc/pcmcia/config.opts (`cardmgr` usually reads this file after `config`). For the most part, the PCMCIA utilities should work fine with the default settings, but the machine- and card-specific options in `config.opts` are at your disposal if your hardware just won't behave.

Of particular interest are the exclude and include keywords that enable you to manually specify IRQs and addresses. For example, you will see the following lines to prevent `cardmgr` from using standard IRQs, regardless of what the kernel may say about their availability:

```
# First built-in serial port
exclude irq 4

# First built-in parallel port
exclude irq 7
```

You can specify per-module options with the `module` keyword. These examples are also from the default `config.opts` file:

```
module "ray_cs" opts "net_type=1 essid=ESSID1"

module "wvlan_cs" opts "station_name=MY_PC"
```

**NOTE** *In normal circumstances, you do not configure wireless options with* `config.opts`, *but rather, with* `iwconfig` *and possibly* /etc/pcmcia/wireless.opts *(see Section 5.15 for more information).*

### Auxiliary Configuration Scripts

Each driver class has a script in /etc/pcmcia. For example, the /etc/pcmcia/network script corresponds to the network class mentioned earlier. `cardmgr` runs the class script after loading and configuring a card's module.

The /etc/pcmcia configuration scripts work like init.d boot scripts, taking an argument to start, stop, reload, or perform other actions:

**start** Activates the device upon card insertion

**stop** Deactivates the device upon card removal

**restart** Reinitializes the device

**check** Verifies the device

**suspend** Deactivates a card, but leaves the driver running

**resume** Picks up at the point where suspend left off, if possible

Just because a script exists in /etc/pcmcia doesn't mean that it actually works. These scripts run through several combinations of distribution-specific configuration files, trying to find the right settings. If your PC Card doesn't auto-configure correctly upon insertion, you may need to modify one of the scripts or its corresponding .opts configuration file.

**WARNING** *You may find it easiest to write your own driver class scripts or modify the existing ones, but remember to make a backup of any script you decide to change. Reinstalling the* pcmcia-cs *package overwrites each script in* /etc/pcmcia *(leaving a backup with a* .0 *extension). The* .opts *configuration files remain in place during a reinstall.*

You should not normally need to call one of the /etc/pcmcia scripts by hand. cardmgr and cardctl (discussed next) do this for you.

## 11.6.2 cardctl

The cardctl utility enables you to alter card settings and display information about cards and sockets. For example, you can view PC Card identifiers with this command:

```
runas cardctl ident
```

The output looks similar to this:

```
Socket 0:
  product info: "Lucent Technologies", "WaveLAN/IEEE", "Version 01.01", ""
  manfid: 0x0156, 0x0002
  function: 6 (network)
```

Notice how this information relates to the configuration data in /etc/pcmcia/config.

Here are some other cardctl commands:

**config** Shows detailed low-level hardware settings.

**status** Displays card or socket status.

**eject** *socket* Shuts down the card in *socket* (use ident to identify the socket number). You should run eject on certain cards, such as SCSI cards and other interfaces that take a long time to initialize, before removing them.

**insert** *socket*   Tells any relevant drivers that you just put a card into *socket*. Like eject, this is not necessary for most cards.

**suspend** *socket*   Attempts to freeze the driver for *socket* and cut the power.

**resume** *socket*   Attempts to recover from a suspend operation.

**reset** *socket*   Resets the card in *socket*.

There are a few more complex options for cards that need to operate in multiple environments (schemes); see the cardctl(8) manual page and the PCMCIA-HOWTO for more information.

**NOTE**   *Most* pcmcia-cs *builds also come with* cardinfo, *a GUI display of the PCMCIA configuration. You may prefer to run this application in place of information commands such as* cardctl status.

## 11.7 Approaching Other Devices

Obviously, the number of devices that you can attach to your PC is enormous, and attempting to write a chapter that covers all of them is next to impossible. However, with what you just learned about SCSI, USB, PCMCIA, and IEEE 1394, along with what you will learn about printers in Chapter 12, Ethernet interfaces, and so on, you should be well equipped to take on almost anything. For example, you know how to identify a USB scanner; it's just a matter of installing the appropriate drivers and software (the most popular Unix scanning system is called SANE, if you are interested).

This book isn't finished with devices just yet, though. In particular, Chapter 13 has information about tape drives, and Chapter 17 contains tips on how to purchase hardware so that you can avoid Linux compatibility nightmares.

# PRINTING

The printing process on Unix works roughly as follows:

1. An application generates a document to print.
2. You or the application sends the document to a print server by means of a print client program.
3. The print server puts the document on a queue.
4. When it is the document's turn to print, the print server sends the document through a print *filter* program.
5. The print filter changes the document to make it acceptable to a printer.
6. If the printer does not understand PostScript (the standard document format in Unix), another print filter must *rasterize* the document into a bitmap form that the printer understands.
7. The print server sends the result to the printer device.

Making your printer work on a Unix system can be a trying experience. There are several problems:

- There are few standards.
- Each stage of the process can present any number of errors.

- There are several different client, server, and filter packages for printing.
- It's sometimes difficult to determine the purpose of each printing system component.
- The existing software never seems quite satisfactory, so upgrades are frequent.
- Security holes run rampant in network print servers.
- There are two basic ways to configure network printing: one where all computers send their documents directly to a printer, and the other where all computers send their documents to a print server, which then talks to the printer. It can be confusing when you have a network full of machines that use both approaches.

With all of this said, you may not even want to bother to learn how printing works. To be perfectly honest, if your distribution's printer setup tool works for you, it may not be worth going any further, as long as you know how to firewall the print server's network port. However, when things don't work according to plan, the information in this chapter will help you find out where the problem lies.

This chapter first explains the pieces of the printing system on Linux and then shows you how to put everything together using CUPS (Common Unix Printing System). The best place to start is the print code that applications create, PostScript.

## 12.1 PostScript

Unix applications that print generate PostScript files as output. PostScript is not a simple file format; rather, it is a *page description language.* Therefore, PostScript documents are programs, so you need an interpreter to view or read them. Most mid- to high-end laser printers understand PostScript, as do certain inkjet printers, but the cheapest printers do not. If you have such a printer (and who doesn't like to buy cheap hardware?), your computer must perform the extra step of rasterization before the document is sent to the printer.

When you rasterize a PostScript file, you convert its vector graphics into a bitmap. On Linux, the Ghostscript program does this work. Ghostscript can produce output for almost any printer on the market, but it also has many other uses because it is a full-featured PostScript interpreter. See Section 12.6 for more information.

If you are interested in PostScript as a programming language, *PostScript Language Tutorial and Cookbook* [Adobe 1985] is a good introduction to the language, and *PostScript Language Reference Manual* [Adobe 1999] serves as a comprehensive guide to the language features. However, if you just want an example PostScript file for tests, use a Web browser's print-to-file feature.

## 12.2 Print Servers

There are several different Unix print servers. Here are just a few:

**Berkeley LPD (Line Printer Daemon)**   One of the oldest print servers around, this system is fairly stable, but is somewhat sparse on features and can be difficult to configure. Many network-capable printers have integrated LPD servers.

**LPRng**   This new spin on LPD has many new features, but in all honesty, is not any easier to configure. You may also see a related package named PLP (Portable Line Printer).

**lpsched**   This is the System V printing system. If you're lucky, you'll never have to see it.

**CUPS (Common Unix Printing System)**   Sooner or later, someone was bound to get so fed up with the ugly state of printer clients and daemons on Unix that they wanted to rip everything to pieces. CUPS is the latest entry in the Unix printing field, and it may prove to be the most successful. Its internals and protocol departs from the older printing systems, but it still has a server (called the scheduler) and print filters. In addition, the client commands are mostly identical to the lpsched commands, with LPD-compatible substitutes as well.

This chapter concentrates on CUPS, which is quickly gaining popularity because it is definitely much easier to configure and use than the alternatives. In particular, CUPS offers a Web-based interface for many of the more mundane printing tasks.

## 12.3 Print Filters

Two print filters dominate Unix printing:

**Foomatic**   This print filter works with almost any print server, and on the command line. Foomatic can call Ghostscript for printers that do not understand PostScript.

**ifhp**   This is a general-purpose filter for PostScript printers. ifhp is an older print filter that works well with the Berkeley LPD-style servers.

## 12.4 Print Clients

There are two traditional clients that send data to a print server:

**lpr**   This is the matching client for Berkeley LPD-based servers. Associated programs include lpq (to view the current printer job queue) and lprm (to remove a job from the queue).

**lp**   Both CUPS and System V lpsched use the lp interface to print (CUPS also has limited lpr capability). The lpstat command shows printer jobs, and cancel removes a print job.

On traditional Linux systems, you send a PostScript job to the printer named *printer* with a command like this (you do not need -P*printer* if you want to send the job to the default printer):

```
lpr -Pprinter file
```

For CUPS, you may also use the lp program (-d *printer* is optional if you are sending to the default printer):

```
lp -d printer file
```

Commands like lpr and lp let you send any PostScript file or data pipeline directly to a printer. However, one of the biggest problems with this model is that users have no idea that the print server expects PostScript (in fact, most users have no idea what PostScript is). In response, administrators change their print filters to automatically convert plain-text input files to PostScript so that users can use lpr to send either a PostScript or plain-text file to the printer without worrying about conversions.

Other operating systems don't usually let you get very close to the printer; instead, they make you print through an application that produces the correct output. Unix has these applications, too (such as gimp and its gimp-print counterpart), but Unix also lets you get very close to the printer with lpr.

Users tend to want to print pictures and various other kinds of data. If you send a JPEG file or other file to a printer with lpr, it may do the right thing if the administrator set up the print filter to recognize and filter the file. More often than not, though, the print system either rejects the file or prints endless pages of junk, because the system tried to convert the binary file into PostScript using the text filter.

Therefore, it is extremely important that you know *where* the system converts your file into PostScript. This is not a problem if you primarily use graphical applications to print, because these programs normally generate PostScript and send the result to a command such as lpr. However, if you like to use the command line, you must be very careful about what you send to the printer.

CUPS is fairly smart about document conversions because it attempts to determine the MIME type of any input data before sending it to the printer. Furthermore, the system verifies that it can convert the data to something that the printer understands. If CUPS doesn't know how to convert the data, the CUPS server rejects the document rather than passing the printer data that it won't understand.

### 12.4.1 Network Printing

You should have an idea of how network printing clients send data to print servers:

- Berkeley LPD clients send data to TCP port 515 on a print server.

- CUPS uses the Internet Printing Protocol (IPP). IPP is a TCP protocol that looks like HTTP (Hypertext Transfer Protocol). The standard IPP port is 631, but CUPS also comes with a daemon that accepts the LPR protocol on port 515.

- Most network-ready PostScript laser printers allow you to connect to TCP port 9100 and talk directly to the print engine. Most network-aware print filters use this port to send data.

Regardless of the protocol, you should be especially vigilant with respect to open network ports on print servers. Filter out or firewall any open ports. There have been serious vulnerabilities in print servers in the past, and you can expect that many more will crop up in the future, especially with a system as new as CUPS. This also holds true for network-aware printers. You do not want an intruder to waste the money that you spend on printer supplies.

# 12.5 CUPS

With these preliminaries out of the way, let's look at CUPS. CUPS has several interfaces, including a Web-based status and administration tool. The Web interface is very good for normal maintenance and operation, but unfortunately, if your needs lie outside the abilities of the interface, you still have to know how the system works and where the various configuration files reside.

You can install CUPS anywhere you like. Most distributions use a /usr installation prefix, so the clients are in /usr/bin, the system programs are in /usr/sbin, and so on. This book assumes that your directory prefix is /usr. Here are the directory locations and contents:

**/usr/sbin**   The cupsd server and administration programs

**/usr/bin**   User-level clients, including lpr and lp substitutes

**/etc/cups**   Configuration files

**/usr/lib/cups**   Filters, backends, network frontends, and Web interface scripts

**/var/log/cups**   Printer log files

**/var/spool/cups**   Spooled print jobs

**/usr/share/cups**   PPD file sources, fonts, and other program data

**/usr/share/doc/cups**   Online documentation

## 12.5.1 Configuring cupsd

The central server and scheduler in CUPS is named cupsd, and the central configuration file is cupsd.conf. You normally do not need to do anything to get a working cupsd, but a stock configuration file isn't usually very secure (see Section 12.5.2).

Examine the configuration file to get an overview of the things you can change. If you have ever configured the Apache Web server, you will immediately observe similarities between the `httpd` configuration files and the CUPS files.

Your `cupsd.conf` file contains a lot of information, but first look for the `AccessLog` path and change it if you want the log file in some other place:

```
AccessLog /var/log/cups/access_log
```

The default IPP port is 631, so you should see the following line:

```
Port 631
```

You should not need to change this. However, you may wish to add more ports with the `Listen` keyword.

The following parameters select the user and group that run all tasks *except* the `cupsd` server. You likely do not need to change these, but you may need to add the user and group to your system:

```
User lp
Group sys
```

## 12.5.2 CUPS Security

Before you start CUPS, you should get a handle on security matters. Configured and installed from source code, CUPS does not have an enviable level of security, and you should do something about that before you even start the server. If your CUPS installation came with a Linux distribution, you should still take a look through this section to verify that you have a practical level of security.

This section covers how to configure *digest* authentication, the most useful type of authentication available for the CUPS Web administration interface. Run through the following steps on a new installation:

1. Scan your `cupsd.conf` for a section that looks like this:

```
<Location /admin>
AuthType Basic
AuthClass System

## Restrict access to local domain
Order Deny,Allow
Deny From All
Allow From 127.0.0.1
#Encryption Required
</Location>
```

2. Change `AuthType Basic` to `AuthType Digest`. Basic authentication sets up a Web browser to send Unix user passwords as plain text. As earlier in the networking chapters, this is a really bad idea.

3. Run the following command to add an `admin` user to the CUPS digest password file (`/etc/cups/passwd.md5`):

```
lppasswd -a admin
```

4. When prompted, choose a password containing at least six characters and one number.

### Certificate Authentication (for Command-Line Utilities)

You are now set up to use the CUPS Web interface securely. However, you will inevitably turn to command-line administration programs such as `lpadmin` when managing CUPS. These utilities also require authentication because they operate through the same network port as the Web interface. However, you may notice that you don't need a password to run these command-line programs as the superuser. Why is this so?

The answer is that CUPS has another form of authentication called *certificate* authentication, used primarily by the command-line programs and internal server communication. The CUPS scheduler places identifiers in the certificate directory `/etc/cups/certs` for various purposes, but the one you care most about is `/etc/cups/certs/0`. Any user that can read this file can run administrative programs without a password, because these programs send the certificate instead of a username and password.

**NOTE** *Don't use `chmod` to allow administrative access for non-root users because you may inadvertently allow administrative access for anyone on the system. Instead, add the desired users to the Unix group specified by the `Group` directive from Section 12.5.*

## 12.5.3 Starting CUPS

With your security situation now under control, you're ready to start the CUPS scheduler and add some printers. To start CUPS, all you need to do is run `cupsd` as the superuser. If you compile CUPS from source code, you should take careful note that the install procedure modifies your `init.d` and `rc.d` boot directories to make CUPS part of your startup sequence.

To test your installation, access the Web interface by pointing a Web browser to CUPS at this URL (notice that this is the IPP port on your machine):

```
http://localhost:631/
```

This should yield a screen with several printing options. There are no printers in a new CUPS installation, so adding a printer is your first order of business.

### 12.5.4 Adding and Editing Printers

The easiest way to add a printer is with the Web interface (there is an **Add Printer** button on the printer list page). The first time you try to do any administration task, CUPS asks you for a username and password. Use the admin user and password that you configured in Section 12.5.2.

To add a printer with the command-line interface, use the lpadmin command. The bare minimum command for adding a printer without a print filter is as follows:

```
lpadmin -p name -v device
```

Depending on your configuration, you may need the -E option to specify encryption.

#### Adding a Test Printer

As is the case with most Unix utilities, commands like lpadmin do nothing more than modify text files (except that with CUPS, lpadmin opens a network connection to the CUPS server, sends some data, and then the server changes the files). You should know exactly what happens when you run lpadmin.

Add a dummy test printer by going through the following steps:

1. Run lpadmin to add the printer:

```
lpadmin -p test -v file:/dev/null
```

2. Use lpstat to verify that the printer is there:

```
lpstat -p
```

Your new printer should show up as follows:

```
printer test disabled since Jan 01 00:00 -
        reason unknown
```

3. Examine /etc/cups/printers.conf. You should see an entry like this:

```
<DefaultPrinter test>
Info test
DeviceURI file:/dev/null
  ...
  ...
</Printer>
```

4. Activate your printer:

```
lpadmin -p test
```

The `lpstat -p` command should now report the printer as idle rather than disabled.

5. Send a test job to the printer:

```
echo test | lp -d test
```

6. Verify that the job started by looking at `/var/log/cups/error_log`. The filename is somewhat misleading, because `error_log` also contains normal diagnostic messages. You should see some entries that look like this:

```
I [05/Oct/2003:14:44:46 -0700] Started "/usr/lib/cups/cgi-
bin/printers.cgi" (pid=17156)
I [05/Oct/2003:14:46:23 -0700] Adding start banner page "none" to job 1.
I [05/Oct/2003:14:46:23 -0700] Adding end banner page "none" to job 1.
I [05/Oct/2003:14:46:23 -0700] Job 1 queued on 'test' by 'user'.
```

7. The job should also complete. Use the following command to make sure this is the case:

```
lpstat -W completed -l test
```

The output should look like this:

```
test-1                    user            1024   Sun Oct  5 14:46:23 2003
         queued for test
```

8. Remove the test printer when you're finished by using this command:

```
lpadmin -x test
```

This lengthy procedure confirms that your CUPS server is running and that you can add and modify printers.

### Adding a Real Printer

Now that you have some familiarity with the process, you are ready to add a real printer with a particular model using this command:

```
lpadmin -p name -v device -m model
```

The `model` parameter is extremely important because it provides printer-specific information, including the printer driver specification. If you do not use the `-m` parameter, CUPS uses a "raw" print model, sending unfiltered input directly to the printer. You almost certainly do not want this, because printers can generate copious amounts of garbage upon receiving bad input.

If you want to make the new printer the default, run this command:

```
lpoptions -d name
```

For the most part, you provide a PostScript Printer Description (PPD) filename as *model*. You can get a list of PPD files with this command:

```
lpinfo -m
```

However, in a stock CUPS installation, it's unlikely that the output list will contain an appropriate PPD entry for your printer, even though some of the entries may look tempting. Before discussing PPD files (see Section 12.5.6 for more information on those), let's briefly look at how to specify a device for the -v option in the earlier lpadmin command.

## 12.5.5 Printer Devices (Backend Specifications)

As you might surmise from the file:/dev/null specification in the test printer you created, you specify devices with Uniform Resource Identifiers (URIs). You can get a partial list of URI options with the lpinfo command:

```
lpinfo -v
```

The output looks something like this:

```
network socket
network http
network ipp
network lpd
direct parallel:/dev/lp0
direct scsi
serial serial:/dev/ttyS0?baud=115200
serial serial:/dev/ttyS1?baud=115200
 ...
 ...
```

The right-hand column contains backend types and complete URIs. You might see the following backends:

> **parallel**  Most direct connections are still through the parallel port. The port named LPT1 in DOS and Windows is /dev/lp0 on Linux, so the following device specification works fine in most cases:

```
parallel:/dev/lp0
```

> However, you may want to use the bidirectional capabilities of the port for PostScript printers. For example, you may want an accounting program to ask the printer how many pages it prints for each job. Use this device for the bidirectional parallel port:

```
parallel:/dev/parport0
```

**usb**   Newer printers with USB connections use a slightly different back-end than parallel ports do. The URI looks something like the following, although the device filename may not be the same on your system:

```
usb:/dev/usb/lp0
```

**socket**   This is a direct TCP network connection to the print engine of a network printer. Most of these printers listen on TCP port 9100, so you can specify this as follows (since port 9100 is the default, you don't really need the :9100):

```
socket://printer_host:9100
```

**lpd**   If you want CUPS to send jobs to the Berkeley LPD port of a remote print server or printer, use this URI specification:

```
lpd://host/printer_name
```

**smb**   This is for printing to a Windows printer share. You need to use Samba's smbspool program in this case. See Section 14.6.2 for more details on the URI specification and setting up the Samba backend.

**ipp, http**   These are for printing to other network IPP servers (such as remote CUPS servers). Here is an example:

```
ipp://host/printer_name
```

**serial**   In the earlier days of Unix, machines talked to printers with a serial port, and some special-purpose printers still have serial ports. Because serial ports have a more complex system configuration than parallel ports, you often need special parameters to indicate the baud rate and other port settings. At the very least, you should specify the baud rate, as in this example:

```
serial:/dev/ttyS1?baud=38400
```

However, you often need to specify the parity and flow-control settings. Flow-control settings include soft (or xonxoff), dtrdsr, and hard (or rtscts). Use a + sign before each additional setting, as shown in the following example:

```
serial:/dev/ttyS1?baud=38400+size=8+parity=none+flow=dtrdsr
```

**scsi**   SCSI printers are rare, but if you happen to find one, you can print to its generic SCSI device, as in this example:

```
scsi:/dev/sg1
```

> **file**    This prints to a file. By default, CUPS disables printing to any file on the system except /dev/null. You can change this by adding a FileDevice parameter in your cupsd.conf file. Be warned that you risk very serious security breaches if you do so.

CUPS does not let you choose a backend that it knows it cannot reach. For example, if your kernel does not have parallel port support, CUPS does not list parallel ports when you run lpinfo -v. However, the system isn't perfect; a port showing up in the list does not mean that support actually exists.

Each one of these backend specifications uses its own separate backend program located in /usr/lib/cups/backend. The backend comes in at the very end of the print process.

## 12.5.6 PPD Files

After choosing an appropriate device, you can complete the printer definition with a PPD file. CUPS uses PPD files for its printer database.

A PPD file is in plain text and describes a printer's capabilities. CUPS keeps its default PPD files in /usr/share/cups/model; to make the options in a new PPD file available to the CUPS Web interface, put the file in /usr/share/cups/model and send your cupsd a HUP signal. When you import a PPD file into the CUPS PPD file database with lpadmin -m, CUPS makes a copy of the file in /etc/cups/ppd.

The PPD file gives you fine control over printing options. Notice that if you choose the raw interface (that is, no PPD file), you get no options with the **Configure Printer** button in the CUPS Web interface, so you cannot change media, duplex, banner page, and other settings.

Here is the general printer and file information from the PPD file of an Apple LaserWriter 16/600:

```
*FormatVersion: "4.3"
*FileVersion:   "1.1"
*LanguageVersion: English
*LanguageEncoding: ISOLatin1
*PCFileName:    "POSTSCRI.PPD"
*Manufacturer:  "Apple"
*Product:       "(LaserWriter 16/600)"
```

Looking elsewhere in the file, you might see some information on page sizes:

```
*PageSize Letter/US Letter: "<</PageSize[612 792]/ImagingBBox null>>setpagedevice"
*PageSize A4/A4: "<</PageSize[595 842]/ImagingBBox null>>setpagedevice"
```

A standard PPD file should also contain font information:

```
*DefaultFont: Courier
*Font AvantGarde-Book: Standard "(001.006S)" Standard ROM
*Font AvantGarde-BookOblique: Standard "(001.006S)" Standard ROM
```

```
*Font AvantGarde-Demi: Standard "(001.007S)" Standard ROM
*Font AvantGarde-DemiOblique: Standard "(001.007S)" Standard ROM
*Font Bookman-Demi: Standard "(001.004S)" Standard ROM
*Font Bookman-DemiItalic: Standard "(001.004S)" Standard ROM
*Font Bookman-Light: Standard "(001.004S)" Standard ROM
*Font Bookman-LightItalic: Standard "(001.004S)" Standard ROM
*Font Courier: Standard "(002.004S)" Standard ROM
*Font Courier-Bold: Standard "(002.004S)" Standard ROM
```

The preceding excerpts are from a GPL version of a PPD file. PostScript printer manufacturers provide PPD files for their products, and for the most part, these should work fine with CUPS. However, non-PostScript printers do not normally come with PPD files, so they need a third-party PPD file that specifies a print filter to rasterize PostScript. You can get CUPS PPD files at sites such as http://www.linuxprinting.org/.

## 12.5.7 Specifying a Filter

One of the most frequently encountered problems with CUPS is that many of the PPD files you find on the Internet contain CUPS-specific print filter parameters that you may not have on your system. You should be able to recognize these parameters and have an idea of how to correct or delete them as you go.

CUPS filters convert file formats in two ways:

**To a common format** This type of filter converts various file formats into a common format. This common format will be either PostScript or raster data. The `mime.convs` file controls the filters that perform the conversion. For the most part, you should not have to worry about these filters, which are covered in the next section.

**From a common format** A filter specified in the PPD file runs just before the backend to change the common format data into the language that the printer understands. If you have a PostScript printer, you probably do not need this filter in your PPD file. However, if you don't have a PostScript printer, these backend filters require a lot of attention, as you will see.

### CUPS Filters and mime.convs

CUPS comes with a number of filters in `/usr/lib/cups/filter` that transform various intermediate file formats into printer-ready data. However, it is difficult to see where and how CUPS runs these filters.

When you print a file, you can observe something like the following in the log file (this example is for a text file):

```
Started filter /usr/lib/cups/filter/texttops (PID 3999) for job 25.
Started filter /usr/lib/cups/filter/pstops (PID 4000) for job 25.
```

To get this detailed logging, the LogLevel parameter in your cupsd.conf must be a minimum of info. However, info does not log the initial input file type; you need to set the parameter to debug in order to log this additional information.

In the log, you can see some filters running, and from the names of the filters, you know that CUPS has some sort of idea about the job's file type. Unfortunately, the actual workings of the conversion mechanism aren't terribly obvious from the log file output. Here's how the sequence works:

1.  CUPS determines the output format that the backend needs to send to the printer by looking at the PPD file.

2.  CUPS determines the input file type with the help of /etc/cups/mime.types. In the preceding example log output, the application/postscript rule in /etc/cups/mime.types matched.

3.  CUPS looks through the /etc/cups/mime.convs file for a suitable filter to perform the conversion between the input file format and the format that the backend needs. Consider this line from mime.convs that transforms plain-text files to PostScript output:

---

text/plain                  application/postscript  33     texttops

---

The four columns here are the input MIME type, the output MIME type, the estimated cost, and the name of the filter program that converts the input to the output.

4.  CUPS runs the filter or filter sequence required for the printer backend. If there are no suitable entries in mime.convs, CUPS logs this message:

---

Unable to convert file 0 to printable format for job *n*!

---

5.  CUPS runs any necessary additional filter before handing the final output to the backend (see the next section).

### Specifying a Backend Filter in the PPD File

Just before sending the job to the printer backend, CUPS may run a backend filter from the PPD file.

Backend filters are set with the cupsFilter parameter in the PPD file. Here is an example from the PPD file that you saw earlier:

---

*cupsFilter:    "application/vnd.cups-postscript 0 foomatic-rip"

---

As you can see, the cupsFilter parameter's value consists of three parts:

1.  An expected MIME type. In the preceding example, the type is PostScript. The default is application/vnd.cups-postscript.

2.  The relative cost of the filter (set this to 0).

3.  The filter's executable name.

The preceding `cupsFilter` parameter is very typical for printers that do not understand PostScript. Foomatic is a print filter that handles many different kinds of printers.

There are a few gotchas with the `cupsFilter` setting:

- You don't need an extra filter if your printer already understands Post-Script. Many PPD files for PostScript printers that you find on the Web contain filters that don't really do anything, but require extra software configuration. Delete any `cupsFilter` lines in your PPD file if your printer understands PostScript.

- The default PPD files and `mime.convs` file that come with CUPS do not contain the necessary settings to rasterize PostScript files, and it can be somewhat confusing to configure the rasterizer. For example, the generic HP LaserJet PPD files in the CUPS distributions expect raster (not PostScript) input. However, the default `mime.convs` file doesn't contain an active entry for transforming PostScript into raster output. For this reason, you may want to avoid the standard CUPS PPD files and look on the Web for appropriate files.

- To address the problem of rasterization, most PPD files for non-PostScript printers on the Web assume that you have Foomatic as a filter (see Section 12.5.8) with Ghostscript as the rasterization engine. If your printer doesn't understand PostScript, it's unlikely that you will be able to avoid Foomatic.

There is good news, though. Most PPD files that you find on the Web work fine *if* all of your software (Ghostscript, Foomatic, CUPS, and so on) is installed correctly.

### 12.5.8 Foomatic (for Non-PostScript Printers)

If your printer does not have native PostScript support, there may still be one more piece of the puzzle to configure — the rasterizer filter. There are several options here, but the most popular system at the moment is Foomatic.

Before going into details about Foomatic, you should be clear on the end goal here: you want a print filter to run a Ghostscript (gs) command to render PostScript input into bitmap form to send to the printer. The command arguments look something like this:

```
gs -q -dSAFER -dNOPAUSE -dBATCH device_options -sOutputFile=- -
```

This seems simple enough, but unfortunately, *device_options* can be a tremendous mess. There are countless combinations of printer data formats and options. Foomatic attempts to resolve these problems with a database containing options for nearly every printer model out there. You may see references to this database all over the Web but very little information on how to actually *use* the database.

What most documentation fails to mention is that most administrators and users don't even interact with the database. All you need to worry about is building printer configuration data, such as PPD files. In fact, this work is already done for you when you visit http://www.linuxprinting.org/ to get a PPD file for your printer. All of the information that the Foomatic filter program (foomatic-rip) needs is in that PPD file. For example, here is a portion of the HP LaserJet 1100 PPD file that contains Ghostscript arguments:

```
*FoomaticRIPCommandLine: "gs -q -dBATCH -dPARANOIDSAFER -dQUIET -dNOPA&&
USE -sDEVICE=ijs -sIjsServer=hpijs%A%B%C -dIjsUseOutputFD%Z -sOutputFi&&
le=- -"
*End
```

**NOTE** *See Section 12.6.3 for notes on certain HP printer drivers.*

### Testing Foomatic

To use Foomatic as a filter, you need the foomatic-rip program in lib/cups/filter (a symbolic link to another location works fine). You can verify that Foomatic produces the correct printer output by running foomatic-rip on the command line, generating printer output by hand. You can then send this data directly to the printer, bypassing the print spooler.

First, locate your printer's PPD file (*ppd_file*) and find a test PostScript file to test with (*test_file*.ps). Run this command to create printer data in test.prn:

```
foomatic-rip -v --ppd ppd_file test_file.ps > test.prn
```

The -v option specifies verbose operation so that you can see exactly what the filter is doing. If everything goes well, you should see the following at the end of the diagnostic messages:

```
KID4 exited with status 0
Renderer exit stat: 0
Renderer process finished

Closing foomatic-rip.
```

Successful completion also means that test.prn should now be a gigantic (probably binary) file that you can send directly to the printer device.

## 12.5.9 Administrative Command Overview

With the mess of print filters hopefully behind you, it's time to learn some commands for day-to-day tasks. Compared to other Unix server systems, it isn't terribly important that you know the syntax of every last command, because the Web administration interface does an adequate job in most cases (and is sometimes far preferable to the command line — for example, when doing printer media option configuration).

However, you should develop at least a passing familiarity with the following commands (remember that each command has a manual page):

**lpadmin**   Adds, removes, and modifies printers.

**lpinfo**   Displays device and PPD file information (for use with lpadmin).

**lpoptions**   Sets printer options. To display a quick list of options for a particular printer, run this command:

```
lpoptions -p printer -l
```

**lpstat**   Displays printer and job information (after you create printers). To display a printer's job queue, use this command:

```
lpstat -o printer
```

To see the status of every printer on the system, use this:

```
lpstat -a
```

**cancel**   Removes a job. To remove all jobs from a queue, run this command:

```
cancel -d printer -a
```

**disable**   Disables printing (but still possibly allows new jobs on the queue).

**enable**   Enables printing.

**reject**   Disables print queuing.

**accept**   Enables print queuing.

**lppasswd**   Modifies users and passwords (for digest authentication; see Section 12.5.2).

## 12.5.10 Client Access Control

By default, CUPS allows printer and administration access only to localhost. If you have a network of machines that you want to grant access to your CUPS server, then you have to change your cupsd.conf file to reflect this.

To get an idea of how per-client access control works, edit your cups.conf file and search for the line that reads <Location />. It should start with a section that looks like this:

```
<Location />
Order Deny,Allow
Deny From All
Allow From 127.0.0.1
</Location>
```

The `Location /` section defines global access-control parameters for the CUPS server. In the preceding example, the directives work together to give access to localhost (127.0.0.1) and nothing else:

**Order Deny,Allow**   Allows you to specify hosts and networks that are denied and allowed access with the `Deny` and `Allow` directives. Furthermore, it also means that you can override `Deny` directives with `Allow` directives. This is the most useful mode in CUPS, and you should never change it.

**Deny From All**   Denies access to all clients by default. Again, you should not change this.

**Allow From 127.0.0.1**   Makes an exception to the preceding `Deny From All` rule, granting access to localhost.

If you want to allow access for all of your printers to more clients, you can just add another rule directive after the `Allow From 127.0.0.1` line. The following rule directive grants access to the subnet defined by `10.0.1.0/255.255.255.0`:

```
Allow From 10.0.1.0/255.255.255.0
```

You may have as many `Allow From` *client* lines as you like, and you can specify the *client* parameter in several ways. The following five specification types are the most useful:

- Subnet notation, as in the preceding `10.0.1.0/255.255.255.0` example
- IP addresses, such as `10.0.1.3`
- Fully qualified domain names, such as `client.example.com`
- Domain wildcards, such as `*.example.com`
- Network interfaces, such as `@IF(eth0)`

Remember that the `Location /` section is for global access, including printer job control and other client tasks. Administrative tasks, on the other hand, have their own `Location` section (`<Location /admin>`) that specifically excludes connections from all hosts except localhost. In fact, you have already seen this section when you forced CUPS to digest authentication. Search for it in your `cupsd.conf` to verify that it allows administrative access to localhost, and to nothing else.

**NOTE**   *You can specify per-printer client access by adding* `<Location /printers/name>` *access control sections, where* name *is the name of a printer. You'll probably need to experiment for a while to get it to work perfectly.*

## 12.5.11 Auto-Discovery

One of the more interesting CUPS features is automatic network printer discovery. This is called *browsing*. Most CUPS installations have browsing active by default, meaning that CUPS listens for messages from other print servers on the network. The `cupsd.conf` parameter is `Browsing`:

However, without additional help, your CUPS server will likely *not* make itself known to the other print servers on the network. To make your CUPS server broadcast its presence, you need a BrowseAddress broadcast address parameter in cupsd.conf. For example, to send notification packets to as many hosts on the network as possible (essentially, as many as your routers allow), use this parameter:

BrowseAddress 255.255.255.255

You can think of a numeric broadcast address as a sort of inverse subnet combined with an IP address. For example, to send packets to the subnet defined by 10.1.2.0/255.255.255.0, try this:

BrowseAddress 10.1.2.255

This said, the best choice is likely the "local" interface selection that sends broadcast packets out to all network interfaces except PPP links:

BrowseAddress @LOCAL

If you have a server with several Ethernet interfaces, but do not want to broadcast on all of these interfaces, use @IF. For example, here's how to broadcast to eth1:

BrowseAddress @IF(eth1)

## 12.5.12 Running an LPD-Compatible Server

Browsing and broadcasting goes a long way toward allowing communication between various CUPS servers on a network, but if you want older clients running Berkeley LPD printing systems to be able to print to your CUPS server, you need to configure your server to allow jobs from these clients.

To do this, run a special LPD server frontend called cups-lpd located in /usr/lib/cups/daemon. This is an inetd service (see Section 6.3), so you want a line like this in your /etc/inetd.conf (or the xinetd equivalent):

printer stream tcp nowait *cups-user* /usr/lib/cups/daemon/cups-lpd cups-lpd

*cups-user* is your CUPS User parameter from cupsd.conf (usually lp). There is no built-in access control in cups-lpd, but like any other network service, you want to make sure that your firewall rules have adequate coverage; see Section 5.13. Remember that printer is defined in /etc/services as port 515.

## 12.5.13 Troubleshooting CUPS

When you have a problem with CUPS, it's particularly important to take things one step at a time. You may find this sequence helpful:

1. Make sure that CUPS is working properly by creating a test printer with no filters (raw mode) and a device of file:/dev/null. Send a test file to the printer with the Web interface and lp, and verify that the jobs complete with lpstat:

   ```
   lpstat -W completed -o test_printer_name
   lpstat -o test_printer_name
   ```

2. Use your printer's PPD file to activate your filter. See Sections 12.5.4 and 12.5.6 for more detail if something goes wrong. Print more test files, again making sure that the jobs finish.

3. Add the printer's actual device, and then try another test job. If necessary, try printing to a file, then sending the file directly to the printer.

If a test print job fails and stalls, the printer state changes to "not ready," and you need to start the printer again to retry the job or run any new jobs. Do this with enable printer or the Web interface. Before you start changing files around, though, you should look at your log files, which are described in the next section.

### Error Messages

The complex nature of the print spooler and filters makes it crucial that you pay careful attention to your log messages. The most important log file is /var/log/cups/error_log (the name is slightly misleading because the file also contains normal diagnostic messages).

Looking at the log reveals this format:

```
I [timestamp] Started filter /usr/lib/cups/filter/pstops (PID 3434) for job 26.
D [timestamp] ProcessIPPRequest: 10 status_code=0
E [timestamp] [Job 26] unable to open print file - : Permission denied
```

The letter at the start of the line indicates the message severity or priority. The three letters in the preceding example are as follows:

**I** An informational log message. These notices usually indicate some significant event, such as a filter invocation or job submission.

**D** A verbose debugging message. You should not care about these unless you run into a problem.

**E** An error message indicating that something doesn't work. The CUPS scheduler usually keeps running if there is an error. However, you may end up missing a feature or having a stalled printer job.

You can change the log level with the `LogLevel` parameter in the `cupsd.conf` file. The default level is `info` in most installations. If you want the debugging messages, you must use `debug`. If you change your `LogLevel` parameter, remember to reload your configuration file after making any changes by sending a HUP signal to `cupsd`.

## Filter Problems

The first thing you should do after running into trouble in the print filter stage is to make sure that the CUPS filters in `/etc/cups/mime.convs` function properly.

To do this, first disable any filters that you might have in your printer's PPD file so that you can eliminate the backend filter from the list of things that can go wrong. You will probably only have such filters if you are using a non-PostScript printer. If that's the case, edit your printer's PPD file (the one in `/etc/cups/ppd`), looking for a `cupsFilter` parameter (see Section 12.5.7). Comment out the parameter by adding a `%` just after the `*`; for example:

```
*%cupsFilter:    "application/vnd.cups-postscript 0 foomatic-rip"
```

After making this change (and making `cupsd` re-read its configuration with a HUP signal), submit a test job to see if data can make it past the `mime.convs` filter stage to the printer device. Although you are not likely to run into any trouble with the CUPS-supplied filter programs in `mime.convs`, this process may help you uncover spool directory permissions problems (discussed in the next section) because these sorts of problems usually show up in the initial print filter stages.

Having worked out any kinks not involving the `cupsFilter` filter, re-enable this parameter and look for more trouble:

- Verify that the `cupsFilter` filter is in the `lib/cups/filter` directory.
- For the Foomatic filter, use `foomatic-rip -v` manually from the command line to check for valid output (see Section 12.5.8).
- Check that the filter has the correct path for any necessary program.
- If your filter relies on Ghostscript, ensure that you have the required driver by running `gs -help`.

## Spool Directory Permission Errors

Look for this message in your error log:

```
E [timestamp] [Job n] unable to open print file - : Permission denied
```

CUPS normally runs its filters as the pseudo-user lp and the group sys, so this user must have access to the spool directory `/var/spool/cups` in order to access intermediate data. When fixing the permissions, look for these problems:

- Check all component directories of /var/spool/cups. Can the lp user access each of them?
- Make sure that you have the lp user in your /etc/passwd file.
- Verify that lp belongs to the sys group. (Remember that you can change the pseudo-user and group with the User and Group parameters of cupsd.conf.)

### Device Problems

After running through the filter gauntlet, you are ready to send output to devices. Fortunately, there is relatively little that can go wrong at this final stage:

- The lp user must have write access to any printer device directly connected to the system. In addition, check the kernel bootup messages and /proc to ensure that the kernel recognizes the device ports.
- For network printers, make sure that your host can reach the printer. If your device is the socket type on TCP port 9100, test the connection with this command:

```
telnet printer_address 9100
```

Terminate a successful connection by pressing CONTROL-], then CONTROL-D. Unless you know the printer's native language, this connection does little good other than confirming that it can be made.

## 12.6 Ghostscript

If you want to get a handle on printing under Unix, you should get to know Ghostscript. As mentioned before, most Unix programs that print generate PostScript output. Ghostscript is a PostScript interpreter that includes these features:

- Bitmap rendering from PostScript code in several different output formats
- PostScript file filtering
- Reading and writing to PDF format
- Document previewing

To get a feel for how Ghostscript works, run it with a file and no other arguments:

```
gs file.ps
```

In addition to getting a preview window showing the first page of the file, you should also see this message back at your terminal window:

```
>>showpage, press <return> to continue<<
```

As the prompt suggests, pressing RETURN pages through the file. After reaching the final page, you get a GS> prompt; you may press CONTROL-D or CONTROL-C to exit.

There are several frontend programs, such as gv and ggv, that give a nicer interface to the Ghostscript preview. Whether you use one of these frontend programs or not, running a preview can verify that you have a valid PostScript file to begin with. This can go a long way in tracking down problems, especially if your print spooler also uses Ghostscript to rasterize images for the printer.

### 12.6.1 Command-Line Options

A full gs command line such as the one in Section 12.5.8 may seem a bit complicated, especially when it comes to device specification. However, it's not hard to gain enough familiarity to make use of Ghostscript's filtering capabilities.

Take a close look at the following command, which filters *old*.ps to create *new*.ps:

```
gs -q -dNOPAUSE -dBATCH -dSAFER -sDEVICE=pswrite -sOutputFile=new.ps old.ps
```

The first four options are typical for filters that run with no user input. Here's what they specify:

**-q**   Quiet mode; suppress any normal diagnostic output.

**-dNOPAUSE**   Do not wait for the user to press RETURN after each page.

**-dBATCH**   Terminate after interpreting all input.

**-dSAFER**   Disallow file alteration capabilities (to avoid security problems). The -dPARANOIDSAFER option disables file-read capabilities.

The next two options usually go hand-in-hand when creating an output file:

**-sDEVICE=*driver_name***   Use *driver_name* as the output driver. In this context, the term *driver* usually refers to a file format driver rather than a piece of code that manipulates devices, though there are exceptions (such as the x11 driver for the preview window). To see a list of drivers, run gs -help.

**NOTE**   *Some drivers require other command-line parameters to operate correctly. Two notable examples are the* uniprint *and* ijs *drivers. The* uniprint *driver comes with a number of* .upp *files (containing extra parameters) in the Ghostscript library directory. To use these settings, use* @file.upp; *for example:*

```
gs @file.upp -q -dNOPAUSE -dBATCH -sOutputFile=out ...
```

**-sOutputFile=*file***   Write output to *file* (use - for standard output). If you wish to create one file per page of PostScript input, insert %d somewhere into the name of *file*. Ghostscript substitutes the page number for %d.

### 12.6.2 More Ghostscript Tricks

Here are a few more useful things that you can do with Ghostscript:

- To transform a PostScript file into a PDF file, use the `pdfwrite` driver (Ghostscript comes with a `ps2pdf` script that does essentially the same thing):

```
gs -q -dNOPAUSE -dBATCH -dSAFER -sDEVICE=pdfwrite -sOutputFile=file.pdf file.ps
```

- The `pswrite` driver (introduced in the previous section) is an effective way to make somewhat defective files print. If you can view the file with Ghostscript, the chances are good that a file filtered with the `pswrite` driver will print on even a finicky printer.

- You can combine several PostScript or PDF files into one by adding the additional filenames to the end of the command line.

- To change the output resolution (in dots per inch), use the `-rdpi` or `-rxdpixydpi` parameters. The default resolution is usually 72 dpi. These commands generate larger bitmaps:

```
gs -q -dNOPAUSE -dBATCH -dSAFER -r150 -sDEVICE=pnmraw -sOutputFile=- file.ps
gs -q -dNOPAUSE -dBATCH -dSAFER -r300x150 -sDEVICE=pnmraw -sOutputFile=- file.ps
```

### 12.6.3 HP Inkjet Server

If you have an inkjet or non-PostScript laser printer made by HP, then you almost certainly need the HPIJS (HP Inkjet Server) printer driver package. The main part of HPIJS is a program called `hpijs`. You can think of this as a plug-in driver for Ghostscript that translates Ghostscript's internal raster image format into printer formats. This driver is especially important if you are printing photographs or other graphics.

You can tell if you need HPIJS by looking at the PPD file for your printer. If you see `-sDEVICE=ijs` in the `FoomaticRIPCommandLine` parameter, you need the driver. You can install it as a binary package or from source code; the only thing that matters is that Ghostscript can find the command in its path.

**NOTE**   *Current versions of* `hpijs` *come with* `foomatic-rip` *and a set of PPD files. The best output quality likely comes from using these PPD files rather than random ones you see on the Internet.*

## 12.7 Further Printing Topics

This chapter is really only the tip of the iceberg when it comes to printing. Chapter 14 revisits printing to look at details of how to interface CUPS with Samba servers, but among the aspects not touched here are application configuration, complex color graphics support, and advanced PostScript topics, not to mention several other Unix print server packages.

Here are some Web sites that can help you with your quest for Unix printer configuration:

**http://www.linuxprinting.org/** This site has PPD files and documentation on many print servers. It also contains the Foomatic central information site.

**http://www.cups.org/** This is the central CUPS Web site.

**http://www.ghostscript.com/** A good source for Ghostscript software and topics.

**http://gimp-print.sourceforge.net/** Gimp-print is a GIMP plug-in specifically designed for direct color printing. In certain cases, you may want to make gimp-print generate printer-ready data, bypassing Ghostscript rasterization completely with the `lp -oraw` feature. (Gimp-print can also create PostScript output.)

# 13

## BACKUPS

There is no single system for backups on Linux. There are many different kinds of archiving programs and formats. You already saw tar, one of the most popular archivers, in Chapter 1. The good news is that there isn't much more to making backups than what you already know; the bad news is that it's not too clear how you should get the archive to the physical medium.

This chapter takes you through the basics of backups: what data you need to back up, what backup devices are available, what types of backups you can make, how to use the most common archivers, and how to use tape drives.

### 13.1 What Should You Back Up?

Your backup priorities should be as follows:

1.  Home directories. Try to make daily backups of your home directories.
2.  System-specific configuration and data, such as the stuff in /etc and /var. This should include your machine's list of installed packages.

3. Locally installed software (for example, /usr/local). You don't want to lose the work you put into custom software installations, so make a backup every now and then.

4. System software from your distribution. This really is the least of your worries, because you can probably restore this part of the system by reinstalling the operating system. Furthermore, by the time your disk gets around to crashing so hard that you need to restore from backups, you probably want to install a newer version of the operating system anyway.

## 13.2 Backup Hardware

In the formative years of Unix, there was only one reasonable kind of backup hardware: the tape drive. Tapes were inexpensive compared to fixed storage (hard drives), they were fairly reliable, and they could be taken off-site for additional data security.

However, hard disk technology has outpaced tape drive technology in the past ten years. For PCs, tape drives are expensive compared to hard disks (and the tapes themselves are also expensive). In addition, tape drive capacities are far smaller than the disks now on the market.

There are currently two popular backup alternatives to tape drives:

- CD- and DVD-R/RW drives
- An extra hard disk (internal or external)

Both of these work, but you need to improvise, because there aren't any tried-and-true standard solutions for making backups to these devices. You still want to use a traditional backup utility (almost certainly tar) to create archives on the medium, but you need to find a way to manage the archives by yourself.

That said, don't count out the tape drive just yet. A significant portion of this chapter deals with tape drives.

## 13.3 Full and Incremental Backups

Before going into detail about backup hardware and archiving programs, you need to know about the two basic backup types:

**Full backup**   An archive of everything on a filesystem or directory

**Incremental backup**   An archive of all items that have changed since the last full backup

In large-scale operations, there are more kinds of backups, and you may hear of *cumulative* and *differential* backups. These are levels between incremental and full backups — that is, an incremental backup may contain all of the changes since the last differential backup, and the differential backup, in turn, could contain all changes since the last full backup. However, for small systems where you do backups by hand, it is reasonable to deal only with full backups and the incremental backups that build on the full backups.

The advantage to incremental backups is that they usually finish quickly and do not require much storage space. However, over time, the difference between the last full backup and the current state on the disk gets to be so significant that these advantages dwindle: the incremental backups start to take up as much space as the full backups, and it can be very difficult to merge an old full backup and a newer incremental backup if you ever need to restore a full set of files from the backups. In particular, files that you intentionally deleted between the two backups can reappear. Therefore, you need to do a full backups on a regular basis.

Systems administrators generally keep a set of full and incremental backups so that they can restore files that may have only existed for a short period of time. For example, if you have daily incremental backups that go back 30 days and a full backup from at least 30 days ago, you can restore any file that was on the filesystem at backup time during that time period. Of course, if you don't know the exact dates, finding the file can take a little time.

To restore a complete set of files, you need to extract the latest full backup first, then the latest incremental backup (unless, of course, the full backup is by chance newer than the incremental backup).

## 13.4 Using tar for Backups and Restores

In Section 1.18, you learned the basics of tar. As it turns out, you already know nearly all you need in order to do manual backups. If you want a comprehensive list of tar options, you can look at the (gigantic) GNU info documents. However, the good news is that you don't need to know very many options, and after reading this section, you should only need tar --help every now and then as a refresher.

### 13.4.1 Creating Archives

With processors as fast as they are now, and disks getting ever larger, it doesn't make much sense to omit compression for any archive. Recall that you can create a compressed archive of a directory with one command:

```
tar zcvf archive directory
```

A large part of making a backup is figuring out where to put the archive. There are a few choices here:

- For tape drives, see Section 13.6.2 for how to write the archive to the tape device.

- For backing up to a spare disk, you can write the archive as a file on the disk's filesystem.

- If you need to pipe the output to standard output (to feed it to another command, such as cdrecord), use - as the archive name.

Here are some options to consider when running GNU tar:

**--exclude** *file*  Exclude *file* from the archive.

**--exclude-from** *file*  Doesn't include in the archive any of the files listed in *file*.

**--one-file-system**  Archives files from inside a single filesystem. This is handy for breaking up backups by partitions.

**--absolute-paths**  Doesn't strip the leading / from an absolute pathname. This has its uses, but only if you know what you're doing.

**--listed-incremental** *file*  Uses *file* as the incremental state file (see Section 13.4.2).

One tricky part about adding these options to a traditional tar command is that you must insert a - in front of the regular one-character options. Therefore, if you want to create an archive of the misc directory, but exclude misc/scratch, you would have to run the following with -zcvf rather than with zcvf, as you saw in the previous example. Here's how it would look:

```
tar --exclude misc/scratch -zcvf archive misc
```

**NOTE**  *Remember that* tar *strips the leading / from an absolute pathname (unless you specify the* --absolute-paths *parameter). Therefore, to exclude an item, you must match the path that goes into the archive, not necessarily the one on the system. Let's say that you wanted to create an archive of / without /usr. You must remove the / by yourself:*

```
tar --exclude usr -zcvf archive /
```

## 13.4.2 Incremental Backups with tar

To enable incremental backups with GNU tar, you need to create an incremental state file that contains information about each newly archived file. Here's how to do it:

1.  Run the following command to make a full backup in *full_archive* (*state_file* is the name of the state file; you must choose your own name):

    ```
    tar --listed-incremental state_file -zcvf full_archive file1 ...
    ```

2.  Make a copy of the original state file. For example:

    ```
    cp state_file state_file_incr
    ```

3.  When it is time to make an incremental backup, run the same tar command as earlier, but with the state file copy that you created in step 2, *state_file_incr*:

```
tar --listed-incremental state_file_incr -zcvf incremental_archive file1 ...
```

This should produce a much smaller archive than the full backup, because tar compares the time(s) listed in *state_file_incr* (remember, it's a copy of the original *state_file*) against the modification times of the current files on the disk.

4. Repeat steps 2 and 3 for subsequent incremental backups.
5. To do another full backup, delete or rename *state_file* and start at step 1.

You need to make a copy of the original state file before each incremental backup because GNU tar updates the file specified with --listed-incremental after its run. If you were to perform backups with the same state file over and over again, the incremental backups would only record the changes since the last incremental backup, not since the last full backup. Although this would yield a complete set of changes, it would also make it nearly impossible to find a lost file inside a set of incremental backups. Furthermore, to do a complete restore, you would need to use *all* of your incremental backups.

**NOTE** *Remember that incremental backups are only good when accompanied by the previous full backup. Make sure that you don't overwrite your full backup with an incremental backup.*

### 13.4.3 Extracting Archives

Recall from Section 1.18.1 that you can extract files from a compressed archive as follows:

```
tar zxvf archive
```

By default, tar extracts all files in the archive. However, you can limit the extraction to specific files and directories by adding their names to the end of the command line (you may need to run tar ztvf to get a list of filenames):

```
tar zxvf archive file1 file2 ...
```

When extracting system files and home directories as root (for example, from a restore or when moving the things around), it is critical that you use the p option to preserve the original permissions:

```
tar zxvpf archive
```

Otherwise, tar creates files using the current permissions mask (umask). This can be annoying at the very least, and could cause your system to malfunction at the worst.

**WARNING**    *Before extracting an archive, it's very important to check your current working directory against any files that the extraction process might create so that you don't accidentally clobber newer versions of files with older ones from the archive. When doing a partial restore, it's usually a good idea to change to an empty temporary directory first.*

## 13.5 Backups to Non-Traditional Media

Even though you have the ability to create your own filesystems on CD- or DVD-R/RW drives and spare hard disks, you should still stick with an archiver program like tar to make your backups. The primary reason is simple: tar preserves all file attributes, including permissions and ownership. In addition, it is easier to manage full and incremental backups with tar.

If you choose to make backups with cdrecord (see Section 11.2.2, your best bet is probably to write a compressed tar archive directly to the CD or DVD with a command like this:

```
tar zcf - | cdrecord dev=dev cdrecord_args -
```

You may need to experiment with the speed option to cdrecord, because the archiving command may not produce data fast enough for your recorder.

Again, remember that this command does not create a filesystem on the disc. To read from the archive, you can just use the raw device.

### 13.5.1 Backups to Hard Disks

Using a spare hard disk for backups is relatively easy. Create a regular filesystem on the disk and simply write your archives as regular files. You should be able to keep a fair amount of data on the spare disk if you use compression and incremental backups.

## 13.6 Tape Drive Devices

Tape devices are character devices on a Linux system, going by a variety of filenames:

- SCSI tapes use the names /dev/st0, /dev/nst0, /dev/st1, /dev/nst1, and so on. The SCSI tape drive interface and driver is widely regarded as the most reliable, but, of course, SCSI tape drives are also more expensive than others.
- ATAPI tape devices start at /dev/ht0 and /dev/nht0.
- There is limited support for tape drives on the floppy controller at /dev/ft0 and /dev/ntf0.

To identify a tape drive, look in your kernel messages for lines like this:

```
Vendor: HP        Model: C1533A           Rev: 9503
 Type:   Sequential-Access               ANSI SCSI revision: 02
st: Version 20010812, bufsize 32768, wrt 30720, max init. bufs 4, s/g segs 16
Attached scsi tape st0 at scsi0, channel 0, id 4, lun 0
```

There are two versions of each tape device on a Unix system:

- A *rewind* tape device rewinds the tape after every operation. For example, /dev/st0 is a rewind device.

- A *no-rewind* tape device does not rewind the tape after an operation. No-rewind devices start with n; for example, /dev/nst0 is a no-rewind device.

For day-to-day operation, rewind devices are practically useless. You may as well forget that they exist; the next few sections show that you often need to reposition the tape.

When working with tapes, you sometimes need to know the tape block size. Applications tend to write to the tape in a certain block size, and many tape drives do not allow you to read from the tape if you specify the incorrect block size. This is almost never a problem, because you normally write to and read from the tape with the same program. However, if you want to use dd to get direct access to tape files, you may need to specify the block size manually (see Section 13.6.7).

Before you get started with a tape drive, you should set the TAPE environment variable to the no-rewind device name. This variable saves a lot of typing in the long run, in particular, with -f options for the mt and tar commands (which are explained in the next section).

### 13.6.1 Working with Tape Drives

A tape is one of the simplest forms of media available. You can think of a tape as a sequence of files with a *file mark* between each file, as shown in Figure 13-1. Notice how there is no file mark at the beginning of the tape and that the first file is numbered 0.

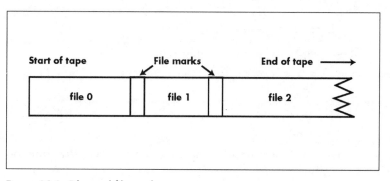

*Figure 13-1: Files and file marks on a tape.*

A tape does not contain a filesystem. Furthermore, there is no information on a tape indicating the name of each file (though automated backup systems usually include a special tape index file at the beginning of the tape). When manually working with a tape, you work with file numbers and file marks, and nothing else.

To access the data on a tape, you must manipulate the tape drive *head*. Figure 13-2 shows the initial position of the tape head. Let's say that your tape device is st0, so you're using the tape device /dev/nst0. First, verify the tape position with the mt status command (the -f *file* option specifies the tape device file; remember that you do not need this if you set the TAPE environment variable):

```
mt -f /dev/nst0 status
```

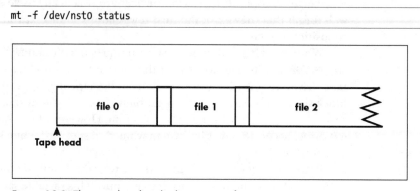

*Figure 13-2: The tape head at the beginning of a tape.*

The output should look like this (the following output is from a DAT drive):

```
SCSI 2 tape drive:
File number=0, block number=0, partition=0.
Tape block size 0 bytes. Density code 0x13 (DDS (61000 bpi)).
Soft error count since last status=0
General status bits on (41010000):
 BOT ONLINE IM_REP_EN
```

There's a lot of information here:

- The current file number is 0.

- The current block number is 0, so the tape head is at the beginning of a file.

- You should ignore the partition; most tape drives don't support it anyway.

- The block size is 0, meaning that the tape drive does not have a fixed block size.

- The density code indicates how much data can fit on the tape.

- The soft error count is the number of recoverable errors that have occurred since the last time you ran mt status.

- General status bits explain more about the state of the tape and tape drive. BOT means "beginning of tape," and ONLINE reports that the tape drive is ready and loaded. See Section 13.6.6 for a full list of mt status bits.

### 13.6.2 Creating Archives on a Tape

It is difficult to understand how a tape drive works by running through various files on a random tape in a collection of backups. Therefore, to explain the process of searching through a tape, this section shows you how to create some archives for yourself before going into the specifics of unarchiving. Once you have learned this, you will be able to play with a tape without significant confusion or worrying about losing data.

Here is a procedure for creating three files on a tape — specifically, tar archives of /lib, /boot, and /dev:

1. Put a new tape in your drive (a blank tape, or one that you don't care about).

2. Make sure that your TAPE environment variable is set to the no-rewind tape device.

3. Run mt status to verify that the tape is in the drive and your TAPE variable is set.

4. Change to the root directory.

5. Create a tar archive of the first file on the tape with this command:

```
tar zcv lib
```

6. Run mt status. The output should look something like the following, indicating that the tape is on the next file (file 1):

```
SCSI 2 tape drive:
File number=1, block number=0, partition=0.
Tape block size 0 bytes. Density code 0x13 (DDS (61000 bpi)).
Soft error count since last status=0
General status bits on (81010000):
 EOF ONLINE IM_REP_EN
```

7. Create an archive of your /boot directory:

```
tar zcv boot
```

8. Create an archive of your /dev directory:

```
tar zcv dev
```

The contents of your tape should now look like Figure 13-3.

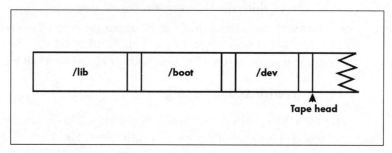

Figure 13-3: The tape containing three archive files with the head at the start of a new file.

### 13.6.3 Reading from Tape

Now that you have some files on the tape, you can try reading the archive:

1.  Change to the /tmp directory to avoid any accidents (in case you accidentally type x instead of t in one of the steps that follow).

2.  Rewind the tape:

```
mt rewind
```

3.  Verify the first file on the tape, the archive of /lib:

```
tar ztv
```

A long listing of the files in the archive should scroll by.

4.  Run mt status. The output should look like this:

```
SCSI 2 tape drive:
File number=0, block number=4557, partition=0.
Tape block size 0 bytes. Density code 0x13 (DDS (61000 bpi)).
Soft error count since last status=0
General status bits on (1010000):
 ONLINE IM_REP_EN
```

The tape is *still* at file 0, the first file on the tape. How did this happen? The answer is that as soon as it finishes reading, tar stops where it is on the tape, because you may want to do something crazy (such as append to the archive). The tape head is now at the very *end* of file 0 (notice the block count in the mt output); see Figure 13-4.

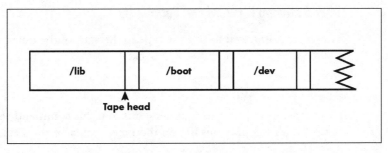

*Figure 13-4: The tape head at the end of file 0.*

The most important consequence of the new tape position is that another tar ztv does not access the next archive on the tape, because the head is not at the beginning of the next file, but rather, it is at the beginning of the file mark. To advance the tape forward to the next file (the /boot archive), use another mt command:

```
mt fsf
```

This command moves the tape so that the head is at the end of the file mark (the beginning of the /boot archive), as shown in Figure 13-5.

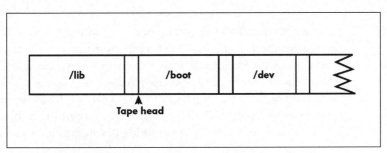

*Figure 13-5: The tape head at the beginning of file 1.*

## 13.6.4 Extracting Archives

To extract archives from a tape, all you need to do is replace the t in the commands in the previous section with xp:

```
tar zxpv
```

As usual, you should double-check your current working directory before extracting any archives.

## 13.6.5 Moving Forward and Backing Up

The `mt fsf` command moves the tape to the start of the next file. There is also a command for moving the tape back:

```
mt bsf
```

However, it is important to understand that this command rewinds the tape to the *end* of the previous file on the tape; that is, to the start of the next file mark that the tape head sees.

Let's say that you are at the start of file 1, as shown earlier in Figure 13-5. Running `mt bsf` reverses the state to that shown in Figure 13-4. Try it for yourself, and then run another `mt status`. The file number should be 0 with a block number of -1 (the driver cannot compute the length of the file by itself).

In general, to get back to the start of the previous file when you are at the start of a file, you need to move back twice and then forward once. Because most `mt` tape movement commands take an optional file count (an example is the 2 here), you can run the following sequence:

```
mt bsf 2
mt fsf
```

However, there's another gotcha here, because the tape in this example is at the start of file 1. Running `mt bsf 2` attempts to move the tape back two file marks. However, the beginning of the tape is not a file mark. Therefore, the `mt bsf 2` in this sequence backs up, passing one file mark, and then hits the beginning of the tape, producing an I/O error. The subsequent `mt fsf` skips forward again, moving the tape back to the beginning of file 1.

Therefore, if you want to get to file 0, you should always rewind the tape instead with `mt rewind`.

**NOTE**    *The Linux* `mt` *includes a* `bsfm` *command that is supposed to take you directly to the start of the previous file. This nonstandard extension does not work quite correctly; if the tape head is at the start of a file,* `mt bsfm` *runs* `mt bsf`, *then* `mt fsf`, *taking you right back to where you started.*

The bottom line is that you need to pay careful attention to the tape head position with respect to the file marks and choose the appropriate command. If it all seems a little ridiculous to you, it's probably not worth sweating over; to get to file *n* on a tape, this always works (though it may be slower):

```
mt rewind
mt fsf n
```

To eject the tape, use the `offline` command:

```
mt offline
```

### 13.6.6 mt Commands and Status

These are the most common mt commands:

**mt status**    Produces a status report.

**mt fsf** *n*    Winds forward to the start of the first block of the next file. The *n* parameter is optional; if specified, mt skips ahead *n* files instead of just one.

**mt bsf** *n*    Winds back to the end of the previous file. The *n* is an optional file count.

**mt rewind**    Rewinds the tape.

**mt offline**    Rewinds the tape, then prepares for tape removal. In some tape drives, the tape drive ejects the tape; in others, the drive unlocks the tape so that you can manually remove it.

**mt retension**    Winds the tape all the way forward and then rewinds. This sometimes helps with tapes that you're having trouble reading.

**mt erase**    Erases the entire tape. This usually takes a long time.

There are countless other mt commands documented in the mt(1) manual page, but they really aren't very useful unless you're trying to extract blocks from the center of a file or to set SCSI tape driver options.

Running mt status yields a number of status bit codes (such as the BOT code from Section 13.6.1). Here are the important codes:

**ONLINE**    The drive is ready with a loaded tape.

**DR_OPEN**    The drive is empty (possibly with the door open).

**BOT**    The current position is the beginning of the tape.

**EOF**    The current position is the *beginning* of a file (the end of a file mark). This is a somewhat misleading code, because you can confuse it with the end of file.

**EOT**    The current position is the end of the tape.

**EOD**    The current position is the end of recorded media. You can reach this by trying to mt fsf past the very last file marker.

**WR_PROT**    The current tape is read-only.

### 13.6.7 Direct File Access

tar isn't the only command that can write archives to a tape. Sometimes you may not know what is on the tape, and even if you do know, you may want to copy a file from the tape to the local filesystem for further (and easier) examination.

Your good old friend dd can do this, as this example for /dev/nst0 shows:

```
dd if=/dev/nst0 of=output_file
```

This doesn't always work — you may get an I/O error because you did not specify the correct block size. The program that writes the archive on the tape usually determines the block size; in the case of tar, the block size is 10KB (specified to dd as 10k). Therefore, because dd defaults to a block size of 512 bytes, you would use the following command to copy a tar archive from the tape to *output_file*:

```
dd bs=10k if=/dev/nst0 of=output_file
```

Block sizes for common programs are listed in Table 13-1 (see also Section 13.7).

**Table 13-1:** Block Sizes for Common Archiving Programs

| Archiver | Block Size | bs Parameter |
|----------|------------|--------------|
| tar | 10KB (20 x 512 bytes) | bs=10k |
| dd | 512 bytes | bs=512 |
| cpio | 512 bytes | bs=512 |
| dump | 10KB (20 x 512 bytes) | bs=10k |
| Amanda | 32KB | bs=32k |

**NOTE** *Unlike* tar, dd *advances the tape head to the next file on the tape, instead of just moving it up to the file mark.*

## 13.7 Other Archivers

Although tar is the most common archiver on Linux systems, there are two other important systems called dump/restore and cpio that you should be aware of. The following sections provide an overview of the most important archiver operations, but they do not go into very much detail.

### 13.7.1 Dump and Restore

The dump/restore system is a throwback to the older days of Unix. Unlike most other archivers, the dump program looks at the internal structure of a filesystem, and therefore it only supports certain filesystem types. On Linux, this list currently includes only the ext2 and ext3 filesystems, and this is unlikely to change, because there is little interest in porting the system to the myriad other filesystems. This inflexibility makes dump/restore a somewhat unattractive backup solution. Still, some people prefer dump (probably because they're too old to learn new tricks, or perhaps that they don't like their backup program to change the access times on their files), so you may be stuck with reading one of these archives.

### Dump

The dump command to back up an entire directory looks like this:

```
dump -0 -f archive directory
```

You can use a tape device as *archive* if you like, or if your tape device is in the TAPE environment variable, you can omit -f *archive* entirely.

The -0 option forces a full (level 0) backup. If you actually intend to use dump to do regular backups, add a -u option to make dump write date information to /usr/etc/dumpdates. With this file and option in place, you can specify backup levels other than 0 (for example, a level 5 with -5).

**NOTE** *When using -u, you must dump the entire filesystem — that is, the directory parameter must be the mount point or the disk device (for example,* /dev/hda4*).*

### Restore

The restore program extracts files and directories from an archive created with dump. If you're only looking for one or a few files, you need to run restore in interactive mode, so follow this procedure:

1. Run the following command, where *archive* is the archive (this can be a tape drive):

```
restore iavf archive
```

2. Wait until restore has read the filesystem index from the archive and prints a restore > prompt.
3. Use the cd and ls commands until you find a file or directory that you want to restore from the archive.
4. Add the file or directory to the extraction list with the add command (add as many files and directories as you like):

```
add file
```

5. Type extract to begin the extraction.
6. After extraction, restore asks this question:

```
set owner/mode for '.'? [yn]
```

If you want to set the current directory's permissions and owner to the same as the root directory in the archive, answer y. This is nearly always a bad choice for an interactive restore, so answer n if you have any doubt. It's not hard to fix this if you do make a mistake, though.

*The root directory in the archive corresponds to the originating filesystem's mount point. Let's say that you dump a partition mounted at /home. None of the paths in the archive would contain /home — that is, /home/user would show up as /user in the archive.*

To forgo interactive mode and restore everything (and set the permissions for the current directory), use the rvf options:

---

restore rvf *archive*

---

## 13.7.2 cpio

Linux administrators rarely use cpio (or its newer, more capable cousin named afio) for backups or other tasks, but you should still have an idea of how this program works so that you can create, test, and extract archives.
cpio has three modes:

- Create, or "copy-out," mode (activated with -o) takes a file list from the standard input, creates an archive from a matching directory hierarchy, and sends the result to standard output or a file.
- Extract, or "copy-in," mode (activated with -i) tests and extracts files from an archive.
- Pass-through mode (activated with -p) copies files. tar and rsync (see Chapter 15) usually do this job better unless you have a very specific list of files. This book does not cover this somewhat obscure cpio mode.

### Creating Archives

Because you are unlikely to have a cpio file lying around on your system, you should experiment by creating one yourself. The cpio copy-out mode requires that you generate a file list first. You can use the output of find to create a file list in a pipeline to cpio.

Let's say that you want to archive /usr/local/bin as a file named local_bin.cpio:

---

find /usr/local/bin | cpio -o > local_bin.cpio

---

On any halfway modern system, the output of this command includes lines like this for every single file created:

---

cpio: /usr/local/bin/*file*: truncating inode number

---

This annoying message isn't anything to worry about; it just means that cpio can't store the full inode number in the limited space available in the archive. The very end of the command should contain a block count (by default, 512 bytes equal one block), as in this example output:

---

20967 blocks

---

*If you need to write an archive to a tape, you have two choices (these are equivalent because the block sizes in* cpio *and* dd *are the same):*

```
cpio -o -O tape
cpio -o | dd of=tape
```

## Testing and Extracting Archives

Now that you have local_bin.cpio, you can list its contents with this command:

```
cpio -i -t -v -I local_bin.cpio
```

The options have the following meanings:

- **-i**    Specifies copy-in mode.
- **-t**    Specifies a test archive.
- **-v**    Sets verbose mode; shows the files as ls -l would. You may omit this option if you don't care.
- **-I** *file*    Reads *file* as the archive (the default file is the standard input).

To extract an archive, replace the -t with -d:

```
cpio -i -d -v -I archive
```

However, this can be dangerous with the local_bin.cpio archive that you created earlier, because that archive contains absolute pathnames. This can be a threat to system stability and security, especially if you extract as root, because the extraction can easily overwrite a file such as /etc/passwd. Use the --no-absolute-filenames option to prevent this:

```
cpio --no-absolute-filenames -i -d -v -I local_bin.cpio
```

Keep in mind that there are a few more cpio options that cpio may need in copy-in mode if it can't figure out some of the format options of the archive for itself:

- **-b**    Switches the byte order. The default cpio format depends on the byte order of the architecture of the CPU that was used to create the archive, so if you have an archive from a completely different kind of machine, you may need this option.
- **-C** *n*    Uses *n* as the archive block size.
- **-H** *name*    Uses *name* as the archive format (valid formats are bin, crc, hpbin, hpodc, newc, odc, tar, and ustar). Note that only GNU cpio supports all of these options.

### 13.7.3 Amanda Tapes

Amanda is an automatic backup system that writes a "hybrid" archive on a tape. That is, the first 32KB block in an Amanda tape contains information about the archive, and the rest of the blocks make up a regular archive in `tar` or `dump` format.

If you come across an Amanda file, do the following to extract the files:

1. Put the first block into a file named `header`:

```
dd if=file of=header bs=32k count=1
```

2. Run `strings header`. The output should look something like this:

```
AMANDA: FILE 20031117 duplex /etc lev 0 comp .gz program /bin/tar
To restore, position tape at start of file and run:
    dd if=<tape> bs=32k skip=1 | /bin/gzip -dc | bin/tar -f... -
```

3. Follow the instructions. Extract the contents from the rest of the file as follows (if you're using a tape drive as *file*, the tape head should already be correctly positioned, so don't use `skip=1`):

```
dd if=file bs=32k skip=1 | unpack_command
```

*unpack_command* should follow the output you got in step 2. For example, if you're dealing with a tar archive, *unpack_command* might look like this:

```
gzip -dc | tar xpf -
```

## 13.8 Further Backup Topics

This chapter covers the basics of manual backups for small systems. However, once you get into larger operations, there is much more to explore:

- Automated backups. Amanda (http://www.amanda.org/) is a popular, powerful, and free automatic network backup package (that is, after you figure out how it works).
- Tape changers. The Linux `mtx` command can operate a tape changer and autoloader.
- Backups with Samba.
- Commercial backup systems such as BRU.
- Database backup systems (Oracle and the like).

A good, comprehensive, and detailed guide to backups (especially for large organizations) is *Unix Backup and Recovery* [Preston].

# 14

# SHARING FILES WITH SAMBA

Your Linux machine probably doesn't live alone on your network. If you have a PC running Windows, it's only natural that you would want to permit access to your Linux system's files and printers from those Windows machines with the standard Windows network protocol, SMB (Server Message Block). Mac OS X also supports SMB filesharing.

The standard filesharing software suite for Unix is called Samba. Not only does Samba allow your network's Windows computers to get to your Linux system, but it works the other way around — you can print and access files on Windows servers from your Linux machine with the included client software.

To set up a Samba server, you need to perform these steps:

1. Create an `smb.conf` file.
2. Add filesharing share sections to `smb.conf`.

3. Add printer share sections to `smb.conf`.

4. Start the Samba daemons: `nmbd` and `smbd`.

A *share* is a resource that you offer to a client, such as a directory or printer.

The discussion of Samba in this chapter is concise, limited to getting Windows machines on a single subnet to see a stand-alone Linux machine through the Windows Network Neighborhood browser. There are countless ways to configure Samba, because there are many possibilities for access control and network topology. For the gory details on how to configure a large-scale server, you will find *How Samba Works* [Lendecke] a much more extensive guide, and there is also information at the Samba Web site, http://www.samba.org/.

# 14.1 Configuring the Server

The central Samba configuration file is `smb.conf`, and it is usually located in Samba's `lib` directory (for example, `/usr/local/lib`). However, some distributions put the configuration file in an etc directory, such as `/etc/samba` or `/usr/local/etc`. The `smb.conf` file breaks down into several sections denoted with square brackets (such as [global] and [printers]).

The [global] section in `smb.conf` contains general options that apply to the entire server and all shares. These options pertain primarily to network configuration and access control. Here is a sample [global] section that shows you how to set the server name, description, and workgroup:

```
[global]
  # server name
  netbios name = name

  # server description
  server string = My server via Samba

  # workgroup
  workgroup = MYNETWORK
```

These parameters work as follows:

**netbios name**  The server name. If you omit this parameter, Samba uses the Unix hostname.

**server string**  A short description of the server. The default is the Samba version number.

**workgroup**  The SMB workgroup name. If you're on a Windows NT domain, set this parameter to the name of your domain.

### 14.1.1 Server Access Control

There are a few options that you can add to your `smb.conf` file to put limits on the machines and users that can access your Samba server. The following list includes many options that you can set in your [global] section, as well as in the other sections that control individual shares (described later in the chapter):

**interfaces**  Set this to have Samba listen on the given networks or interfaces. Here are two examples:

```
interfaces = 10.23.2.0/255.255.255.0
interfaces = eth0
```

**bind interfaces only**  Set this to yes when using the `interfaces` parameter in order to limit access to machines that you can reach on those interfaces.

**valid users**  Set this to allow the given users access. For example:

```
valid users = jruser, bill
```

**guest ok**  Set this parameter to `true` if you would like a share to be available to anonymous users on the network.

**guest only**  Set this parameter to `true` to allow anonymous access only.

**browseable**  Set this to make shares available in Samba's browseable share list. If you set this parameter to `no` for any or all shares, you will still be able to access shares on the Samba server, but they will not be browseable, and therefore you will need to know their exact names.

### 14.1.2 Passwords

In general, you only want to allow access to your Samba server with password authentication. Unfortunately, the basic password system on Unix is different than that on Windows, so unless you specify clear-text network passwords or authenticate passwords with a Windows server, you must set up an alternative password file. This section shows you how.

Assuming that your Samba configuration directory is /etc/samba, you can use these entries in your [global] section to define the Samba password file as /etc/samba/passwd_smb:

```
# use a separate password file for Samba to enable encrypted passwords
security = user
encrypt passwords = yes
smb passwd file = /etc/samba/passwd_smb
```

With these lines in place, you can manipulate the `passwd_smb` password file with the `smbpasswd` program.

**NOTE** *If you have access to a Windows NT domain, you can set* security = domain, *to make Samba use the domain's usernames and eliminate the need for an SMB password file. However, in order for domain users to access the machine running Samba, each domain user must have a local account with the same username on the machine running Samba.*

### Adding and Deleting Users

The first thing you need to do in order to give a Windows user access to your Samba server is to add the user to the `passwd_smb` file with the `smbpasswd -a` command:

```
smbpasswd -a username
```

The *username* parameter to the `smbpasswd` command must be a valid username on your Linux system.

Much like the regular system's `passwd` program would, `smbpasswd` asks you to enter the new user's password twice. If the Samba password file does not exist, `smbpasswd` creates it for you, then confirms that it has created the new user.

To remove a user, use the `-x` option to `smbpasswd`:

```
smbpasswd -x username
```

At times, you may not necessarily want to delete a user, but rather, temporarily deactivate the user. The `-d` option disables a user; and `-e` re-enables the user:

```
smbpasswd -d username
smbpasswd -e username
```

### Changing Passwords

You can change a Samba password as the superuser by using `smbpasswd` with no options or keywords other than the username:

```
smbpasswd username
```

However, if the Samba server is running, any user can change their own Samba password by entering `smbpasswd` by itself on the command line.

## 14.2 Starting the Server

After you add a user and a password, you should probably test your server. To start the server, you need to run nmbd and smbd with the following arguments, where *smb_config_file* is the full path of your smb.conf file:

```
nmbd -D -s smb_config_file
smbd -D -s smb_config_file
```

The nmbd daemon is a NetBIOS name server, and smbd does the actual work of handling share requests. The -D option specifies daemon mode. If you alter the smb.conf file while smbd is running, notify the daemon of the changes with a HUP signal.

## 14.3 Diagnostics and Log Files

If something goes wrong upon starting one of the Samba servers, an error message appears on the command line. However, runtime diagnostic messages go to the log.nmbd and log.smbd log files.

These files are usually in a var directory, but you can change the location to *dir* by specifying the -l *dir* option to smbd and nmbd. However, if you want to override the log directory location (to /var/log, for example), it's usually better to change the log file directory and log filename at once with the log file parameter in smb.conf. You can force the log output from smbd to a file with this line in the [global] section of your smb.conf:

```
log file = /var/log/smb.log
```

Unfortunately, this does not set the nmbd log directory; if you want the log output from both daemons to go to the same file, you must still use nmbd -l /var/log/smb.log.

## 14.4 Sharing Files

To export a directory to SMB clients (that is, to share a directory with a client), add a section like this to your smb.conf file, where *label* is what you would like to call the share, and *path* is the full directory path:

```
[label]
  path = path
  comment = share description
  guest ok = no
  writable = yes
  printable = no
```

These parameters are useful in directory shares:

**guest ok**   Allows guest access to the share. The `public` parameter is a synonym.

**writable**   A yes or true setting here marks the share as read-write. Do not allow guest access to a read-write share.

**printable**   Specifies a printing share; this parameter must be set to `no` or `false` for a directory share.

**veto files**   Prevents the export of any files that match the given patterns. You must enclose each pattern inside forward slashes (so that it looks like */pattern/*). Here's an example that bars object files, as well as any file or directory named `bin`:

```
veto files = /*.o/bin/
```

### 14.4.1 Home Directories

You can put a special section called [homes] in your `smb.conf` file if you want to export home directories to users. The section should look like this:

```
[homes]
  comment = home directories
  browseable = no
  writable = yes
```

By default, Samba reads the logged-in user's `/etc/passwd` entry to determine the user's home directory for [homes]. However, if you don't want Samba to follow this behavior (that is, you want to keep the Windows home directories in a different place than the regular Linux home directories), you can use the %S substitution in a `path` parameter. Here is an example that switches a user's [homes] directory to /u/*user*:

```
path = /u/%S
```

Samba substitutes the current username for the %S.

## 14.5 Sharing Printers

You can export all of your printers to Windows clients with a special [printers] section in your `smb.conf` file. Here's how the section looks when you're using CUPS:

```
[printers]
  comment = Printers
  browseable = yes
```

```
printing = CUPS
path = cups
printable = yes
writable = no
```

To use the printing = CUPS parameter, your Samba installation must be configured and linked against the CUPS library.

As you learned in Chapter 12, there are several other printing systems in addition to CUPS. On Linux, you can set the printing parameter to BSD, LPRNG, PLP, or CUPS. Of these, CUPS is the easiest.

**NOTE**    *Depending on your configuration, you may also want to allow guest access to your printers with the* guest ok = yes *option because you may not want to give a Samba password or account to everyone who needs to access the printers.*

### 14.5.1 Sharing a Single Printer

If you want to export a single printer, you can do so with a printer section that looks like this:

```
[printer_name]
  comment = My printer
  printer name = printer_name
  printing = CUPS
  path = cups
  browseable = yes
  printable = yes
```

You can specify a driver name for Windows clients with the printer driver parameter. For example, to tell a client that the printer is an HP LaserJet 4M, you can use the following in the printer section:

```
printer driver = HP LaserJet 4M
```

## 14.6 Using the Samba Client

Samba comes with a program named smbclient that can print to and access remote Windows shares. This program comes in handy when you are in an environment where you must interact with Windows servers that offer no Unix-friendly means of communication.

To get started with smbclient, use the -L option to get a list of shares from a remote server named *SERVER*:

```
smbclient -L -U username SERVER
```

You do not need -U *username* if your Linux username is the same as your username on *SERVER*.

After running this command, smbclient asks for a password. If you want to try to access a share as a guest, you can press ENTER; otherwise, enter your password on *SERVER*.

Upon success, you should get a share list like this:

```
Sharename       Type    Comment
---------       ----    -------
Software        Disk    Software distribution
Scratch         Disk    Scratch space
IPC$            IPC     IPC Service
ADMIN$          IPC     IPC Service
Printer1        Printer Printer in room 231A
Printer2        Printer Printer in basement
```

Look at the Type field to make sense of each share. You should only pay attention to the Disk and Printer shares (the IPC shares are for remote management). In this list, there are two disk shares and two printer shares. You can use the name in the Sharename column to access the share.

## 14.6.1 Accessing Files

If you need only casual access to files in a disk share, use the following command (again, you can omit the -U *username* if your Linux username matches your username on the server):

```
smbclient -U username '\\SERVER\sharename'
```

Upon success, you will get a prompt like this:

```
smb: \>
```

In this file transfer mode, smbclient is similar to the Unix ftp; you can run these commands:

**get** *file*  Copies *file* from the remote server to the current local directory.

**put** *file*  Copies *file* from the local machine to the remote server.

**cd** *dir*  Changes the directory on the remote server to *dir*.

**lcd** *localdir*  Changes the current local directory to *localdir*.

**pwd**  Prints the current directory on the remote server, including the server and share names.

**!** *command*  Runs *command* on the local host. Two particularly handy commands are !pwd and !ls to determine directory and file status on the local side.

**help**  Shows a full list of commands.

### Using the SMB Filesystem

If you need frequent access to files on a Windows server, you can attach the share directly to your system with the smbmount command:

```
smbmount '\\SERVER\sharename\' -c 'mount mountpoint' -U username -P password
```

To use this command, you must have the smbfs kernel driver loaded as a module or directly compiled into the kernel. In addition, the rest of the Samba programs should be in your path. By default, a Samba installation built from source code does not include the smbmount command. You must specify --with-smbmount when running the Samba configure script to create these extra programs.

## 14.6.2 Printing to a Windows Share

The easiest way to print to a Windows SMB share is through CUPS. Follow these steps to get a printer working:

1. Put the CUPS SMB backend in place. Find the smbspool program in your Samba distribution, and then create a symbolic link named smb in the backend directory to smbspool, like this:

```
ln -s smbspool_path/smbspool cups_prefix/lib/cups/backend/smb
```

2. Restart CUPS.
3. Run lpinfo -v to confirm that the SMB spooler is in the available backends. You should see this in the output:

```
network smb
```

4. Add a new printer as outlined in Chapter 12. If you don't need a password to access the printer, use the following as the printer device path (notice that the backslashes are forward slashes in CUPS):

```
smb://SERVER/sharename
```

If you need a username and password, add them to the front of the server:

```
smb://username:password@SERVER/sharename
```

If your target printer is in a different Windows workgroup, you can specify the workgroup in the first part of the name:

```
smb://username:password@WORKGROUP/SERVER/sharename
```

### Sending Files Directly to a Printer Share

If you have a file that is suitable for a printer (such as a PostScript file that you want to send to a PostScript printer), you can send it directly to the printer share with this smbclient variant:

```
smbclient '\\SERVER\sharename' -U username -P < file
```

This command is particularly useful when testing and troubleshooting printers. Working with CUPS and Samba simultaneously can be difficult, so if you find yourself running into trouble when trying to access a printer on a Windows system, try going through these steps:

1. Use the Windows system to print a test document to a file, then transfer *file* to your Linux system.
2. Run the command in the preceding example to attempt to print the test *file*.
3. If the file does not print, you have a problem on the Samba side. Otherwise, the problem lies with CUPS.

# NETWORK FILE TRANSFER

This book's primary focus is the single-machine environment. However, any modern machine is on a network. Eventually, you will want to transfer files from one Unix machine to another. There are many ways to move files around, but the choices usually come down to these:

- Using a simple command such as scp if you need to transfer just a few files.
- Using an archiving program such as tar through an ssh pipeline to transfer a directory hierarchy. Here is an example:

```
tar cBvf - directory | ssh remote_host tar xBvpf -
```

This old method gets the job done, but it is not very flexible. In particular, after the transfer completes, the remote host may not have an exact copy of the directory. If *directory* already exists on the remote machine, and it contains some extraneous files, those files persist after the transfer.

- Using a synchronizer system that duplicates an entire directory structure on the remote host. The two most popular synchronizer utilities are rsync and rdist.
- Using old, clunky, insecure programs like ftp that you should not use.

This chapter explains the rsync system. The main advantages of rsync over other systems are these:

- There is only one command to learn, rsync, which has a relatively simple syntax.
- It offers relatively good performance.
- It has multiple operating modes.

## 15.1 rsync Basics

The base requirement of the rsync system is that you install the rsync program on the source and destination hosts. The easiest way to transfer files is to use a remote shell account. This section assumes that you want to transfer files to or from a machine to which you have SSH access.

On the surface, the rsync command is not much different than scp or rcp. In fact, you can run rsync with the same arguments as those utilities. For example, to copy a group of files to your home directory on *host*, you can run this command:

```
rsync file1 file2 ... host:
```

However, given your current system and rsync configuration, this command probably will not work, because the rsync program defaults to using rsh as the remote shell, and as you saw in Section 6.7, you shouldn't use something this insecure. To get around this, you can tell rsync to use ssh with the --rsh option:

```
rsync --rsh=ssh file1 file2 ... host:destination_dir
```

Look out for this error message:

```
rsync not found
rsync: connection unexpectedly closed (0 bytes read so far)
rsync error: error in rsync protocol data stream (code 12) at io.c(165)
```

This notice says that your remote shell can't find rsync on its system. If rsync isn't in the remote path but is on the system, use --rsync-path=*path* to manually specify its location.

If you don't want to type --rsh=ssh every time that you invoke an rsync command, set the RSYNC_RSH environment variable to ssh. The remainder of the commands in this chapter assume that you have done this.

If your username is different on the remote host, add *user@* to the hostname, where *user* is your username on *host*:

```
rsync file1 file2 ... user@host:destination_dir
```

With no extra options, rsync copies only files. In fact, if you specify just the options described so far and you supply a directory *dir* as an argument, you will see this message:

```
skipping directory dir
```

To transfer entire directory hierarchies, complete with the same symbolic links, permissions, modes, and devices, use the -a option, as in this example:

```
rsync -a dir host:destination_dir
```

If you're not too sure what will happen when you transfer the files, use the -n option to operate rsync without actually copying any files. The -n option implies the -v (verbose mode) option, showing details about the transfer and the files involved:

```
rsync -na dir host:destination_dir
```

The output looks like this:

```
building file list ... done
ml/nftrans/nftrans.html
[more files]
wrote 2183 bytes  read 24 bytes  401.27 bytes/sec
```

## 15.1.1 Making Exact Copies of a Directory Structure

By default, rsync copies files and directories without considering the previous contents of the destination directory. For example, if you transferred the directory d containing the files a and b to a machine that already had a file named d/c, the destination would contain d/a, d/b, and d/c after the rsync. To make an exact replica of the source directory, you must delete files in the destination directory that do not exist in the source directory, such as d/c in this example.

Use the --delete option to remove files from the destination that don't reside in the local directory, like this:

```
rsync -a --delete dir host:destination_dir
```

**NOTE**  *Again, if you're not certain about your transfer, use the -n option to tell you if rsync wants to delete any files before it actually performs the removal.*

You may also wish to use --max-delete=*n* to make sure that rsync deletes no more than *n* files in the target directory. This option essentially amounts to a last-ditch effort not to delete large numbers of files when there's some problem on the source side. However, it will still delete files until reaching *n* deleted files, and in fact, you may notice that your version of rsync might have a bug, where it deletes one more than *n* files.

## 15.1.2 Using the Trailing Slash

You have to be particularly careful when specifying a directory as the source in an rsync command line. Consider this command:

```
rsync -a dir host:dest_dir
```

Once this command completes, you will have a directory *dir* inside *dest_dir* on *host*. However, adding a slash (/) significantly changes the behavior:

```
rsync -a dir/ host:dest_dir
```

Here, rsync copies everything *inside* dir to *dest_dir* on *host* without actually copying the *dir* directory itself. The *dir* directory will not exist on *host* after the operation. Therefore, you can think of a transfer of *dir/* as an operation similar to cp *dir/* *dest_dir* on the local filesystem.

Let's consider an example. Say that you have a directory d containing the files a and b (d/a and d/b). You run the following command to transfer them to the c directory on *host*:

```
rsync -a d/ host:c
```

After the transfer completes, the directory c contains copies of a and b, but *not* d. If, however, you had omitted the trailing / on d, c would have gotten a copy of d, with a and b inside, so that as a result of the transfer you'd have files and directories named c/d/a and c/d/b on the remote host.

When transferring files and directories to a remote host, accidentally adding a / after a path would normally be nothing more than a nuisance; you could then go to the remote host, add the *dir* directory, and put all of the transferred items back in *dir*. Unfortunately, you must be careful to avoid disaster when combining the trailing / with the --delete option. If you use the --delete option to transfer *dir* to *dest_dir* without the slash, rsync ignores everything in *dest_dir* except *dir*. Using *dir/*, on the other hand, makes rsync compare the contents of *dir* against *dest_dir* and makes *dest_dir* look exactly like *dir*. Therefore, you can accidentally delete a whole bunch of files in *dest_dir*.

**WARNING** *Be wary of your shell's automatic filename completion feature. GNU readline and many other completion libraries tack a trailing slash onto a completed directory name.*

### 15.1.3 Excluding Files and Directories

One very important feature of rsync is its ability to exclude files and directories from a transfer operation. Let's say that you would like to transfer a local directory called src to *host*, but you want to exclude anything named RCS. You can do it like this:

```
rsync -a --exclude=RCS src host:
```

It's important to note that this command excludes *all* files and directories named RCS because --exclude takes a pattern, not an absolute filename. If you want to exclude only one specific item, specify an absolute path that starts with /, as in this example:

```
rsync -a --exclude=/src/RCS src host:
```

**NOTE**    *The first / in /src/RCS in this command is not the root directory of your system, but rather, the very base directory of the transfer.*

Here are a few more tips on exclude patterns:

- You may have as many --exclude parameters as you like.
- If you use the same patterns time and again, place those patterns in a plain-text file (one pattern per line), and then use --exclude-from=*file*.
- To exclude directories named *item* but include *files* with this name, use a trailing slash: --exclude=*item*/.
- The exclude pattern is based on a *full* file or directory name component and may contain simple wildcards. For example, t*s matches this, but does not match ethers.
- If you exclude a directory or filename, but find that your pattern is too restrictive, use --include to specifically include another file or directory.

## 15.2 Checksums and Verbose Transfers

The rsync command uses file checksums (near-unique signatures) to determine whether any files on the transfer source are already on the destination.

The first time you transfer an entire directory hierarchy to a remote host, rsync sees that none of the files already exist at the destination, and it transfers everything. Testing your transfer with rsync -n verifies this for you.

After running rsync, try running it again, but this time as rsync -n or rsync -v. This time, no files should show up in the transfer list because an exact copy of the file set exists on both ends, so the file checksums are the same.

However, when the files on the source side are not identical to the files on the destination side, rsync transfers the source files and overwrites any files that exist on the remote side. There are a few options that override this checksum behavior:

**--ignore-existing**   Does not clobber files already on the target side.

**--backup (abbreviation: -b)**   Does not clobber files already on the target, but rather renames these existing files by adding a ~ suffix to their names before transferring the new files.

**--suffix=*s***   Changes the suffix used with --backup from ~ to *s*.

**--update (abbreviation: -u)**   Does not clobber any file on the target that has a later date than the corresponding file on the source.

With no special options, rsync operates quietly, only producing output when there is a problem. However, you can use rsync -v for verbose mode, and if you need even more output, rsync -vv gives yet more details. (You can tack on as many v options as you like, but two is probably more than you need.) For a comprehensive summary after the transfer, use rsync --stats.

## 15.3 Compression

Many administrators always use -z in conjunction with -a to compress the data before transmission:

```
rsync -az dir host:destination_dir
```

Compression can improve performance in certain situations. For example, if you are uploading a large amount of data across a slow connection (such as the slow upstream link on many DSL connections), or if the latency between the two hosts is high, it helps. However, across a fast 100 Mb/s local area network, the two endpoints can spend more time compressing and decompressing data than the network takes transmitting the uncompressed files.

## 15.4 Limiting Bandwidth

It's easy to clog the uplink of DSL and cable modem connections when uploading a large amount of data to a remote host. Even though you won't be using your (normally large) downlink capacity during such a transfer, your connection will still seem quite slow if you let rsync go as fast as it can, because outgoing TCP packets such as HTTP requests will have to compete with your transfers for bandwidth on your uplink.

To get around this, you can use --bwlimit to give your uplink a little breathing room. For example, to limit the bandwidth to 10000 kilobytes per second, you might do something like this:

```
rsync --bwlimit=10000 -a dir host:destination_dir
```

## 15.5 Transferring Files to Your Computer

The rsync command isn't just for copying files from your local machine to a remote host. You can also transfer files from a remote machine to your local host by placing the remote host and remote source path as the first argument on the command line. Therefore, to transfer *src_dir* on *host* to *dest_dir* on the local host, run this command:

```
rsync -a host:src_dir dest_dir
```

**NOTE**    *If you omit* host:, *you can use* rsync *for making duplicates of directories on your local machine.*

## 15.6 Further rsync Topics

rsync can do many more things that are beyond the scope of this book. One of its most significant abilities is acting as a network server. Such a server offers several modules that you can call by symbolic names instead of pathnames. You can also offer public read-only access to the modules; this is a nice alternative to anonymous FTP.

Another important feature is rsync batch mode operation. Although it is fairly easy to write scripts containing rsync commands to do network file distribution, rsync can also employ a number of auxiliary files related to command options, logging, and transfer state. In particular, the state files make long transfers faster, and easier to resume when interrupted.

There are also many more command-line options than those described in this chapter. To get a rough overview, run rsync --help. There is more detailed information in the rsync(1) manual page as well as at the rsync home page: http://samba.anu.edu.au/rsync/.

# 16

## USER ENVIRONMENTS

This book's focus is on the Linux system that normally lies underneath a user's interactive session. Eventually, the system and the user have to meet somewhere. You saw plenty of commands and shell features in Chapter 1 and Chapter 7, but there's still one little piece missing: the startup files that set defaults for the shell and other programs.

Most users do not pay close attention to their startup files. Over time, the files become cluttered, containing unnecessary environment variables and tests that can lead to annoying (or quite serious) problems. Worse still, operating system vendors usually do not consider the consequences of what they put in the default startup files, packing them full of items that may even confuse the user.

Keeping in tune with the shell-oriented theme of this book, this chapter focuses specifically on shell startup files. If you have ever received a Unix account in the past, it may have come with a bafflingly large array of startup files, sometimes called *dot files* because they nearly always start with a dot (.). You may be surprised to learn that it really isn't necessary to have so many startup files.

# 16.1 Appropriate Startup Files

When designing startup files, you should keep the user in mind. If you are the only user on a machine, you don't have much to worry about — if you make an error, you're the only one affected, and it's easy enough to fix. However, if your new startup files are to be the defaults for all new users on a machine or network, or if you think that someone might copy your files for use on a different machine, your task becomes considerably more difficult. If you make an error in a startup file for ten users, you might end up fixing this error ten times. That's annoying, to say the least.

There are two essential goals to keep in mind when creating startup files for other users:

**Simplicity**  Keep the number of startup files small, and keep the files as small and simple as possible so that they are easy to modify but hard to break. Each item in a startup file is just one more thing that can break.

**Readability**  Use many comments in the files, so that the users get a good picture of what each part of a file does.

# 16.2 Shell Startup File Elements

What goes into a shell startup file? Some things may seem obvious, such as the path and a prompt setting. But wait, what exactly *should* be in the path, and what does a reasonable prompt look like? And how much is too much to put in a startup file?

The next few sections outline the essentials of a shell startup file, covering the command path, manual page path, prompt, aliases, and permissions mask.

## 16.2.1 The Command Path

The most important part of any shell startup file is the command path. The path should cover the directories that contain every application of any general interest to a regular user. At the very least, the path should contain these components, in this order:

```
/usr/local/bin
/usr/bin
/usr/X11R6/bin
/bin
```

This order ensures that you can override standard default programs with site-specific program variants located in /usr/local.

It's important to make every general-use program on the system available through one of the directories listed above (for example, using the Encap system described in Section 9.4). If the general-use programs are located in more than just these four directories, it probably means that your system is getting out of control. Don't change the path in your user environment to accommodate a new system directory. In fact, in the interest of minimizing the number of directories in the command path, some administrators prefer to fold the programs in /usr/X11R6/bin into /usr/local/bin or /usr/bin with the help of symbolic links or a different installation prefix.

Many users use a bin directory to store their own shell scripts and programs, so you may want to add this to the front of the path:

```
$HOME/bin
```

If you are interested in systems utilities (such as traceroute, ping, and lsmod), add the sbin directories to your path:

```
/usr/local/sbin
/usr/sbin
/sbin
```

### Adding Dot (.) to the Path

There is one small but controversial command path component to discuss: the dot. Placing a dot (.) in your path allows you to run programs in the current directory without using ./ in front of the program name. This may seem convenient when writing scripts or compiling programs, but it is a bad idea for two reasons:

- It can be a security problem. You should *never* put a dot at the front of the path. For example, an attacker could put a Trojan horse named ls in an archive distributed on the Internet. Even if a dot is at the end of the path, you are still vulnerable to typos such as sl.

- It is inconsistent and can be confusing. A dot in the path can mean that a command's behavior can change according to the current directory.

## 16.2.2 The Manual Page Path

Your manual path (the MANPATH environment variable used by man) should match your command path, except that each directory in the manual page path variable should end in a /man directory rather than /bin.

Here is the manual page path that corresponds to the command path listed in Section 16.2.1:

```
/usr/local/man:/usr/man:/usr/X11R6/man:$HOME/man
```

## 16.2.3 The Prompt

Avoid a long, complicated, useless prompt. For whatever reason, many administrators feel the need to drag in everything, including the kitchen sink. Just because you *can* place the current working directory, hostname, username, and fancy decorations in a prompt, it doesn't mean that you *should*.

Above all, avoid strange characters, such as these:

---
{ } = & < >

---

**NOTE** *Take special care to avoid >. This can cause erratic, empty files to appear in your current directory if you accidentally copy and paste a section of your shell window, because > redirects output from a file.*

Even a shell's default prompt isn't ideal. For example, the default bash prompt contains the shell name and version number, and the default tcsh prompt includes the hostname, the current working directory, and a >.

Here is a simple prompt setting for bash that ends with the customary $ (the traditional csh prompt ends with %):

---
PS1='\u$ '

---

The \u is a substitution for the current username (see the PROMPTING section of the bash manual page). Other popular substitutions include the following:

\h    The hostname (the short form, without domain names)

\!    The history number

\w    The current directory (this can become somewhat long; you can display only the final component with \W)

\$    $ if running as a user account, and # if root

### 16.2.4 Aliases

Among the stickier points of modern user environments is the role of aliases, a shell feature that substitutes one string for another before executing a command. At one time, these were efficient shortcuts intended to save some typing. However, aliases also have these drawbacks:

- They have balky syntax, especially when manipulating arguments.
- They are confusing; a shell's built-in which command can tell you if something is an alias, but it won't tell you where it was defined.
- They are frowned upon in subshells and non-interactive shells; they do not work in other shells.

With all of these disadvantages, it makes sense to avoid aliases whenever possible, because it's easier to write a shell script (see Chapter 7). Modern computers can start and execute shells so quickly that the difference between an alias and an entirely new command should not mean anything to you.

However, there is one particular instance where aliases do come in handy — when you wish to alter a part of the shell's environment. You can't change an environment variable with a shell script, because scripts run as subshells.

### 16.2.5 The Permissions Mask

As described in Section 1.17.1, a shell's built-in umask (permissions mask) facility sets your default permissions. You should run umask in one of your startup files to make certain that any program you run creates files with your desired permissions. However, you may wonder what the best choice is, especially if you have a stand-alone machine with no other users.

The two reasonable choices break down as follows:

**077**    This is the most restrictive permissions mask; it does not give any other users access to new files and directories. This is appropriate on a multi-user system where you do not want other users to look at any of your files.

**022**    Gives other users read access to new files and directories. This is more useful than you may initially presume on a single-user system, because many daemons that run as pseudo-users would not be able to see files and directories created with the more restrictive 077 umask.

**NOTE**    *Certain applications (mail programs in particular) override the* umask, *changing it to 077 because they feel that their files are the business of no one but the file owner.*

## 16.3 Startup File Order and Examples

Now that you know what to put into shell startup files, it's time to see some specific examples. Surprisingly, one of the most difficult and confusing parts of creating startup files is determining which of several startup files to use. The next sections cover the two most popular Unix shells, bash and tcsh.

### 16.3.1 The bash Shell

In bash, you have these startup filenames to choose from: .bash_profile, .profile, .bash_login, and .bashrc. Which one of these is appropriate to use for your command path, manual page path, prompt, aliases, and permissions mask? The answer is that you should have a .bashrc file accompanied by a .bash_profile symbolic link pointing to .bashrc.

The reason for this setup is that there are several different kinds of bash shell instance types, as follows:

**Interactive shell**    The is the type of shell that you use to run commands from a terminal. There are two subtypes of interactive shells:

*Login shell*    This is traditionally invoked by /bin/login; for example, when getty or sshd starts /bin/login. The exact circumstances that determine an interactive shell are a little strange (the first character of a login shell's invocation name is a -), but the basic idea is that the login shell is an initial shell. When bash runs as a login shell, it looks for a user's .bash_profile, .bash_login, and .profile files, running the first one that it sees.

*Non-login shell*   This is any other interactive shell. Windowing system terminal programs (xterm, GNOME Terminal, and so on) start non-login shells unless you specifically ask for a login shell. bash reads from .bashrc upon startup of a non-login shell.

**Non-interactive shell**   This is a shell that doesn't require input from a terminal.

The reasoning behind the two different startup file systems is that in the old days, users logged in through a traditional terminal with a login shell, then started non-login subshells with windowing systems or the screen program. It was deemed a waste to repeatedly set the user environment and run all sorts of wasteful programs in these subshells. With login shells, you could run fancy startup commands in a file such as .bash_profile, leaving only aliases and other "lightweight" things to your .bashrc.

That's a nice theory, but in these modern times, nearly everyone logs in through a graphical display manager that never starts a login shell. Therefore, you need to set up your entire environment (path, manual path, and so on) in your .bashrc, or you would never see any of your environment in your terminal window shells. However, you *also* need a .bash_profile if you ever want to log in on the console or remotely, because these are login shells, and they don't ever bother with .bashrc.

None of the issues described in the previous two paragraphs should matter, because it's never a good idea to make a complicated mess of your startup files, and modern hardware is so fast that a little extra work for every new shell shouldn't cause much of a performance hit anyway.

Here is a very elementary (yet perfectly sufficient) .bashrc that you can also share with your .bash_profile:

```
# Command path.
PATH=/usr/local/bin:/usr/bin:/bin:/usr/X11R6/bin:$HOME/bin

# Manual page path.
MANPATH=/usr/local/man:/usr/man:/usr/X11R6/man:$HOME/man

# PS1 is the regular prompt.
# Substitutions include:
# \u  username       \h  hostname       \w  current directory
# \!  history number  \s  shell name      \$  $ if regular user
PS1='\u\$ '

# EDITOR and VISUAL determine the editor that programs such as less
# and mail clients invoke when asked to edit a file.
EDITOR=vi
VISUAL=vi

# PAGER is the default text file viewer for programs such as man.
```

```
PAGER=less

# These are some handy options for less.
LESS=mei

# You must export environment variables.
export MANPATH EDITOR VISUAL PAGER LESS

# By default, give other users read-only access to most new files.
umask 022
```

As described earlier, you can share this .bashrc file with .bash_profile via a symbolic link. One (possibly better) alternative is to create .bash_profile as this one-liner:

```
. $HOME/.bashrc
```

## Checking for Login and Interactive Shells

Now that your .bashrc matches your .bash_profile, you can no longer run extra commands for login shells. Therefore, if you want to define different actions for login and non-login shells, you can add the following test to your .bashrc, which checks the first character of the shell's $0 variable for a - character:

```
case $0 in
  -*)   command
        command
        ...
        ...
        ;;
esac
```

If, for whatever reason, you want to run certain commands only if a shell is interactive, use a construct like this in your .bashrc:

```
case "$-" in
  *i*)  command
        command
        ...
        ...
        ;;
esac
```

Normally, bash doesn't read startup files at all for non-interactive shells. The preceding code only applies if you set the BASH_ENV environment variable to a startup filename.

## 16.3.2 The tcsh Shell

The standard csh on virtually all Linux systems is tcsh, an enhanced C shell that popularized features such as command-line editing and multi-mode filename and command completion. Even if you don't use tcsh as the default new user shell (this book suggests using bash), you should still provide tcsh startup files in case your users happen to come across tcsh.

You don't have to worry about the difference between login shells and non-login shells in tcsh. Upon startup, tcsh looks for a .tcshrc file. Failing this, it looks for the csh shell's .cshrc startup file. The reason for this order is that you can use the .tcshrc file for tcsh extensions that don't work in csh. You should probably stick to using the traditional .cshrc instead of .tcshrc; it's highly unlikely that anyone will ever use your startup files with csh. And if a user actually does come across csh on some other system, your .cshrc will work adequately.

Here is sample .cshrc file:

```
# Command path.
setenv PATH /usr/local/bin:/usr/bin:/bin:/usr/X11R6/bin:$HOME/bin

# Manual page path.
setenv MANPATH /usr/local/man:/usr/man:/usr/X11R6/man:$HOME/man

# EDITOR and VISUAL determine the editor that programs such as less
# and mail clients invoke when asked to edit a file.
setenv EDITOR vi
setenv VISUAL vi

# PAGER is the default text file viewer for programs such as man.
setenv PAGER less

# These are some handy options for less.
setenv LESS mei

# By default, give other users read-only access to most new files.
umask 022

# Customize the prompt.
# Substitutions include:
# %n   username        %m  hostname           %/  current directory
# %h   history number  %l  current terminal   %%  %
set prompt="%m%% "
```

# 16.4 Default User Settings

The best way to write startup files and choose defaults for new users is to experiment with a new test user on the system. Create the test user with an empty home directory. Then, most importantly, refrain from copying your own startup files to the test user's directory. Write the new startup files from scratch.

When you think you have a working setup, log in as the new test user in all possible ways (on the console, remotely, and so on). Make sure that you test as many things as possible, including windowing system operation and manual pages. After you're happy with the test user, create a second test user, copying the startup files from the first test user. If everything still works fine, you now have a new set of startup files that you can distribute to new users.

The following sections outline reasonable defaults for new users.

## 16.4.1 Shell

The default shell for any new user on a Linux system should be bash. In the old days, the Bourne shell (sh) was more difficult to use in interactive mode than alternatives such as the C shell (csh), so users typically had a login shell that was different than the standard system shell. This changed when bash arrived on the scene, for it had all of the features of csh and its enhanced version (tcsh).

There are several good reasons for using bash on a Linux system:

- Users interact with the same shell that they use to write shell scripts (csh is a notoriously bad scripting tool; please, don't even think about it).

- bash is standard on Linux systems; tcsh is sometimes not.

- bash uses GNU readline, and therefore, its interface is identical to many other tools. tcsh has a powerful command-line editing system, but it takes some time to learn.

- bash gives you finer control over I/O redirection and file handles.

However, you can't teach an old dog new tricks, and many seasoned Unix wizards use csh and tcsh simply because they can't bear to switch. Of course, you can choose any shell you like, but my opinion is that you should choose bash if you don't have any preference, and you should also use bash as the default shell for any new user on the system (if they have another preference, they will be able to change their own shell with the chsh command).

**NOTE**   *There are plenty of other shells out there (rc, ksh, zsh, es, and so on). But just because they exist does not mean they are suitable beginner shells.*

### 16.4.2 Editor

The default editor should be `vi` or `emacs`. These are the only editors virtually guaranteed to exist on nearly any Unix system, and they will therefore cause the least trouble in the long run for a new user.

As with shell startup files, avoid large default editor startup files. A little `set showmatch` in the `vi` `.exrc` startup file never hurt anyone, but steer clear of anything that significantly changes the editor's behavior or appearance, such as the `showmode` feature, autoindentation, and wrap margins.

### 16.4.3 Pager

It is perfectly reasonable to set the default `PAGER` environment variable to `less`, because it is very easy to use.

## 16.5 Startup File Pitfalls

There are a few things you really should avoid in startup files (many have to do with the X Window System):

- Don't put X commands in a shell startup file.
- Don't set the `DISPLAY` environment variable in a shell startup file.
- Don't set the terminal type in a shell startup file.
- Don't skimp on descriptive comments in default startup files.
- Don't run commands in a startup file that print to the standard output.
- *Never* set `LD_LIBRARY_PATH` in a shell startup file (see Section 8.1.4).

## 16.6 Further Startup Topics

Because this book deals only with the underlying Linux system, this chapter does not cover windowing environment startup files. This is a large issue indeed, because the display manager that logs you in to a modern Linux system has its own set of startup files, such as `.xsession`, `.xinitrc`, and the endless mess of GNOME- and KDE-related items.

The windowing choices may seem bewildering, and this isn't far from the truth, because there isn't even one single common way to start a windowing environment in Unix. However, once you determine what your system does, you may get a little carried away with the files that relate to your graphical environment. This is fine, but don't carry it over to new users. The same tenet of keeping things simple in shell startup files works wonders for GUI startup files too.

# BUYING HARDWARE FOR LINUX

Computers are frustrating. Simply shopping for one is enough to drive a sane person mad, and if you want a Linux machine, you might as well sign up for therapy now. Aside from relatively low hardware prices, the cards are stacked against you. A confusing barrage of specifications and incompatibilities awaits you in your quest, and along the way, you must often confront extremely lame advertising for what are often the ugliest examples of industrial design in history.

This chapter is a field guide to hardware selection. Although hardware is in a constant state of flux, the good news is that an old adage applies: The more things change, the more they stay the same. If you can see computer hardware in more abstract terms, you have everything you need to make an educated purchase. Despite the constant escalation of specifications, a computer still has a processor (CPU), random-access memory (RAM), secondary storage, and some

I/O devices. Every now and then, some underlying technology may change, but nothing is going to stop memory from doing anything other than storing a bunch of ones and zeros.

Here are three guidelines that you should remember:

**Know what you want, and don't lose sight of it**   This usually comes down to a price versus performance trade-off, but details such as ergonomics can be just as important.

**Don't listen to vendors**   They generally want to sell you the most expensive thing in the store even though it may not even work correctly. In addition, these people are trained to sell systems for Windows users — in most cases they're not aware of hardware issues important to Linux users.

**You often get what you pay for**   However, refer to Rule 1 first: is the more expensive hardware what you really need and want?

## 17.1 Core Components

The discussion in this chapter focuses on desktop computers. With the exception of notebooks, I build my machines from components. The goal is not to save money; in fact, the finished system often costs more than similarly outfitted pre-assembled computers. The advantage is that there are fewer headaches with custom configurations. If you know exactly what goes into your computer, you will have no surprises, and in this territory, surprises only come in the unpleasant variety. You don't want hardware that Linux doesn't support, and an unreliable piece of hardware can seriously degrade your quality of life.

Assembling a computer is easy, but it isn't for everyone. It takes time and a certain amount of dexterity to avoid hurting yourself on sharp electronic pieces. If you don't want to go for an off-the-shelf model that may contain unknown components, and you also don't want to assemble your computer yourself, you still have two choices. You can find out exactly what is in that off-the-shelf model that you're looking at, and then determine whether the parts will work with Linux. Reputable manufacturers list this information and do not substitute parts. Your other choice is to buy custom parts and then have a small computer shop or friend assemble them for you. If you go to a shop, make it clear that component substitution is unacceptable.

You need the following components:

- A motherboard. Modern motherboards have integrated hard drive interfaces, as well as USB and many other I/O ports.
- A processor (CPU).
- Random-access memory (RAM).
- A hard disk.
- An Ethernet NIC card (optional).

- A graphics card.
- A case to hold the components. The case usually includes a power supply.

### 17.1.1 Processor and Motherboard

Virtually all IA32-like (x86 PC) central processing unit (CPU) models work with Linux. The kernel and gcc compiler support many vendor-specific CPU optimizations, and features such as multiprocessing also work well with Linux.

Two important considerations when choosing a processor should be power consumption and heat. CPUs that consume more power also generate a substantial amount of heat. To handle the extra heat, you need a lot of fans. *Never overclock a processor running Linux,* unless you like to see your computer crash.

**NOTE** *If you are interested in taming the usual din that a computer makes, a great place to start is the power supply. Most power supply units included with PC cases are of the very cheapest sort, with loud, unreliable cooling fans. You can easily replace the power supply with a low-noise premium model from a third party. It will not be cheap, but if noise irritates you, it is worth every penny.*

Although nearly all CPU models will work with Linux, some care must be taken when choosing the CPU's home — the motherboard. You should consider your motherboard, processor, and memory as a single unit, and you may even want to choose your motherboard first and find a CPU to fit. After all, it is possible that your motherboard will cost more than the CPU!

Pick a motherboard that has been available for a reasonable amount of time. Three or four months should be sufficient. Often, initial releases of motherboards have bugs that cause mysterious hardware failures. Avoid fancy (untested) new features. Linux doesn't immediately support each new bell and whistle that comes off the assembly line, and these unusual features may interfere with normal system operation. Watch out for brand-new processor models that require you to purchase a new motherboard chipset, as these can be expensive nightmares.

Modern motherboards come with a number of integrated peripherals. They normally include two ATA disk interfaces, plus parallel, serial, and USB ports. Some motherboards come with additional hardware, such as integrated SCSI controllers, video chips, and sound. These integrated features can save you space on the motherboard and the hassle of installing your own components, but if you buy separate plug-in components, you can perhaps save a little money and a compatibility headache. The advantages of integrated motherboard components are somewhat dubious in the case of most components except SCSI controllers. If, like many people, you choose a motherboard with integrated video, find out what chip it uses and make certain that the XFree86 server has support for it (see http://www.xfree86.org/ and http://www.xouvert.org/).

## 17.1.2 Memory

The third guideline from the beginning of this chapter ("you often get what you pay for") is most important when buying memory. Name-brand memory is only marginally more expensive than generic labels, and it can save you many headaches. A Linux machine exhibits odd behavior if it has bad memory. If a program seems to crash often, look for these symptoms:

- The crash happens in the same place every time.
- Rebooting makes the problem go away.
- The operating system appears unaffected, and other programs run fine.
- It happens during frequent disk access.

You should consider buying ECC (error-correcting code) memory. It is a little more expensive than standard memory, and not all motherboards support it (read your motherboard manual carefully), but ECC memory practically ensures that you never have a memory problem.

A Linux system automatically uses extra memory for disk cache, and this can substantially improve performance for applications that use large files (or several small files). However, for many users, there is a point where more memory adds little or no benefit because the system has already cached nearly everything. You can briefly check the state of a system's memory utilization with the free command; the information in /proc/meminfo has a little more detail.

## 17.1.3 Hard Disk

The old "IDE versus SCSI" question was once one of the bigger debates surrounding hard disks. However, if you want to build a desktop computer, the debate means little, because you will likely choose an ATA (IDE) disk out of cost concerns. In the old days, power users considered ATA disks to be performance dogs, and there wasn't a large disparity in price when compared against SCSI disks. Improvements in CPU speeds, caching, memory cost, the interface, and hard disk manufacturing techniques have made ATA perform tolerably well for a desktop system with a single disk — even Apple switched its desktop disks to the ATA type.

A disk has two primary specification numbers: average access time (measured in milliseconds, or ms) and rotation speed (measured in rotations per minute, or RPM). In general, a faster (lower) access time is the more important consideration for Unix, because the system spends a lot of time looking at a bunch of small files. If you are a software developer, this is particularly important because compilers and scripting languages use many file accesses on a single invocation. On the other hand, if you have big files (movies, music, whatever), a higher rotational speed gets this stuff off the hard disk faster.

There usually isn't a trade-off between rotational speed and access time because they are linked. More RPMs mean that the disk head takes less time to pass over the proper place on the disk platter for the next access, hence a lower average access time.

Higher performance, however, comes at a price above and beyond the sticker price. The fastest-spinning disks are usually noisy and generate more heat. I'll spare you the "hard disks I have hated in the past" war stories, but if you want a quiet disk, look for one with a fluid bearing system (sometimes called FDB). These drives use liquid instead of solid ball bearings for their platters, and they are a big improvement for your ears.

Any ATA disk should work in a Linux system. The kernel disk drivers are fast, and they support special features with the hdparm command. If you run into compatibility issues, they will likely be between your motherboard and the disk (in particular, some older motherboards do not support disks larger than 32GB; look for jumpers on the disk to "clip" the disk, limiting it to a lower capacity).

If you put two ATA disks in the same system, put them on different interfaces (your motherboard should have primary and secondary ATA interfaces), which should improve concurrent access slightly. If you purchase an add-in ATA interface card, you may need extra drivers. When considering one of these cards, look for drivers in the **ATA support** menu described in Section 10.4.1.

### 17.1.4 Network Cards and Infrastructure

The Linux kernel supports most wired PC Ethernet devices (also known as NICs, or network interface cards), but you should check any card against the compatibility list in a current Linux kernel. Don't believe a manufacturer's claim of compatibility in this case — the manufacturer may require you to install a special kernel driver before the device works. Keep in mind that the kernel drivers that come from vendors often don't work correctly.

Most cable and DSL adapters require an Ethernet card. You should be able to use any supported Ethernet card regardless of the protocol that you use, provided that Linux supports the protocol. You may need to use a funny protocol like PPPoE for your provider (see Section 5.9).

Current networks of 100Base-T (100 megabits per second, or about 12 megabytes per second) are more than adequate for most purposes. They are also very inexpensive. To attach several machines to a home network, you need a hub or switch (it is possible to connect two machines directly with an Ethernet crossover cable, but this isn't really worth the trouble).

The most significant differences between using a hub and a low-end switch is that a switch can send and receive signals at the same time and therefore has a potential of faster throughput and lower latency. However, unless you have a habit of sending large files around your network simultaneously, you won't notice much of a performance difference between the two. On the other hand, the difference in price between hubs and switches is also fairly small. Whether you purchase a hub or a switch, pick a model that has ports for each of your computers, plus a few extra. Also, make sure that the hardware supports the older 10Base-T standard. This feature is often called *10/100*, and it provides the most convenient way to move files from an old computer with a 10Base-T interface.

### Wireless Ethernet

You may want to consider wireless Ethernet for a notebook, even if you don't plan to use Ethernet when you're on the go. There are several advantages:

- It is one less cable to connect. This saves time as well as wear and tear on the machine.
- Visitors with wireless cards can connect to your network without much hassle.
- Some PDAs can connect to a network with wireless Ethernet.
- You may need to connect to a foreign network at some time.

There are also some disadvantages:

- It is more expensive.
- Security can be a hassle (see Section 5.15.1).
- There are some really annoying twerps who think that wireless Ethernet makes them the coolest people on the planet.

To make wireless Ethernet work, you need a wireless access point along with the network card (some notebooks come with integrated cards). Many access points come in units that also provide a broadband router and an integrated switch. Even if you don't have a broadband connection or choose not to use the routing feature, the switch can still be useful for connecting desktop computers.

For notebook Ethernet cards, see Section 11.6. For information on how to set up a wireless client, see Section 5.15.

## 17.1.5 Graphics Hardware

Your primary concern in choosing a video card should be compatibility with XFree86. Although you can inspect the list of compatible cards at http://www.xfree86.org/ and http://www.xouvert.org/, it is unfortunately not always easy to identify a card because manufacturers have a habit of not changing product names while altering hardware significantly.

As with the motherboard, a good method for ensuring that your graphics hardware is compatible with your system is to identify a brand or particular graphics chip that has consistent support and then find a video card that isn't cutting-edge. If a card has been available for some time, there is a much greater chance of XFree86 support. Regarding performance, quick video hardware often means very little under Linux; in fact, the fastest 3-D hardware may not be optimal for normal tasks in XFree86.

XFree86 supports multi-output video cards and additional cards that can drive multiple monitors, sometimes called *multiple heads*. If you value your onscreen workspace, this is worth looking at because the emergence of LCD displays makes it feasible to have two large monitors without a desk the size of an aircraft carrier. You can also combine multiple displays into one big virtual display with the Xinerama extension.

# 17.2 Other Hardware Components

Now it's time to move beyond the essential components and look at your choices for the other parts that you can attach to a computer.

## 17.2.1 Monitors

Because you will work with the shell interface more under Unix than other PC operating systems, you should choose a monitor that displays crisp text. In addition, high resolution is important in a monitor because you want the ability to display at least two shell or text editor windows at once, so that you can quickly switch between them. However, you can only take resolution so far. To the beginner, it is always tempting to reduce the font size to accommodate more windows, but because this increases eye strain, there is no real substitute for a large display.

Traditional Unix workstations like Sun SPARCstations usually came with very large, heavy, expensive cathode ray tube (CRT) monitors offering some of the highest resolutions commercially available. CRT displays are now lighter and carry the lowest price tags of high-end displays. However, you should avoid them whenever possible. Above all, an LCD display offers a razor-sharp text display that is impossible on any CRT. This advantage, combined with a very light weight, small footprint, and lack of a flyback transformer makes a good case for an LCD display for all but the most special-purpose applications. (At some point in the not-so-distant future, a CRT will not even be a consideration, rendering this paragraph a historic curiosity.)

As mentioned above, traditional monitors that came paired with Unix machines had fairly high resolutions. The minimum that Sun and NeXT used was around $1152 \times 900$ (often called *megapixel displays*), and most users found it comfortable (you won't find this option on modern LCD displays). $1024 \times 768$ is a little cramped but passable if you can keep a minimal desktop. It also may be the only option if you are shopping for a notebook. A $1280 \times 1024$ display is the next step up and it is often ideal; if you happen to have just a little extra money and are itching to spend it on something worthwhile, this is it. Higher resolutions such as $1600 \times 1200$ are good if you have large graphics to display. However, if you want to increase your workspace, especially for text, it's better to buy a second monitor and use the multi-monitor support mentioned in Section 17.1.5. A multi-monitor configuration costs less than a single huge monitor and gives you more effective onscreen space due to the layout of the monitors.

## 17.2.2 Keyboards

Choose your keyboard wisely, because you'll use it more than you ever imagined in Linux. First, check the basics of the layout. Is the ESC key in a reasonable place, and is it a normal-sized key? This is extremely important for vi users, who press ESC on a regular basis. Where are the tilde-backtick (~ `) and pipe-backslash (| \) keys? These characters come up frequently in shell commands. (To those using non-U.S. keyboards, you might want to ask a friend about good key layouts and mappings.)

If you intend to run only Unix on your computer, keys other than those immediately around the alphanumerics aren't very important. You don't really need a numeric keypad or 37 function keys. Arrow keys are also slightly less important when running Unix unless you're playing a game. Nearly every program that takes text input accepts CONTROL-P, CONTROL-N, CONTROL-B, and CONTROL-F (up, down, left, and right, respectively). In vi, you will make use of h, j, k, and l (left, down, up, and right).

One little thing to watch out for is the CAPS LOCK key. On virtually every keyboard made today, it is next to the A key. This is wrong; the CONTROL key belongs there. Philosophical issues aside, see if the CAPS LOCK key is large enough and doesn't have an overly weird shape. You should remap the CAPS LOCK key to CONTROL and use it that way.

## 17.2.3 Mice

Other than your personal preferences and testing, there is only one important thing to remember when buying a mouse: *Make sure your mouse has at least three buttons.* The third (middle) button in X Window System applications does a paste operation; you don't want to be without it. You can even use it to paste a URL into a browser window. Also, clicking on a link in Mozilla with the middle button makes the link appear in a new window or tab.

In a modern mouse, the scroll wheel usually doubles as the third button when pressed down. The scroll wheel is more difficult to press than a real button, and many Unix veterans dislike this. However, there may be some merit to it, because clumsy fingers on traditional three-button mice have been known to paste strange commands into Unix shells and editors.

## 17.2.4 Modems

Most fax modems and many voice modems work with Linux. There is only one very important rule when buying a modem for Linux: *Never buy a Winmodem.* These devices require complicated software drivers to do signal processing. There are some straggling Linux drivers for certain Winmodems out there, but you shouldn't bother. You don't want to waste time trying to set this up, and you don't want the extra strain on your kernel. It is unfortunate that many notebooks come with Winmodems; if you have a Winmodem in your notebook, your only option is usually to get a PC Card modem.

That said, for desktops you have a choice between internal and external modems. Internal modems are cheaper, do not have external power supplies, and need no cords other than the telephone line. Unfortunately, they may also require some Plug-and-Play manipulation or disabling of built-in serial ports. You may be able to use an external USB modem, but make sure that there's a Linux driver before you buy.

### 17.2.5 Printers

Because Unix printer drivers generate the PostScript page description language, the easiest way to get a Linux-compatible printer is to buy one that supports PostScript. Many laser printers and some inkjet printers come with this capability. Unfortunately, these printers are also more expensive than those with simpler imaging technology.

Linux also supports printers that don't understand PostScript by using Ghostscript to transform the PostScript generated by the printer drivers into something that these printers understand. However, this adds an extra step to the printing process inside your machine, and it can be difficult to configure (see Chapter 12).

There are three common ways to connect a printer to a Linux system: using a parallel port, using a USB port, or adding the printer to a local area network. The parallel port is an old and somewhat primitive method, but it works well. USB is the newest method and should work as well as your USB drivers do (see Section 11.3). Printing over the network is fast, it requires no extra kernel drivers, and it is often the easiest to configure. Most network-capable printers also support PostScript, but they are considerably more expensive than their non-networked counterparts.

## 17.3 A Word About Hardware Upgrades

Before we look at how you can save money, you should know something about upgrades. For many people, some kinds of products seem more appealing because you can upgrade them somewhere down the line. This may work for old tools and kitchen appliances, but the computer industry doesn't think that way. They want you to buy something, use it for a year, throw it away, and then buy the newest model because they wouldn't make any money if they actually had to offer upgrades for the dinosaurs of the past. Really, computers just aren't designed like the Stanley #5 jack plane, which was offered in the same basic form for 115 years.

If you see something advertised as being upgradable to some future specification with some extra piece of hardware, it probably isn't going to do you a whiff of good, especially if that extra piece of hardware doesn't exist yet. It usually means that the company has a newer product that isn't quite ready, and therefore, the marketing department is trying to think of ways to milk an old product. If that little upgrade actually does appear, it will most likely be crippled because the old and new technologies are so different that the engineers had to do some really bogus stuff to get the things to talk to each other. I could bring up countless examples, many involving CPUs, but you should take my word on this one.

So what can you upgrade, and what kinds of parts can you carry from an old computer to a new one? Disks, for one, are always fairly easy to add to a machine, whether a disk is new or used. Memory is a little more complicated. For the most part, you can always add more memory to your existing system, but keep in mind that you may need to remove some of your old memory to make room for the new stuff.

You should regard the motherboard, processor, and memory as one unit when purchasing hardware. Don't even think of carrying just one of these components over to a newer system (well, this is a slight fib; sometimes you can keep your memory, but it's very rare). You may also need a new power supply, case, or graphics card when you upgrade other hardware on your system, because the standards for these components are not terribly stable.

Peripherals and USB devices are easier to carry from system to system. There really isn't any need to change peripheral devices (like printers) if what you have works. And if you have a keyboard or mouse that you like a lot on your old system, then in the name of your own sanity, don't get rid of it. I hate to say this, but they just don't build keyboards like they used to. It might be worth buying a special adapter to make an old keyboard compatible with a new system (for example, to convert an AT keyboard to USB).

Upgradable firmware (embedded software) in external hardware components (such as modems) is also a good thing, because it's much easier for a company to write software to support new protocols than to develop and produce hardware fixes.

## 17.4 Saving Money

Axiom 3 in the introduction to this chapter stated that you often get what you pay for; in other words, you might need to pay for a system that works and works well. However, there's no injunction against saving money. If you don't have an obsession with the very latest products, and you know what to look for, you can look for slightly older stuff and save a substantial sum.

## 17.4.1 CPU

Although it is true that your CPU does most of the work on a Linux system, the CPU normally spends most of its time doing absolutely nothing. The uptime command usually reveals that the processor isn't running any jobs. If processor speed is important to you, you'll know it from the type of computing that you do, be it graphics or numerical analysis. But for the vast majority of users, there are many features more important than CPU speed, and carefully choosing a processor is one of the best ways to save money on a new computer.

Nowhere does price so wildly diverge as among processors. A vendor's list at the time of this writing shows one price for its fastest CPU. The next step down is 50 percent of that price, but it is still 91.5 percent as fast as the top model. A slower processor costing 25 percent of the top model retains 78 percent of the performance. Now you may ask yourself, maybe I need that extra 22 percent of power? For comparison, I am typing this on a computer that is only 12 percent as fast as the top processor in that list, and I have no complaints.

The trick to selecting a processor is to pick a spot on the performance/price curve that looks good. Figures 17-1 and 17-2 show plots of ten processors. Figure 17-1 shows how quickly the price rises as the processor speed reaches the fastest available. In Figure 17-2 on the next page, you can see how much performance you get for each dollar that you spend for the same set of processors.

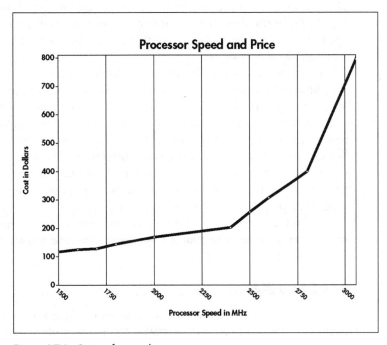

Figure 17-1: Costs of several processors.

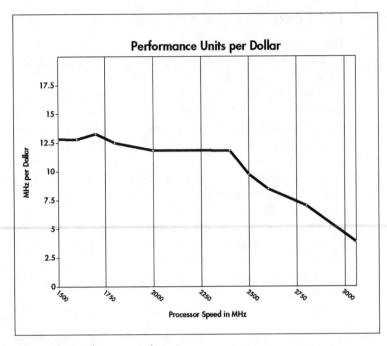

*Figure 17-2: Performance value.*

If you are strictly interested in getting the most bang for the buck, the best choice is the CPU represented by the maximum in the graph on the right. However, keep in mind that you may want to go for one of the CPUs with slightly faster numbers because it may cost only a few dollars more, or you might be able to buy a CD or something else with the savings from choosing a marginally slower option.

You must be cautious in measuring the performance of a processor. The only halfway precise way to compare processors is to compare different clock speeds of the *same model.* Looking at the megahertz (MHz) numbers of two different models, even from the same manufacturer, is comparing apples and oranges. The benchmark results you read about are also unreliable because operation speeds vary among different processors. Unless you know exactly what you're looking for, benchmarks are next to useless. Decide on a price first, and then look for the best deals among the models that fall within your price range.

If you find any of this economic analysis remotely interesting, you might want to read the first chapter of *Computer Architecture: A Quantitative Approach* [Hennessey].

## 17.4.2 Hard Disk

More expensive hard disks often provide more space for the money. For example, a certain hard disk may offer 100 percent more space over another model for only 33 percent more money. But if you're running Linux, which is an operating system with relatively low system storage requirements, is "supersizing" really worth it? Considering how much a modern hard disk can store, will you actually use that extra space before you buy another disk?

By the time you need to purchase another disk, you may find that the cost per megabyte on a new disk is far lower, or that there are desirable technology improvements that may just make you want to decommission your old disk. Remember that the hard disk still has moving parts, and it is therefore one of the least reliable components in a computer.

### 17.4.3 Computer Case

Ugly cases with unrefined power supplies and unsophisticated internal structures are cheaper. If you're not picky and can put up with the hassle, this could be worth it (that is, you're a graduate student and know what it means to have something "cheap but somewhat functional if not kind of annoying"). Also, you might be able to get a used case for free. Be careful, though: a secondhand power supply may not work with your motherboard, and it may not work at all.

### 17.4.4 Video Card

Sometimes you can get a graphics card that the vendor targets for office users. These cards are often less expensive than others. Also, old or discontinued models on clearance won't hurt performance on Linux.

## 17.5 Notebooks

It is difficult to balance Linux compatibility with the latest features on notebook computers. The most common problems with notebooks are built-in video chipsets that XFree86 does not support. Other components that tend to lack drivers are modems, Ethernet interfaces, sound cards, and CD-ROM drives.

The online community is a good place to look for information on Linux notebook compatibility. The http://www.tuxmobile.org/ site is a clearinghouse of links to people who are running Linux on nearly all common notebook models. However, these pages are often out of date, and the driver configuration or bug fixes described may not be necessary with current Linux drivers.

## 17.6 Smaller Designs

Once upon a time, if you wanted a PC, your options were limited to large machines. Because interchangeable parts were so important to build the PC as a commodity, manufacturers were reluctant to design anything smaller because the form factor would change and be incompatible with everything on the market. Very small Unix machines were on the market, such as the Sun SPARCstation IPC and IPX, but they were expensive.

This is changing. Increased demand from consumers, small dimensional standards taken largely from notebook computers, and special applications have created a market for a new class of machines. Form factors such as Mini-ITX are now on the market. They aren't the fastest computers around, and they aren't overly expandable, but they have big advantages. They are small, quiet, use less power, generate less heat, and are astonishingly inexpensive. Linux has made a contribution to the increasing popularity of these machines. Whereas a computer with relatively low processor power stood no chance against a market using Microsoft's resource-hungry operating systems, the ever-increasing population of Linux users does not care. Manufacturers know this and make sure that their products support Linux.

The current small machines are hybrids. The motherboards can still fit into standard cases, use normal-size memory, and often have a single PCI slot. They accept standard PC components, even the power supply. However, because many of the components are self-contained and generate little heat (including power supplies), it has become fashionable to custom-build smaller enclosures. These machines really shine when placed in special small cases that will not accept larger components.

One common example of this is the CD-ROM drive. On a regular desktop computer, these devices are gigantic because they fit into a half-height 5 1/4-inch drive bay. To make them fit in a smaller machine, an easy substitution for the normal size CD-ROM drive is a notebook CD-ROM drive. Like the embedded processors found on many small motherboards, a notebook CD-ROM drive may not be as quick as its larger cousin, but it is a fraction of the size.

# 18

## FURTHER DIRECTIONS

There's a lot to Linux. This book can only go so far, and although it's time to wind down, this chapter will give you an idea of what lies beyond the fundamental topics covered in this book.

## 18.1 Additional Topics

Most (but not all) of these topics are network related. Furthermore, none are specific to Linux; you can carry the knowledge you have of them to and from other Unix systems.

**Electronic mail**   Email is a big topic. Chapters 5 and 6 talked a little about the SMTP port (25) used for mail transfer, and they briefly mentioned Postfix and qmail, the two most viable mail transfer agents (MTAs) available now. There's more behind the MTA: for example, if you want to run an IMAP (Internet Message Access Protocol) server, you probably want the Cyrus package.

**Domain Name Service (DNS)**   Setting up a client is easy, as you saw in Chapter 5, but setting up a DNS server is trickier. The most common DNS server is BIND (Berkeley Internet Name Domain), but a newer DNS server named djbdns is also gaining popularity.

**Web servers**   In the Unix world, "Web server" usually means Apache, the most popular Web server in the world. However, many scripting languages and other tools have embedded Web server features that can aid debugging, status monitoring, and other tasks not directly related to serving Web pages to the general public.

**Virtual private networks (VPNs)**   A VPN allows you to connect several widely dispersed machines in a virtual network (for instance, a single subnet). Administrators typically create a VPN in conjunction with the IPSec protocol so that they can disperse sensitive data (that might otherwise be behind a network firewall) through an encrypted network channel across a possibly insecure link.

**The screen program**   Did you ever want to take your shell session wherever you go? You can do it with the screen program, a terminal multiplexer that supports multiple shells, disconnection, reconnection, scrollback, cut and paste, and more. This utility is a perennial favorite among seasoned Unix wizards. If you want some of the same functionality with a windowing system, check out VNC (Virtual Network Computing).

**DB files and DBM files**   When using many larger servers, you will encounter binary DB and DBM files. These files are very small databases that store blocks of data keyed by small strings, usually as some kind of hash table. For whatever reason, there are an absurd number of different DB/DBM file formats (DB, GDBM, NDBM, and SDBM, to name a few). Most packages that use DBM-style files come with their own manipulation utilities (for example, the postalias command that comes with Postfix), but scripting languages such as Perl include powerful interfaces that you can use if you need to do something beyond the ordinary with these database files.

**Relational databases**   You can run the powerful MySQL and PostgreSQL database servers on Linux. There are several commercial servers as well, but this book intentionally avoids talk of commercial software products.

**RCS and CVS**   The Revision Control System (RCS) is a way to track file revisions. Originally meant for software development, many systems administrators use RCS to control important system files so that they have a record of who made each change (and in theory, so that they can back out of harmful changes, though this rarely comes up in practice). The Concurrent Versions System (CVS) is a network-extensible revision control system that can handle several versions of the same package at once.

**Pluggable Authentication Modules (PAM)**   If you don't like the system of passwords in /etc/passwd, you can replace it with a PAM module that supports some other scheme.

**Network Information Service (NIS)**  NIS is a terrifying combination of RPC and DBM files, used by many systems to provide networked information such as `passwd` and `group`. It is an old system that isn't particularly robust, secure, or pleasant, but it is supported by most Unix platforms.

**Kerberos**  This is a powerful network authentication system.

**Lightweight Directory Access Protocol (LDAP)**  LDAP serves a bunch of data entries to network clients (as NIS does), except that where NIS allows only a single key per data entry, LDAP supports a hierarchy of keys for entries. LDAP is very extensible; OpenLDAP is a popular open source LDAP server.

**Network File System (NFS)**  This is the traditional method of sharing files across a network on a Unix cluster. NFS is a somewhat clunky system that is still in use because most Unix systems support it. Plus, the alternatives such as AFS (Andrew File System), DFS (Distributed File System), and 9P are too expensive, difficult to configure, and not terribly well understood.

**Secure Sockets Layer (SSL)**  Many network servers now offer SSL support to authenticate and encrypt individual TCP connections with the same technology used for secure Web sessions. If you want to set up a server that supports SSL, be prepared to learn all about public keys, private keys, certificates, signing, and more.

## 18.2 Final Thoughts

One of the difficulties of Linux is that, like most software, certain technical details change all of the time because software maintainers change, they implement new features, and they can be just plain fickle. Although this book strives to cover topics that have some degree of stability, it's impossible to tell the future. The good news is that the base system really doesn't change much. Concentrate on what the system components *do*, not the details of every strange little option. Remember that the online documentation is always there. In many cases, learning the correct terminology is more important than learning the actual details, because it's the terminology that helps you in your search for the documentation.

Linux (and Unix in general) doesn't exist in a vacuum. There are a lot of people out there who can help you. A few examples are IRC channels, mailing lists, user groups (check http://www.linux.org/groups/), and the USENIX/SAGE organizations (http://www.usenix.org/). USENIX has been around since the early days of Unix (incidentally, if you're interested in "the old days," you should read *A Quarter Century of UNIX* [Salus]).

Keeping your system simple and clean helps when tracking problems. Don't get obsessed with it, though — zealously removing "errant" files can be harmful.

Finally, don't be afraid to try new stuff!

# COMMAND CLASSIFICATION

This appendix is a guide to the common standard commands. They are organized in the following tables:

**Table A-1:** File Management Commands

| Command | Description |
| --- | --- |
| chgrp | Changes a file's group |
| chmod | Changes a file's permissions |
| chown | Changes a file's user ownership |
| cp | Copies a file |
| dd | Converts and copies |
| df | Displays disk usage statistics |
| du | Displays directory space usage |
| file | Identifies a file type |
| find | Searches for a file |
| ln | Creates a symbolic or hard link |
| ls | Lists files |
| mkdir | Creates a directory |
| mkfifo | Creates a named pipe |
| mknod | Creates a special file |
| mv | Renames or moves a file |
| rm | Removes a file |
| touch | Creates a file or updates a file's timestamp |

**Table A-2:** Text Processing and Scripting Commands

| Command | Description |
| --- | --- |
| awk | The awk general-purpose text processing language |
| basename | Strips extensions and directories from filenames |
| cat | Displays and concatenates files |
| cmp | Compares binary files |
| cut | Extracts columns of lines |
| diff | Compares text files |
| dirname | Extracts the directory from a filename |
| echo | Prints text |
| ed | A classic line-based text editor |
| egrep | Extended grep |
| ex | A newer line-based text editor |
| expr | Evaluates a mathematical expression |
| false | Returns a nonzero exit code |
| fmt | Breaks long lines and reformats text |
| grep | Searches for lines matching a regular expression |
| groff | A multi-purpose typesetting utility |
| head | Displays the first lines of a file |
| ispell | A spelling checker |

**Table A-2:** Text Processing and Scripting Commands (continued)

| Command | Description |
| --- | --- |
| less | Displays a text file |
| more | Displays a text file |
| nroff | Formats roff documents for text display |
| patch | Incorporates changes into files; the opposite of diff |
| perl | A general-purpose scripting language |
| sed | A stream editor |
| sort | Sorts lines in a file |
| split | Chops a file into pieces |
| tail | Displays the last lines of a file |
| tee | Duplicates a file stream |
| test | ([) Checks a condition |
| tr | Translates (or substitutes) characters |
| true | Returns an exit code of 0 (true) |
| uniq | Removes duplicate adjacent lines |
| vi | A visual full-screen editor |
| wc | Counts words, lines, and characters in a file |
| xargs | Executes a command repeatedly with arguments from the input stream |

**Table A-3:** Online Documentation Commands

| Command | Description |
| --- | --- |
| info | Displays GNU-style documentation |
| man | Displays the traditional Unix online manual |

**Table A-4:** Process and System Utility Commands

| Command | Description |
| --- | --- |
| at | Runs a program at a certain time |
| chfn | Changes finger information |
| chsh | Changes shells |
| crontab | Runs a periodic job |
| groups | Shows group membership |
| id | Shows the current user ID |
| kill | Sends a signal to a process |
| logger | Records a message to the system logger |
| login | Allows a user to login |
| lsof | Lists open files and other information |
| mount | Attaches a filesystem to a directory tree |
| newgrp | Changes the current default group |

**Table A-4:** Process and System Utility Commands (continued)

| Command | Description |
| --- | --- |
| nice | Runs a process with a suggested priority |
| passwd | Changes a password |
| printenv | Prints environment variables |
| ps | Displays processes |
| renice | Changes the suggested priority for a process |
| reset | Attempts to reset the terminal |
| strace | Traces system calls |
| su | Switches users |
| sync | Writes kernel buffers to disk |
| time | Displays how much processor and system time a process takes |
| top | Shows the processes with the most resource consumption |
| umount | Detaches a filesystem from a directory tree |

**Table A-5:** System Information Commands

| Command | Description |
| --- | --- |
| arch | Displays the system architecture |
| df | Displays disk usage statistics |
| dmesg | Displays buffered kernel messages |
| finger | Displays user information |
| free | Displays free memory statistics |
| hostname | Displays the current host's name |
| last | Shows the last users who logged in |
| tty | Displays the current terminal name |
| uptime | Displays system load and how long the system has been running |
| vmstat | Displays virtual memory statistics |
| uname | Displays kernel identification information |
| w | Displays uptime information and current users |
| who | Displays current users |
| whoami | Displays the current user |

**Table A-6:** Archival and Compression Commands

| Command | Description |
| --- | --- |
| bunzip2 | A decompression program |
| bzip2 | A decompression program |
| cpio | An archival program |
| gunzip | A decompression program |

**Table A-6:** Archival and Compression Commands (continued)

| Command | Description |
| --- | --- |
| gzip | A compression program |
| tar | An archival program |
| uncompress | A decompression program |
| unshar | A de-archival program |
| uudecode | A decoding program (the counterpart of uuencode) |
| uuencode | Encodes binary file into a text file |
| zcat | Decompresses into a file stream |

**Table A-7:** Miscellaneous Utility Commands

| Command | Description |
| --- | --- |
| bc | A simple calculator |
| cal | Shows a calendar |
| date | Displays the current date |
| dc | Runs the RPN calculator |
| pwd | Prints the working directory |
| script | Starts a shell where all output is recorded in a file |
| sleep | Pauses for a specified number of seconds |
| strings | Attempts to show any text embedded in a binary file |
| yes | Prints an endless stream of lines |
| which | Displays the first matching program in the current path |

**Table A-8:** Development Commands

| Command | Description |
| --- | --- |
| ar | A library archiver |
| as | An assembler |
| c++ | A C++ compiler |
| cc | A C compiler |
| cpp | A C preprocessor |
| g++ | A C++ compiler (see c++) |
| gcc | A C compiler (see cc) |
| gdb | The GNU debugger |
| install | Copies a file into a location with certain parameters |
| ld | linker |
| ldd | Displays dynamic libraries |
| make | A package-building tool |
| perl | A general-purpose scripting language |

**Table A-9:** Shells

| Command | Description |
| --- | --- |
| bash | The Bourne Again Shell |
| csh | The C Shell |
| ksh | The Korn Shell |
| sh | The Bourne Shell |
| tcsh | The TC Shell |

# INDEX

## Symbols

# THE LINUX COOKBOOK, 2ND ED
## Tips and Techniques for Everyday Use

*by* MICHAEL STUTZ

*The Linux Cookbook* is your guide to getting the most out of Linux. Organized by general task (such as working with text, managing files, and manipulating graphics), each section contains a series of step-by-step recipes that help you get your work done quickly and efficiently, most often from the command line. Perfect as an introduction to Linux and the command line, or as a desktop reference for the seasoned user. Covers the major Linux distributions.

APRIL 2004, 576 PP., $39.95 ($57.95 CAN)
ISBN 1-59327-031-3

# WICKED COOL SHELL SCRIPTS
## 101 Scripts for Linux, Mac OS X, and UNIX Systems

*by* DAVE TAYLOR

This cookbook of useful, customizable, and fun scripts gives you the tools to solve common Linux, Mac OS X and UNIX problems and personalize your computing environment. Among the more than 100 scripts included are an interactive calculator, a spell checker, a disk backup utility, a weather tracker, and a web logfile analysis tool. The book also teaches you how to write your own sophisticated shell scripts by explaining the syntax and techniques used to build each example scripts. Examples are written in Bourne Shell (sh) syntax.

JANUARY 2004, 368 PP., $29.95 ($43.95 CAN)
ISBN 1-59327-012-7

# HACKING
## The Art of Exploitation

*by* JON ERICKSON

A comprehensive introduction to exploitation techniques and creative problem-solving methods known as "hacking." Explains technical aspects of hacking such as stack based overflows, heap based overflows, string exploits, return-into-libc, shellcode, and cryptographic attacks on 802.11b.

"the seminal hackers handbook" – SecurityForums.com

NOVEMBER 2003, 264 PP., $39.95 ($59.95 CAN)
ISBN 1-59327-007-0

# THE LINUX ENTERPRISE CLUSTER

*by* KARL KOPPER

*The Linux Enterprise Cluster* explains how to take a number of inexpensive computers with limited resources, place them on a normal computer network, and install free software so that the computers act together like one powerful server. The book includes information on how to build a high-availability server pair using the Heartbeat package, how to use the Linux Virtual Server load balancing software, how to configure a reliable printing system in a Linux cluster environment, and how to build a job scheduling system in Linux with no single point of failure.

MAY 2004, 456 PP., $49.95 ($72.95 CAN) W/CD
ISBN 1-59327-036-4


# THE BOOK OF WEBMIN
## ...or How I Learned to Stop Worrying and Love Unix

*by* JOE COOPER

A comprehensive guide to Unix system administration with Webmin, the Open Source system administration tool. Everything you need to know about Webmin's unique features, including the standard system features (network configuration, disk configuration, users and groups, etc.) and how to integrate the most popular services (Apache, BIND, Sendmail, and more). Tutorials show how to accomplish common tasks with each service.

JULY 2003, 312 PP., $34.95 ($52.95 CAN)
ISBN 1-886411-92-1

**PHONE:**
1 (800) 420-7240 OR
(415) 863-9900
MONDAY THROUGH FRIDAY,
9 A.M. TO 5 P.M. (PST)

**FAX:**
(415) 863-9950
24 HOURS A DAY,
7 DAYS A WEEK

**EMAIL:**
SALES@NOSTARCH.COM

**WEB:**
HTTP://WWW.NOSTARCH.COM

**MAIL:**
NO STARCH PRESS
555 DE HARO ST, SUITE 250
SAN FRANCISCO, CA 94107
USA

# UPDATES

Visit **http://www.nostarch.com/howlinuxworks.htm** for updates, errata, and other information.